BEYOND TRADE

Cultural Roots of India's Ocean

Himanshu Prabha Ray

Aryan Books International
New Delhi

Beyond Trade
CULTURAL ROOTS OF INDIA'S OCEAN

ISBN: 978-81-7305-540-9

Published in **2015** by
Aryan Books International
Pooja Apartments, 4B, Ansari Road, New Delhi - 2
Tel.: 23287589, 23255799; Fax: 91-11-23270385
E-mail: aryanbooks@gmail.com
www.aryanbooks.co.in

Designed and Printed in India by
ABI Prints & Publishing Co., New Delhi

Preface

The book draws on research undertaken for almost three decades while teaching courses on Maritime History and guiding doctoral students as a member of the faculty of Centre for Historical Studies, Jawaharlal Nehru University, New Delhi. This interest continued on joining the National Monuments Authority in 2012 and was further revived when the Ministry of Culture decided to launch *Project Mausam* in 2014 with Indira Gandhi National Centre for the Arts as a nodal agency. As a member of the Executive Committee of IGNCA and as Academic Director of *Project Mausam*, it was my proud privilege to present *Project Mausam* at UNESCO's 38th World Heritage Committee Meeting at Doha, Qatar in June 2014. The enthusiastic response to the presentation further spurred me to work on a book to introduce the theme to the interested reader.

I am thankful to Mr. Vikas Arya for translating my ideas into an elegantly produced volume. The maps were drawn by Uma Bhattacharya in her usual efficient style. Chandan Ray not only provided total support but also contributed the photographs for the book.

Contents

Preface *v*
List of Illustrations *ix*

1. Introduction 1
2. Royal Power: Conceptualization of Maritime Space 15
3. Contextualizing Nagapattinam: Chola Naval Expedition against Sriwijaya 47
4. The Indian Ocean Network: An Overview 75
5. Narratives of Travel and Ship-wreck: Maritime Orientation of Coastal Shrines 103
6. Multiple Partners across the Indian Ocean 127
7. From Global to Local: Early Medieval Gujarat and Konkan Coast 155
8. The Sailing Ship: Connecting the Sea Lanes of the Indian Ocean 183
9. Preserving Maritime Heritage: The Path Ahead 207

Bibliography 221
Index 237

List of Illustrations

		Page No.
1.	Map of Dhow ports on Aden-Mangalore route, 1976 (after Map collection, Perry Castañeda Library, University of Texas).	3
2.	Caves at Nasik with royal inscriptions [courtesy American Institute of Indian Studies (AIIS)].	18
3.	Façade of cave 3 at Nasik (courtesy AIIS).	19
4.	Back wall of cave 3 at Nasik (courtesy AIIS).	20
5.	Valahassa Jataka from Mathura, showing merchants confined to a tower.	21
6.	Valahassa Jataka from Mathura, depicting the white horse as saviour.	22
7.	Valahassa Jataka at Neak Pean.	23
8.	Memorial stone from Goa Museum.	25
9.	Memorial stone from Goa Museum.	26
10.	Temple at Gop.	31
11.	Distribution map of Maitraka temples.	33
12.	Plan of Junagarh.	35
13.	Khapra Kodia cave at Junagarh.	36
14.	Chandor excavations.	39
15.	Port sites along the East Coast of India.	50
16.	Buddhapada from Kaveripumpattinam now in the site museum.	51

17. Stone Buddha images from Pushpavanam, Nagapattinam district. 52
18. 11th century Buddha image from Madagaram now in Thanjavur Art Gallery. 53
19. Bronze image of seated Buddha from Nagapattinam (courtesy Government Museum, Chennai). 57
20. 16th century Lokesvara image from Vellipalayam Nagapattinam district (ht. with pedestal: 105 cms). 58
21. Buddhist bronze of Jambhala and Vasudhara from Nagapattinam now in the Government Museum, Chennai (ht. with pedestal: 9 cms). 59
22. Gopuram of Kayarohanaswami temple at Nagapattinam. 63
23. Kayarohanaswami temple at Nagapattinam, showing earlier sculptures and inscription embedded in the wall. 64
24. Pillars of Kayarohanaswami temple at Nagapattinam. 65
25. Buddhagupta's inscription now in the Indian Museum. 86
26. Xuanzang Memorial at Nalanda. 90
27. Location of coastal Buddhist sites in Odisha. 108
28. Astamahabhaya Tara from Ratnagiri now in the Patna Museum. 116
29. Stucco from Nakorn Pathon showing Supparaka Jataka. 120
30. Map based on the *Periplus Maris Erythraei*. 130
31. Clay bullae made in imitation of Roman coins found in India. 135
32. Map of the island of Socotra. 139
33. Letter from Khalaf b. Isaac to Ben Yiju regarding ship-wrecked goods (after Goitein and Friedman, 2008). 147
34. Indian localities mentioned in the Geniza letters (after Goitein and Friedman, 2008). 148
35. Distribution of sites in Gujarat. 157
36. Map showing find spots of Silahara inscriptions in north Konkan (after Mirashi, 1977). 160
37. The richly sculpted wall of Rani ki Vav, Patan. 164
38. Potsherd from Alagankulam on the Tamil coast with ship symbol. 187
39. Frontispiece to James Rennell's *Memoir of a Map of Hindoostan*. 200
40. Map of Indian Ocean 'World' marking UNESCO's World Heritage Sites. 210

1

INTRODUCTION

Introduction

The history of India's ancient past written in the post-Independence period has been studied largely through the perspective of agrarian expansion and the caste structure, the latter often seen as inhibiting travel across the ocean. In this book, however, the focus is on the relationship between the sea and the land, which underlines the centrality of the coast; the communities who inhabited the space between the ocean and the hinterland; their histories and attempts at constructing their cultural environment. An important component of this cultural landscape is religious architecture and its inter-linkage with travelling groups who moved both across the sea, as well as on routes into the interior. The Indian Ocean is perhaps one of the few regions where this concept can be applied for an understanding of maritime history and archaeology on account of the continued survival of maritime regions (Figure 1). These regions have participated historically in the Indian Ocean network and in several cases are characterised by local traditions of boat building and navigation, architectural features and archaeological sites, as well as narratives of the central experience of trans-locality of maritime communities. Thus it is important to comprehend conceptions of the sea by people who lived along its coasts and traversed it for a variety of reasons.

This book is a part of an ongoing dialogue among scholars and researchers from different disciplines on maritime cultural landscapes as

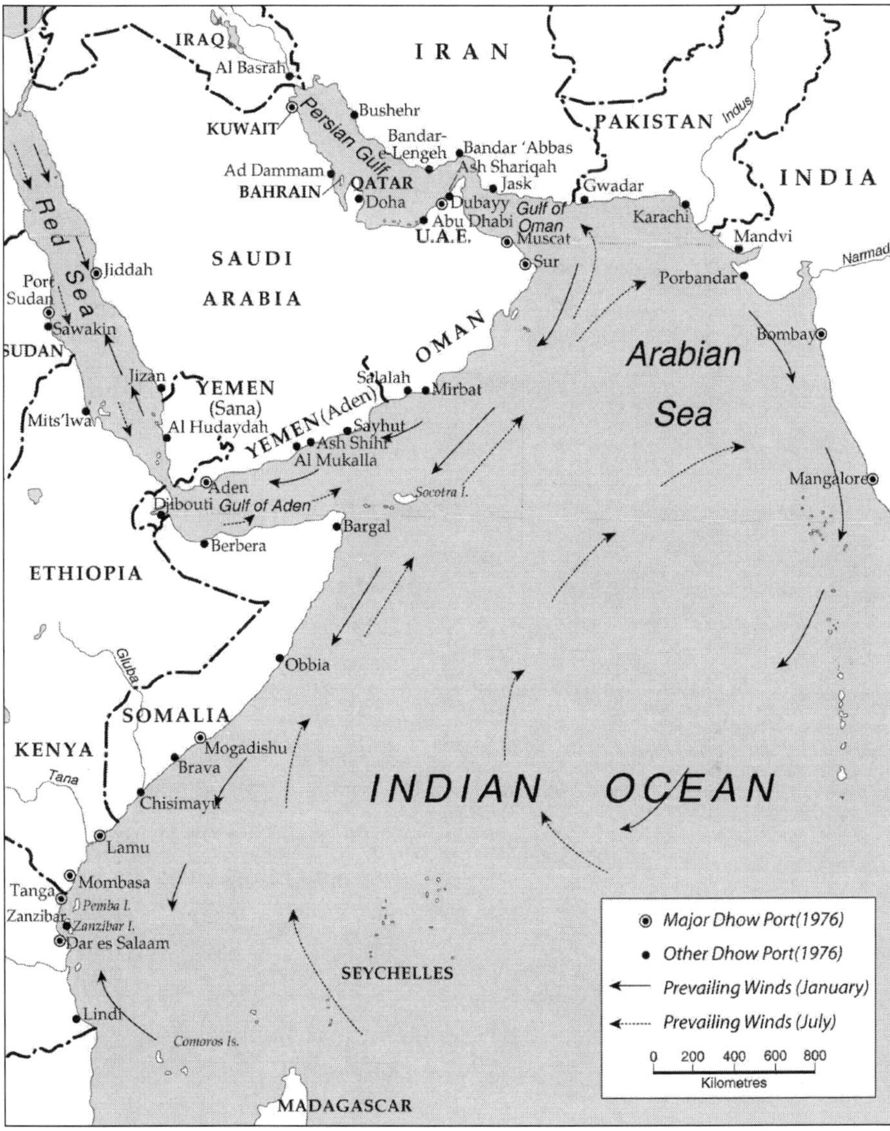

1. Map of Dhow ports on Aden-Mangalore route, 1976.

they evolved across the Indian Ocean both spatially and historically.[1] A common concern that all chapters share is with definitions of maritime spaces; different articulations of social and political power; regional and local nautical traditions; and diverse environmental niches. Thus the study positions itself at two levels: at the macro level it aims to re-connect and re-establish communications between countries of the Indian Ocean world, which would lead to an enhanced understanding of cultural values and concerns; while at the micro level the focus is on understanding national cultures in their regional maritime milieu. This two-fold emphasis is important if issues related to local communities, regional governance and the management of heritage sites are to be included in the discussion.

HISTORIOGRAPHY: MARITIME HISTORY IN THE ANCIENT PERIOD

In their search for the ancient past of the new nation state, historians have tended to marginalize contributions of coastal communities and sailing networks. Three broad trends have influenced historical studies on ancient India: one is the Marxist school, which supports the Indian Feudalism theory.[2] The paradigm opposing the theory of Indian Feudalism emphasizes the centrality of the political structure in initiating change and suggests three discontinuous phases of urbanization around which other economic activities coalesced. These phases have been defined as the Harappan (3rd–2nd millennium BCE), Early Historic (600 BCE to 3rd–4th centuries CE) and Early Medieval (6th–7th to 12th–13th century) periods.[3] Three major historical processes have been postulated for the Early Medieval period within this framework: expansion of state society; assimilation and acculturation of tribal peoples; and integration of local religious cults and practices.

A third model for understanding the development of trade is evident in the writings by André Wink. He argues against the decline of Roman trade, since Greek-Byzantine traders again became active in the India trade from the 4th to 6th centuries.[4] In the 5th–6th centuries Persian commerce synchronized with the ascendancy of the Sasanian Empire, and with the coming of Islam there was an increase in trading networks in the Indian Ocean. André Wink suggests that control of trade was a motivating factor in the Arab conquest of Makran, Sindh, Kathiawar and Kachchh. The period until Arab and Persian settlements along the Indian Ocean littoral and the emergence of an integrated Muslim trading empire marked the 10th century. Furthermore, Buddhism largely disappeared from India in the Early Medieval period, though it continued to flourish in Gujarat until the 9th century. Finally, due to restrictions stipulated in the Law Books or the *Dharmasastras* on maritime travel, the Hindu population turned to "agrarian pursuits and production, away from trade and maritime transport".[5]

A pioneering work on shipping in the Indian subcontinent that is yet to be replaced is Radha Kumud Mookerji's study of 1912 titled *Indian Shipping*. A comprehensive survey of textual and archaeological sources, the work encompasses a time span truly monumental—extending from the Vedic period to the early 20th century. Though the study has been criticized on account of its claim for Hindu Imperialism, its major contribution was to provide a comprehensive compilation of textual references to seafaring, including the use of the Sanskrit work, *Yuktikalpataru*, a treatise on ship-building attributed to King Bhoja and dated to the 11th century. It is significant that in the 11th century, these instructions should have been incorporated in a work on statecraft and attributed to the authorship of a king. In the wider context of South Asian maritime history, it is from the 9th and 10th centuries onwards that there are increasing references in inscriptions to fishing rights; duties levied on commodities brought through the water-routes; and to revenue being obtained from taxes on fishing. This is also a period of expanding maritime networks both in the western Indian Ocean, as also in the Bay of Bengal.

Fishing and sailing communities formed a distinct group and were the crucial components of all sea travel. Fishing was the traditional occupation of coastal groups in several pockets of the Indian Ocean and this is an adaptation that dates to at least the 5th millennium BCE in several areas.[6] These maritime communities are to be distinguished from merchants and traders involved in oceanic trade.[7] Merchants and traders in some cases certainly owned ships and water-craft, but they neither manned nor sailed these. More often, however, goods and cargoes were entrusted to the skipper of the vessel who was then responsible for their sale and profit. The secondary literature on these communities is increasingly expanding and will not be repeated here[8]; instead we would like to shift to the terrain of coastal sites and architecture that linked the hinterland to the sea.

Maritime trade has conventionally been viewed as trade in luxury items, which was controlled by the state and functioned in accordance with the requirements of the ruling elite. In the context of ancient Indian history, the emphasis has been on trading networks, which are accepted as having proliferated during certain historical periods, and declined thereafter, such as Indo-Roman trade in the early centuries CE, Arab trade from the 8th century onwards, Chola trade in the 10th and 11th centuries and so on.[9] No continuity is accepted between the protohistoric Harappan-Mesopotamian contacts and subsequent developments in the Early Historic period.[10] Similarly, the rise of Islam from the 7th–8th centuries onwards is seen to mark the beginning of a new phase of expansion and integration.[11] This is in contrast to raids of the Chola dynasty on Sri Lanka and on south Thailand in the 10th to 12th centuries, which are viewed as a central aspect of Indian kingship.[12] Few monographs devoted to South and Southeast Asian contacts have appeared in recent years.[13]

Implicit in the conventional pattern has been the assumption that maritime trade was sporadic. Similarly contentious is the claim that this trade emerged as a result of the surplus generated by agrarian expansion. Or that the participation of local trading communities of the Indian subcontinent in this network was minimal, especially in the western Indian Ocean, since it was the foreign demand for luxuries that triggered it. In the context of Bengal, for example, the fluvial network not only provided a distinctive environment throughout the early history of Bengal, but it also linked Bengal to the larger Ganga and Brahmaputra valley networks on the one hand and the east coast and Bay of Bengal systems on the other.[14]

The *Periplus Maris Erythraei* perhaps provides the first detailed description of local boats in the Indian Ocean in the early centuries CE and several types extending from the East African coast to the west coast of India are referred to. This text, by an anonymous author compiled during the period of the Roman Empire, was appropriated in the discourse on trade and Empire during the 19th century, a masterly rendition being E.H. Warmington's, *The Commerce between the Roman Empire and India* published in Cambridge in 1928, as also the 1916 study of H.G. Rawlinson titled *Intercourse between India and the Western World from the Earliest Times to the fall of Rome*, published in Cambridge. Unfortunately, this colonial legacy continues to be taken recourse to in the post-colonial period with constant invocations of Indo-Roman trade.[15]

It is becoming increasingly clear that the bulk of the supposed 'Roman' pottery is in fact of indigenous origin. From a study of the distribution pattern of the Red Polished and Rouletted Wares, it is obvious that these ceramics can only be used to demarcate the extent of internal networks, rather than for providing a chronological framework of maritime contacts.[16] Similarly, Roman coin finds in the Indian subcontinent also need to be studied in the wider context of trade in metals and of monetary reform in the Roman Empire. Recent archaeological evidence from south India, especially Tamil Nadu, confirms the existence of an indigenous exchange network in centuries prior to the Common Era that extended along the Kaveri river system and linked the Malabar coast through the Palghat gap to the fertile delta on the east. References in Sangam literature of the early centuries of the Common Era describe the different chiefdoms in the region. Archaeologically, contemporary habitation is indicated by Iron Age Megalithic remains and though correspondence between the two has been far from established, results from the excavations at Kodumanal in Coimbatore district indicate the participation of the site in coastal networks.

Pattanam is at present a land locked rural hamlet located 25 km north of Kochi in Ernakulam district of Kerala and extends over a 45 hectare area. Archaeological excavations since 2007 have revealed the ancient origins of Pattanam, which is said to have been first occupied around 1,000 BCE and continued to be active until the 10th century CE. The major structural remains identified at the site date to the medieval period and include architectural remains of religious architecture and fortification walls.[17] It is within this regional network outlined above that finds of foreign pottery and Roman coins need to be analysed.

There is little evidence of state sponsored trade, though rulers were constantly devising means for taxing and controlling the lucrative business. Trade involved a complex hierarchy of transactions, such as gifts to those in authority, barter and monetary exchanges at the local and regional level. Only commodities required by powerful groups were controlled. It is significant that while archaeological data and distribution networks of ceramics indicate local, regional and oceanic interaction, starting from the 3rd–2nd millennium BCE onwards, inscriptions are largely silent about trading activities until well into the 5th and 6th centuries CE, when trade becomes profitable enough to be taxed. From this period onwards inscriptions reflect an increasing complexity in commodities traded and in the nature of transactions conducted.[18]

Dionisius Agius shows that with the spread of Islam, Arabic was enriched by borrowings from Aramaic, Persian, Greek, Sanskrit and other Indian languages. He also cautions against equating religious with ethnic identity as Arabic sources do not make this distinction and label as Muslim all non-Arab foreigners who converted to Islam, irrespective of their ethnic background.[19] There are nevertheless exceptions. For example, the historian and geographer al-Mas'udi (d. 345/956–7) writing in the 10th century states that the Sirafis and Omanis were the leading seafarers of the time, thereby highlighting regional coastal identities.

The Tang Annals (618–907) from China, on the other hand, make a distinction between Persian and Arab traders, the former termed Po-ssu and the latter Ta-chi or To-che, and do not refer to religious affiliations. In contrast, 13th–14th century writers such as Ibn Jubayr (d. 614/1217) and Ibn Battuta (d. 770/1368–9 or 779/1377) apply the name Muslim in a religious context to distinguish communities from others which were not Islamic, such as Christians, Jews, Hindus and Zoroastrians.[20] This is an important issue which has implications not only for the terms used to label medieval trade and the religious or ethnic identities attributed to the seafarers, but more significantly to comprehend emerging religious identities in the Indian Ocean region and the ways in which these were formulated.

Scholars such as Haraprasad Ray[21] and Tansen Sen[22] have studied commercial exchanges between India and China on the basis of references in Chinese literature. They have suggested direct links between the two countries and bilateral relations, as also the fact that these exchanges had a tremendous impact on intermediary states. In place of earlier Buddhist networking, the Tang and Song governments took greater interest in commercial rather than religious exchanges with the regions to China's south and trade networks proliferated. Recent writings, especially by Kenneth Hall, have however, questioned the notion of bilateral Indo-China trade in which "Southeast Asian societies are portrayed as bystanders, contented agriculturalists who were members of communal agricultural and tribal societies, who were hosts and/or marginal participants in the international trade."[23] Hall underscores the participatory nature of Indian Ocean networks in the ancient period and their reliance on economic and cultural dialogue rather than hegemony and dominance.

OUTLINE OF THE BOOK

As stated in the revised Preface to *Tradition and Archaeology*, archaeological research has pushed back the reliance on fishing as a subsistence strategy to very early beginnings. Archaeological excavations conducted at sites on the south-western headlands of Ra's al-Hamra, a promontory situated 13 kilometres east of Muscat along the Oman coast, indicate the existence of this adaptation to a marine environment as early as the 4th millennium BCE. At the other end of the Indian Ocean, Khok Phanom Di, a site on the Bang Pakong River in central Thailand was occupied between 2000 and 1500 BCE.[24] The coastal site contains a cemetery, and evidence of fishing, shell-harvesting, and shell-jewellery production, with some evidence of rice cultivation including possible farming tools out of shell. What role did such small-scale fishing communities play in the history of the Indian Ocean?

The beginnings of exchange and trade contacts across the Bay of Bengal are dated to around 1000 BCE, while in the western Indian Ocean these date to the 3rd–2nd millennium BCE. Ceramics, beads and plant remains that traversed the sea lanes have been identified and discussed in secondary writings. In spite of the increase in data-base, there have been few changes in the framework within which maritime activity is studied, especially in the pre-14th century period. The focus continues to be on exchange and trade, ports and on luxury goods, with little discussion on the making of maritime landscapes; utilization of seascapes; partnerships between different trading groups; legal structures; and the role of religious centres that dot the coastline. It is these issues that will be discussed in the following chapters in the period from the 4th century BCE to the 14th century CE.

The first issue that the book addresses relates to the conceptualization of maritime space by kings and royalty as evident from inscriptions. The fact that in the early centuries of the Common Era, many of these inscriptions were located within Buddhist monasteries provides insights into the close relationship between the kings and the Buddhist Sangha. Another indicator of the visual topography of the ocean is provided by coastal architecture, such as forts and *viragals* or memorial stones set up for those who died in sea battles. Contestation also took the form of attacks on coastal centres, especially in Gujarat, as is evident from the data from Vallabhi, the prosperous trade centre and capital city at the head of the Gulf of Khambat. Chapters II and III discuss the complex relationship between kings, merchant guilds, warriors often associated with these and religious shrines with reference to control over maritime routes and enclaves. The site of Nagapattinam on the Tamil coast is examined with reference to the naval expedition said to have been conducted across the seas by the Imperial Cholas who ruled from the 9th to 13th centuries CE. The focus on Nagapattinam, a coastal town on the Tamil coast, as a case study stresses the intertwined spaces of politics, trade and culture in the ancient world.

In order to highlight the deep engagement that communities living along the coasts had with the sea and to emphasize the cultural milieu which promoted trans-oceanic travel, the fourth chapter titled the Indian Ocean Network: an Overview, presents a brief survey of textual accounts in Sanskrit, Tamil and Arabic relating to travel across the Ocean, as also inscriptions from Southeast Asia relating to networks across the Bay of Bengal. The last two sections of the chapter deal with evidence for contacts with China as indicated by finds of Chinese ceramics at coastal sites and transformations in the 13th century. The next chapter provides an overview of religious architecture along the coasts, as also religious pilgrimage to many of these. The focus shifts to understanding dangers at sea and representations of a saviour from ship-wreck.

The attempt in the first five chapters is to stress the deep and complex engagement of communities with the waters of the Indian Ocean, but travel for trade and economic gain cannot be excluded from this, as discussed in the sixth and seventh chapters, where the focus is on coastal centres and ports, as also on trading partners. While Chapter 6 highlights events in the Arabian Sea, Chapter 7 shifts the discussion from the Ocean to the region of Gujarat and the Konkan coast. Two issues remain: one, relates to the mode of transportation across the seas; and the second records transformations within the maritime network, especially the irreversible changes that have taken place over the last three to four hundred years. Chapter 8 provides evidence for shipping and draws on developments in the 18th and 19th century to discuss change and transformation in the Indian Ocean as a result of colonial intervention.

The final chapter highlights the need to move beyond national histories; and to document and preserve maritime heritage for posterity.

NOTES AND REFERENCES

1. In the 1950s, the Swedish maritime ethnologist Olof Hasslof introduced the term *sjobruk* or maritime cultural landscape signifying demarcation and utilisation of maritime space by communities for settlement, fishing, shipping, pilotage, etc. C. Westerdahl, The Maritime Cultural Landscape, *International Journal of Nautical Archaeology*, 21, 1, 1992: 5.
2. This credits the introduction of iron around 1000 BCE with expansion of agriculture and production of a 'surplus' in the middle Ganga valley. This surplus was then invested in trading ventures, which emerged around the middle of the 1st millennium BCE. Trade with the Roman Empire led to the development of urban centres in the early centuries of the Common Era, but with the decline of the Roman Empire and consequently its trade with India, these towns and cities were abandoned. A period of agrarian expansion and self-sufficient village economy followed, lasting until 1000 CE when foreign trade revived under the Arabs. R.S. Sharma, *Indian Feudalism c. AD 300 – 1200*, New Delhi: Macmillan, 1965.
3. B.D. Chattopadhyaya, *The Making of Early Medieval India*, New Delhi: Oxford University Press, 1994, p. 167. The period between the 6th-7th and 12th-13th centuries showed developments vastly different from the society of the earlier period. "State formation was a crucial agent of change in this respect, in the sense that it brought a measure of cohesion among local elements of culture by providing them a focus" (p. 35). While urban centres were characterized as centres of political power, surrounded by large agricultural hinterlands and located along trade routes in the Early Historic period, the character of these urban centres changed in the early medieval period into "nodal points in local exchange networks". Chattopadhyaya, *Early Medieval India*, p. 181.
4. A. Wink, *Al-Hind: The Making of an Indo-Islamic World*, New Delhi: Oxford University Press, 1990, pp. 45-64.
5. Ibid., p. 72.
6. Himanshu Prabha Ray, *The Archaeology of Seafaring in Ancient South Asia*, Cambridge World Archaeology Series, Cambridge University Press, 2003, chapter II.

7. This is an argument that figures in several papers in Himanshu Prabha Ray and Jean-François Salles (eds.), *Tradition and Archaeology*: *Early Maritime Contacts in the Indian Ocean*, New Delhi: ISEAS Publishing & Manohar Publishers, 1996; reissued 2012.
8. Kenneth McPherson, Maritime Communities: An Overview, in Himanshu Prabha Ray and E.A. Alpers (eds.), *Cross Currents and Community Networks: The History of the Indian Ocean World*, New Delhi: Oxford University Press, 2007, chapter II, pp. 34-49. Himanshu Prabha Ray, Shipping in the Indian Ocean: An Overview, in David Parkin and Ruth Barnes (eds.), *Ships and the Development of Maritime Technology in the Indian Ocean*, London: Routledge and Curzon, 2002, pp. 1-27.
9. Ranabir Chakravarti edited, *Trade in Early India*, New Delhi: Oxford University Press, 2001. Ranabir Chakravarti, *Trade and Traders in Early Indian Society*, New Delhi: Manohar, 2002. R. Champakalakshmi, *Trade, Ideology and Urbanization: South India 300 BC to AD 1300*, New Delhi: Oxford University Press, 1996, chapter 3. B.D. Chattopadhyaya, *The Making of Early Medieval India*, New Delhi: Oxford University Press, 1994, chapter 6.
10. S. Ratnagar, *Encounters: The Westerly Trade of the Harappa Civilization*, New Delhi: Oxford University Press, 1981. S. Ratnagar, *The End of the Great Harappan Tradition*, New Delhi: Manohar, 2000. Also see for a counter-position, Dilip K. Chakrabarti, *The External Trade of the Indus Civilization*, New Delhi: Munshiram Manoharlal, 1990.
11. V.K. Jain, *Trade and Traders in Western India*, New Delhi: Munshiram Manoharlal, 1990, chapter 4.
12. G.W. Spencer, The Politics of Plunder: The Cholas in Eleventh Century Ceylon, *Journal of Asian Studies*, 1976, 35: 403-19.
13. J.G. De Casparis, *India and Maritime Southeast Asia: A Lasting Relationship*, Third Sri Lanka Endowment Fund Lecture, 1983. D. Devahuti, *India and Ancient Malaya*, Singapore: Eastern Universities Press, 1965. Himanshu Prabha Ray, *The Winds of Change: Buddhism and the Maritime Links of Early South Asia*, New Delhi: Oxford University Press, 1994/2000. I.C. Glover and P. Bellwood, *Southeast Asia: From Prehistory to History*, London – New York: Routledge Curzon, 2004. K.R. Hall, *Maritime Trade and State Development in Early Southeast Asia*, Honolulu: University of Hawaii Press, 1985. H. Kulke, *Kings and Cults: State Formation and Legitimation in India and Southeast Asia*, New Delhi: Manohar Publishers, 1993. Hermann Kulke, K. Kesavapany and Vijay

Sakhuja (eds.), *Nagapattinam to Suvarnadwipa: Reflections on the Chola Naval Expeditions*, Singapore: Institute of Southeast Asian Studies, 2009. Satish Chandra and Himanshu Prabha Ray (eds.), *The Sea, Identity and History: From the Bay of Bengal to the South China Sea*, New Delhi: Manohar Publishers, 2013. Himanshu Prabha Ray, Multi-religious Maritime Linkages across the Bay of Bengal, in Nicolas Revire and Stephen Murphy (eds.), *Before Siam: Essays in Art and Archaeology*, Bangkok: River Books & The Siam Society, 2014, pp. 132-51.

14. Himanshu Prabha Ray, The Archaeology of Bengal: Trading Networks, Cultural Identities, *Journal of the Economic and Social History of the Orient*, Volume 49, Number 1, 2006, pp. 68-95.
15. Roberta Tomber, *Indo-Roman Trade: From Pots to Pepper*, London: Duckworth, 2008.
16. Himanshu Prabha Ray, *The Archaeology of Seafaring in Ancient South Asia*, Cambridge World Archaeology Series, Cambridge University Press, 2003.
17. P.J. Cherian, Pattanam Excavations and Explorations 2007 & 2008: An Overview, in Stefano Campana, Maurizio Forte and Claudia Liuzza (eds.), *Space, Time and Place*, Oxford: BAR International Series 2118, 2010, pp. 269-74.
18. V.K. Jain, *Trade and Traders in Western India*, New Delhi: Munshiram Manoharlal, 1990, p. 56.
19. Dionisius A. Agius, *Classic Ships of Islam: From Mesopotamia to the Indian Ocean*, London – Boston: Brill, 2008, pp. 10-11.
20. Ibid., pp. 11-12.
21. Haraprasad Ray, *Trade and Diplomacy in India-China Relationship: A Study of Bengal during the Fifteenth Century*, New Delhi: Radiant Publishers, 1993.
22. Tansen Sen, *Buddhism, Diplomacy and Trade: The Realignment of Sino-Indian Relations 600-1400*, New Delhi: Manohar, 2004.
23. Kenneth R. Hall, Local and International Trade and Traders in the Straits of Melaka Region 600-1500, *JESHO*, Volume 47, 2, 2004, pp. 213-60.
24. Himanshu Prabha Ray and Jean-François Salles (eds.), *Tradition and Archaeology: Early Maritime Contacts in the Indian Ocean*, New Delhi: ISEAS Publishing & Manohar Publishers.

2

ROYAL POWER

Conceptualization of Maritime Space

Royal Power: Conceptualization of Maritime Space

Traditionally the Indian coasts have been portrayed as inhospitable regions in historical writing, lacking natural harbours and afflicted with a shallow continental shelf and turbulent swells of waves. Did this deter travel across the ocean and attempts to control the waters? Based primarily on architectural and archaeological evidence and inscriptions, this chapter presents an overview of conceptualization of maritime space by royalty in the period from 2nd century BCE to 14th century CE. An analysis of the textual accounts of traditional sailing together with the ethnographic data establishes that the same watercraft was used for multiple purposes—including cargo carrying, carrying of passengers, and taking on protective roles in times of attack. Two issues are highlighted in this chapter: one the attempted control of the seas that is found in royal inscriptions from the beginning of the Common Era onwards, as also references to sea battles in the period prior to 14th century CE; and the second relates to the location of forts, especially from the 9th century onwards. As mentioned in the previous chapter, the attempt is to incorporate the intertwined strands of politics, culture and economy in an understanding of the maritime history of early India.

THE OCEAN AS CONTESTED SPACE

Two names are used for the Indian subcontinent in early sources: the 4th century BCE Minor Rock Edict I of Asoka at Brahmagiri and elsewhere refers to Jambudvipa or 'island of the rose-apple tree' and the same term occurs in the *Mahabharata*;[1] and *Bharatam varsam*[2] or *Bharadhavasa*, which occurs in the Hathigumpha inscription of Kharavela from Bhubaneshwar in Odisha dated to the 2nd century BCE.[3] The Minor Rock Edicts of Asoka describe the king's noble deeds through which the people of Jambudvipa were united with the world of the *devatas* or gods. The conceptualization of the Indian subcontinent as an island continues to occur in later centuries. A 1st century CE inscription on a limestone slab found in a vihara at the Buddhist site of Phanigiri in Nalgonda district reads '*Jambudvipa mile vagu*'.[4]

By the 2nd–1st century BCE, royal inscriptions initiate the practice of defining territory under control of the king and the Buddhist caves in the hills at Nasik, on the river Godavari, are especially significant in this regard. The caves are locally known as Pandulena and are situated 8 kilometres west of Nasik town about 60 to 70 metres up the hill on a rock scarp (Figures 2-4). The monastic establishment had one *cetiyaghara* (cave 18), eighteen *lenas* or caves, including three unfinished ones, one *matapa* or hall and three cisterns, though more water cisterns are also known from the vicinity of the hill.[5] The twenty-six inscriptions from the caves are significant not only for an understanding of the chronology of the Satavahana and Kshatrapa rulers of the region, but for the relationship between royalty and Buddhist monastic centres. The earliest record of the ruler Kanha of the Satavahana-*kula* is inscribed on the upper part of the right window of vihara 19 at Nasik.[6] The vihara appears to be the earliest excavation at the site that came into existence because of the generosity of the king.

On the back wall of the veranda in cave 3 above the entrance is the record of Balasiri, mother of Gotamīputa Siri Satakani. While recording the gift of a cave to the Buddhist Sangha, the record also contains a

2. Caves at Nasik with royal inscriptions.

eulogy of her son Gotamiputa whose honorific titles indicate his sovereignty over a vast territory stretching until the three oceans (line 3 – *savarajaloka-madala-patigahita-sasana... ti-samuda-toya-pitavahana*). The king is described as a unique brahmana, equal in prowess to the Epic heroes Rama, Kesava, Arjuna and Bhima.[7] Thus the inscription is valuable as the earliest evidence of royal control of the oceans, but what is intriguing is its location in a Buddhist *vihara* and the inclusion of epic heroes as role models for the king. No doubt cave 3 was an unusual setting for the Queen's inscription.[8] It consists of a large hall with eighteen cells around it, five to the left, six at the back and seven to the right. There are two additional cells in the veranda in front. A beautiful relief of a stupa was cut in the back wall of the hall between doorways to the third and fourth cell. There are three additional royal inscriptions engraved in the veranda.

This wealth of inscriptional data undoubtedly accords a special place to the Buddhist monastic centre at Nasik and to Satavahana claim for

3. Façade of cave 3 at Nasik.

control of the three oceans. How is this royal power of control over the oceans represented in sculpture? No depictions are to be found at Nasik; instead the Simhala vijaya narrative and its somewhat later 5th century representation at Ajanta cave 17, a cave "fit for the king" elaborate this concept of conquest across the Ocean. Along with caves 2 and 26, the epigraph in cave 17 celebrates the cave's patron, his genealogy and social position. In his inscription in the cave, a local ruler, Upendragupta, admits to having expended enormous wealth to adorn the earth with stupas and viharas. Not all inscriptions, however, commemorate royal power and authority. Inscription 3 in cave 2 states that wherever a holy man of outstanding character chooses to settle, the place becomes an object of pilgrimage.[9] It is these two aspects of Buddhist sites that are important to this Chapter.

Walter Spink suggests that the depiction at Ajanta follows the *Divyavadana* version of the narrative Simhala vijaya,[10] though various versions are to be found in the Theravada Pali Valahassa Jataka,[11] the *Karandavyuha sutra* and the Lokottara Mahasanghika *Mahavastu* where Gautama identifies himself as the winged horse.[12] In one of his previous births, Sakyamuni Gautama was born as Simhala, a merchant who led five hundred others on a seagoing venture to Tamradvipa or Sri Lanka. They were ship-wrecked, but eventually saved from the man-eating ogresses by the horse Balaha, who rose majestically into the sky with Simhala on his back. The ogresses, however, followed him back to his kingdom. Simhala once again rose to the occasion and saved the kingdom from being devoured by them. Simhala was crowned king and Tamradvipa was renamed Simhaladvipa.[13]

The story of Simhala can be read at different levels: at one level, it is about the defeat of evil worldly forces by dharma and "articulates the Mahayana notion that in order to reach the further shore of nirvana, one must rely upon the *sambhogakaya* power of a saving bodhisattva", while at another it refers to physical dangers such as those encountered by the 5th century Chinese pilgrim Faxian off the coast of Sri Lanka, who saved himself by calling upon Avalokitesvara.[14] Simhala vijaya takes on a political character in the *Mahavamsa*, which records that Sri Lanka was uninhabited by humans until it was colonized by Vijaya and his followers in the middle of the 1st millennium BCE.[15] Composed by bhikkhus in the 4th–5th century CE, the *Mahavamsa* was probably

4. Back wall of cave 3 at Nasik.

5. Valahassa Jataka from Mathura, showing merchants confined to a tower.

6. Valahassa Jataka from Mathura, depicting the white horse as saviour.

compiled from earlier sources and chronicles the island's past from its colonization by Prince Vijaya in the 4th or 5th century BCE to the reign of Mahasena (r. 274–301 CE).[16]

The winged horse as saviour is sculpted on a 2nd–3rd century railing pillar recovered from Bhuteshwar mound in Mathura, which shows a standing female figure on the back of a dwarf and on the backside is sculpted the Valahassa Jataka in three compartments (Figures 5-6).[17] Outside the subcontinent, the Valahassa Jataka found popularity in the Buddhist world and it was painted in the caves in Kizil, as also on scrolls in Japan. Representations also occur in the Anand temple at Pagan and in Tibet.[18] Representations of sea travel from Neak Pean in Angkor (Figure 7) may be relevant for this paper. Neak Pean is a small island temple located in the middle of the last baray (the Preah Khan Baray or Jayatataka) constructed by a Khmer king in the Angkor area. The temple is faced by a much damaged sculpture of the horse, Balaha, saving drowning sailors.

The 1st century Greek text *Periplus Maris Erythraei* (sec.44) nevertheless contains references to the conflict between the Satavahanas and the Kshatrapas and the ruling dynasty's attempts at control of incoming traffic at coastal centres. It mentions "...local fishermen in the king's service [who] come out with crews of long ships, the kind called *trappaga* and

7. Valahassa Jataka at Neak Pean.

kotymba, to the entrance as far as Syrastrene [Saurashtra] to meet vessels and guide them up to Barygaza [Bharuch or Broach at the mouth of the river Narmada]."

The practice of claiming control of the seas is a practice that continued into later periods, the only difference being that the inscriptions were now written on copper-plates or stone slabs, rather than being located within religious architecture. Thus, while describing the history of the early Chalukyas, the 7th century inscription refers to king Mangalisa, whose army was powerful enough to invade all islands and who crossed the ocean by bridges of boats and effected the plundering of the island of Revati.[19] Or the following verse in praise of the 11th century Western Chalukyan ruler Tribhuvanamalla:

> May the king Tribhuvanamalla, by the ocean of whose spotless fame the world is encircled, render subject to his control the bride, which is the earth girt about as if by a zone, with the ocean, which is marked with sea-monsters, both male and female resembling elephants.[20]

Of interest to this chapter is the rule of the Kadambas of Goa. The original kingdom of the Kadambas of Goa was the country to the south of the island of Goa including a part of Salsette and perhaps a strip of land extending towards the Western Ghats. The earliest chieftain of the Goa Kadambas was Kantakacharya as mentioned in the Marcella plates who is described as one "whose fame went beyond the seven seas." The record compares him to the epic hero Arjuna and extols his powers that surpassed those of Indra. He was an ally of kings reigning in countries extending to the sea – the kings referred to being the Silaharas who ruled further north on the Konkan.[21]

The Silahara kings who ruled over the region around the present city of Mumbai from 810 to 1240 regularly referred to themselves as lord of the western ocean and rulers of the Konkan region and prided themselves on defeating the attacking mlecchas and yavanas.[22] Inscriptions from north Konkan dating to the reign of the Silahara ruler Aparadityadeva in the 12th century graphically portray an active engagement with the sea. In the Panhale plates, Aparadityadeva is described as having bathed in the western ocean at the holy place of Marut on the occasion of a lunar eclipse and gifted the village Khairadi with orchards of areca-nut trees and all royal privileges to a learned brahmana.[23] The Thana Stone Inscription of Aparaditya II refers to him as having bathed in the excellent tirtha of the great sea, donated a share of four drammas out of the proceeds of an orchard in Sthanakiya-pattana and in addition twenty-four drammas out of the produce of the whole rice-field for the worship of the divine Somanathadeva in Saurashtra.[24]

To what extent did attempts to enforce political authority lead to conflict across the Ocean? A response to this issue is evident from an examination of *viragals* or hero stones found in Maharashtra and Karnataka on the west coast of India. These were raised in memory of those who lost their lives in sea-battles and are dated from 12th to 15th century CE. Three of the hero stones are known from Eksar, Borivili near Mumbai and show "well ordered lines of vessels crowded with warriors

8. Memorial stone from Goa Museum.

armed with bows and spears, propelled by banks of oars."[25] Though the stones carry inscriptions these are now illegible.

Four more hero stones are housed in the Archaeological Museum of Goa. These are dated from 10th to 14th century and depict double-ended vessels propelled by oars, very similar to those known from the region at present. The ships are crowded with soldiers armed with bows and engaged in fights (Figures 8-9).

Writing in the 17th and 18th centuries, Capt. Alex Hamilton referred to the 'lair of the Vagher pirates of Okhamandel', who 'admit no trade but practice piracy ... they being confident in their numbers, strive to board all ships they can come at by sailing' (1727). During a visit to Kathiawar in Gujarat, James Hornell described the memorial set up by the Vaghers, a lawless and turbulent tribe:

9. Memorial stone from Goa Museum.

By far the most interesting of the memorial stones set up to bygone heroes in Kathiawar is one of a small group outside the walled town of Aramra, once of much importance as the last halting place of Hindu pilgrims on their way to the holy shrine of Krishna across the channel of the Beyt Island. On this stone, instead of the conventional horseman there is carved in strong relief, the representation of a square-rigged vessel, evidently of considerable tonnage and well-armed, for a row of rectangular gun-ports are conspicuously shown, extending from stem to stern along the side.

The vessel has all the distinguishing characteristics of an East Indiaman of the latter half of the 17th century. On enquiring from the headman what is the significance of this sculpted ship, so unlike any ordinary type of Indian sea-craft, he summoned a villager of the boat-building caste, people who serve also as seamen on coasting vessels. The villager stated that the hero commemorated was a pirate of great renown in his day, the captain of a great pirate ship manned by kinsmen of the Vagher tribe; he met his death during an attack upon a large European ship. Whether the foreign

> ship was taken or the attack beaten off he could not say; he maintained, however, that the ship represented was the identical one commanded by his ancestor.[26]

The Gujarat coast was prone to attack from the sea. The first Arab raids on Thana and Bharuch were launched in the 7th century from Bahrain. The Kavi plate of Jayabhata IV dated 736 CE eulogises the ruler as one who vanquished the Tajikas or Arabs who greatly oppressed all the people in the city of the lord of Vallabhi.[27] Though these proved to be unsuccessful, later attacks on Vallabhi in the 8th century destroyed the town. As the Persian Muslim scholar Alberuni (973–1048 CE) wrote in the 11th century: "So he [lord of al Mansura] made a night-attack upon the king Vallabha, and killed him and his people, and destroyed his town. People say that still in our time there are such traces left in that country as are found in places which were destroyed by an unexpected night attack."[28]

It is suggested that attacks on Vallabhi resulted in the shifting of the coastal centre to Cambay or Stambhatirtha at the head of the Gulf of Khambat, as it was considered safe from attacks.[29]

There are several references in inscriptions from the west coast to the local polity such as that of the Kadambas of Goa who ruled from 10th to 14th century being involved in sea-battles. The ruling family had marital relations with the Silaharas further north. The inscriptions speak of king Guhalla Deva of the Goa Kadambas undertaking a pilgrimage to Somnath in Saurashtra, but hardly had he reached halfway, when the mast of his ship broke and he was forced to take shelter with a ruler friendly to him. This was the port of Goa where a rich Muslim merchant by the name of Madumod of Taji origin and the wealthiest of all the seafaring traders, came to the help of the king. In return the king gave him much wealth. This record tells us for the first time of Arab traders settled on the Goa coast in 11th century CE.[30]

Clearly then, maritime space formed an integral part of political thinking and conceptualization of the inhabited world—a world that was certainly claimed, but not always controlled. At the same time regional kingdoms had to fend off attacks by sea and we have referred to shifts in political capitals in Gujarat on account of attacks by sea. This is an issue that is discussed at length in the next section, which focuses on the city of Vallabhi located at the head of the Gulf of Khambat. Vallabhi was also the capital of the ruling dynasty of the Maitrakas (493–776 CE) and the core area for religious consolidation. Bhattaraka is mentioned as the founder of the Maitraka dynasty in inscriptions, though none of his own records are known. He is credited with the acquisition of royal power (*rajyasri*) through the strength of his hereditary servants, friends and guilds (*maula-bhrta-mitra-sreni*). The phrase used in the inscriptions is borrowed from the *Arthasastra* (*maula-bhrta-sreni-mitramitra-atavibala* 9.2.1) and is an indication of armed soldiers maintained by trading groups.[31] This association of trade networks, armed soldiers maintained by merchant groups and guilds and legitimization of political authority through religious consolidation by the Maitrakas is described in detail in the next section.

THE EMERGENCE OF VALLABHI: CAPITAL, PORT TOWN & RELIGIOUS CENTRE

The history of hostilities and invasions in western India mentioned above goes back to an earlier period. In the 5th century CE, the Junagarh inscription refers to hostile invasions during the early years of Skandagupta's reign, but these were finally repulsed.[32] Under the early Maitraka rulers, the capital was shifted from Junagarh or Girinagara to Vallabhi and the records of the early Maitraka rulers such as Dronasimha and Dhruvasena I were issued from Vallabhi, e.g. the Bhamodra Mohota plate of Dronasinha (year 183 or 502 CE).[33] The list of administrative personnel of the Maitrakas is fairly large[34] and an important source of state revenue was *sulka* or tolls and the person in-charge of collection is referred to as *sulkika*.[35]

Contemporary Sanskrit literature such as the *Dasakumaracaritam* by Dandin describes Vallabhi as a prosperous trading centre.[36] References to its wealthy resident and travelling communities of traders (*vaniggrama*) are found in the copper plate donations from Toramana's reign dating to the late 5th–early 6th centuries CE.[37] The self-assurance of its trading community is evident from the charter of Visnusena of 592 CE, which reiterates the customary practices followed by the group and the acceptance of these by the ruler. This consolidation of economic activity along with expansion of political authority and increasing involvement of brahmanas and Buddhist viharas in agrarian intensification marks a departure from the trading patterns of earlier periods.

Three copper plates dated in the reign of the Huna Toramana (5th–6th centuries CE) record gifts made to the temple of Jayaswami or Narayana belonging to the queen mother by the trading community of Vadrapalli. Maharaja Bhuta and Maharaja Matrdas also made donations of certain villages to the temple. The main commodities referred to in the plates are molasses, salt, cotton and grain and a detailed list of revenues transferred is also enumerated. These revenues were calculated on the basis of vessel load, donkey load and cart load of the produce. Vadrapalli was probably located 8 kilometres to the west of Sanjeli and signatories to the donation included traders from Ujjain, Kannauj, Mathura and perhaps Mandasor. A goldsmith constructed a lake near the temple.[38]

Of interest to this discussion is the charter of Visnusena dated to 592 CE, issued from Lohata in the Kathiawar region. This charter is addressed to a list of officials as is usual in Maitraka records. The charter assures protection to the community of merchants (*vaniggrama*) established in the region and endorses their continued functioning.[39] It provides a detailed list of seventy-two trade regulations or customary laws to be followed. Some of the regulations are of great interest to this discussion. For example, it is specified that merchants staying away for a year were not required to pay an entrance fee on their return. Other clauses specify duties that were to be paid. A boat full of containers (*bhanda-bhrta-*

vahitrasya) was charged 12 silver coins, but if the containers were for religious purposes, they were charged only one and a quarter silver coin. In the case of a boat carrying paddy it was half this amount. Other items which were frequently transported by boat included dried ginger sticks, bamboo, wine, leather, buffaloes, camels and bulls.[40]

Indigo or *nila* is mentioned as one of the items exported from areas such as Gujarat and the charter of Visnusena mentions a tax on the pressing of the indigo dye. Indigo figures as one of the items of trade from India westward to Egypt handled by the business house of Ibn 'Awkal in the period from 980 to 1030 CE.[41] One of the three varieties mentioned includes Sindani indigo – Sindan/Sandan being identified with the Konkan coast of the subcontinent.

The variety of taxable objects mentioned in the inscription is an indication of the diverse nature of trade in the region. These included oil mills, sugarcane fields, wine, cumin seed, black mustard and coriander. The inscription also refers to a tax on dyers of cloth, weavers, shoemakers and retailers hawking goods on foot. Others such as blacksmiths, carpenters, barbers, potters, etc. could be recruited for forced labour under the supervision of officers.[42] Clearly, the Maitrakas were attempting to widen their resource base. A parallel process that is evident at this time relates to changes in the religious topography of the region – a religious topography that continued to be varied and diverse, with little evidence of assimilation or acculturation within the ideological framework of a State system. On the contrary, the rulers provided patronage for several local cults.

GUJARAT: RELIGIOUS TRANSFORMATION & RITUAL SPACE

Perhaps one of the earliest shrines in Gujarat was excavated at the site of Padri in the Talaja tahsil of Bhavnagar district of Gujarat, hardly 2 kilometres from the Gulf of Khambat and was dedicated to a fertility deity termed *lajja-gauri*.[43] Two terracotta plaques of the fertility goddess *lajja-gauri* were found on the floor of the structure, while a square slate plaque with the image of *lajja-gauri* was found on the surface. Other images included sandstone figures of Ganesa and Visnu.[44] 6th and 7th century *lajja-gauri* figurines have been reported from a number of sites in Gujarat and the worship of the goddess continued into a later period.[45]

Evidence for the worship of another non-Sanskritic local goddess comes from the record of one of the early Maitraka rulers, Dronasinha. He donated a village for providing sandalwood, incense, lamps, oil and garlands to the shrine of the goddess Panduraja, otherwise not known from textual sources. Dronasinha also built a temple to Kottammahika devi within the boundary of Trisangamaka identified with Tarsamia, about 5 kilometres from Bhavnagar and the grant to the goddess was resumed by Dhruvasena II (639–40 CE).[46]

The sectarian affiliation of the Maitrakas is evident in the 6th century, when Dhruvasena I (519–549) refers to his predecessors as worshippers of Siva (*parama-mahesvara*) and himself as worshipper of Visnu (*parama-bhagavata*). These epithets appeared in a grant of land to Buddhist viharas.[47] Thus even here there is no evidence of unambiguous sectarian affiliation of the rulers, nor of grants made to temples with the objective of legitimizing their rule. In most cases donations are made for repair and worship of existing temples, e.g. the copper plate of Siladitya I (599–614). The ruler made a grant of two pieces of land along with a tank (Yamala vapi) for repair of a temple of Siva as well as for worship of the deity. Worship of the deity involved bathing (*snapana*) of the image, application of pounded sandalwood (*gandha*), incense (*dhupa*), flowers (*puspa*), garland (*malya*), lighting of lamps (*dipa*), and performance of music (*gita*) and dance (*nrtya*).[48]

The earliest temple contemporary to the Maitrakas in Saurashtra is the temple of Gop located around 65 kilometres from the coast and dated to the late 6th–early 7th centuries CE (Figure 10). In the next 100 years a large number of temples were constructed mainly along the coastline, but none of these bear any inscriptions or are associated with royalty. A distribution map of the temple sites indicates a clustering of temples at

10. Temple at Gop.

Khimesvara located between the Vartu and Bhadar rivers and a physical disjunction between the coastal religious centres and the political centre at Vallabhi at the head of the Gulf of Khambat (Figure 11).

A distinctive aspect of the temples of western and central India at this time was their dedication to Surya worship. The Bhadreniyaka grant of Siladitya I (circa 610–611) records the donation of two hundred *padavarttas* of land in the village of Bhadreniyaka for worship (*puja*) of the sun god (*Aditya deva*) established in that village. Worship involved bathing of the image, application of sandal paste, flowers, lighting of oil lamps and performance of vocal and instrumental music and dances, cost of sacrifices and offerings (*bali-caru-satra*) and maintenance of servants of the gods.[49]

The Mandasor stone inscription of the time of Kumaragupta I and the Indore copper plate grant of Skandagupta show that sun worship in

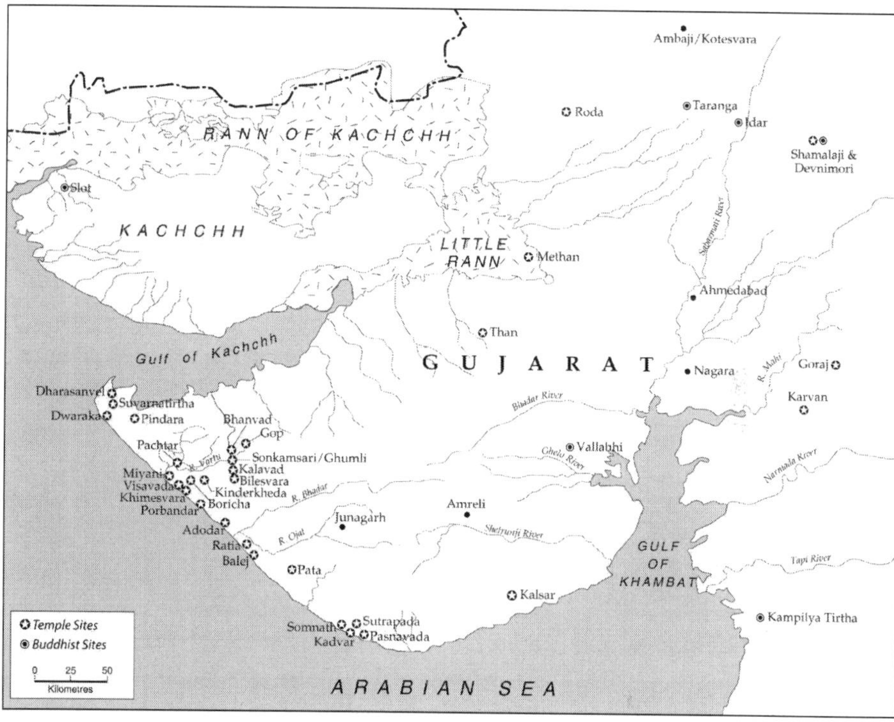

11. Distribution map of Maitraka temples.

central India was patronized by guilds, but similar epigraphic information is not available for temples in Gujarat. The copper plates of Toramana refer to rest houses attached to temples where medicinal diet and therapy was provided to mendicants, to men and women in the service of the deity and to devotees and disciples. This is in addition to the lake referred to above and other grants made to the temple. Archaeological exploration around Sanjeli led to the discovery of a large number of bricks, but no specific structures could be identified.[50] Thus, in addition to being a religious centre, the temple was linked to services provided to the community at large.

The setting up of the lake at Junagarh at the foot of Girnar hills in Gujarat is often quoted as an example of centralized Mauryan control, but what is seldom discussed is the religious landscape around the site

(Figure 12). Though no structures contemporary to the Asokan edicts at Girnar have so far been identified, the earliest remains are of a spacious monastic complex at Intwa on a hill 3 kilometres north of Girnar. An inscribed sealing found in a cell dates the monastery to the reign of Rudrasena I (199–222 CE).[51] The religious monuments at Junagarh include three sets of rock-cut caves: the Khapra Kodia caves (Figure 13); the Baba Pyara caves and the caves at Uperkot. In addition to these, a Visnu temple was established at the site in the Gupta period.

Another extensive site was located 3 kilometres south of the foot of Girnar at Boria amidst thick jungle, while a somewhat later 4th to 6th century CE site was excavated further inland at Devnimori in the Meshvo valley, 120 kilometres east of Ahmedabad. At a distance of about 600 metres to the east of the site was a small mound containing bricks and a small Siva-*linga*, suggesting that it was a Saiva temple.[52]

Though there is no mention of Jainism in the nearly 100 copper plate grants of the Maitraka period, Jain literature describes Vallabhi as a great pilgrimage centre (*tirtha*) and archaeological data provides evidence of earlier shrines. Jain metal and stone images stylistically dated to circa 500–600 CE were found at Akota near Vadodara and from Khedbrahma in north Gujarat. Around the same time Jain rock-cut caves were excavated at Dhank in Saurashtra. Somewhat later in the 8th century, a Jain monastic settlement of Digambara affiliation is known to have existed at Nagasarika or Navsari in southern Gujarat.[53]

As compared to that of the Jains, there is abundant Buddhist presence both archaeologically and in inscriptions, though no structures contemporary to the Asokan edicts have so far been identified. But perhaps the most prolific references to Buddhist monastic establishments occur in the Maitraka inscriptions, which locate these around Vallabhi, though there are no surface indications of any structures at the site.[54] Clay seals with the Buddhist formula "*Ye Dharma Hetu Prabhava*" were, however, found in archaeological excavations at Vallabhi.[55] The inscriptions record among others the names of two merchants Kakka and Ajjita who were

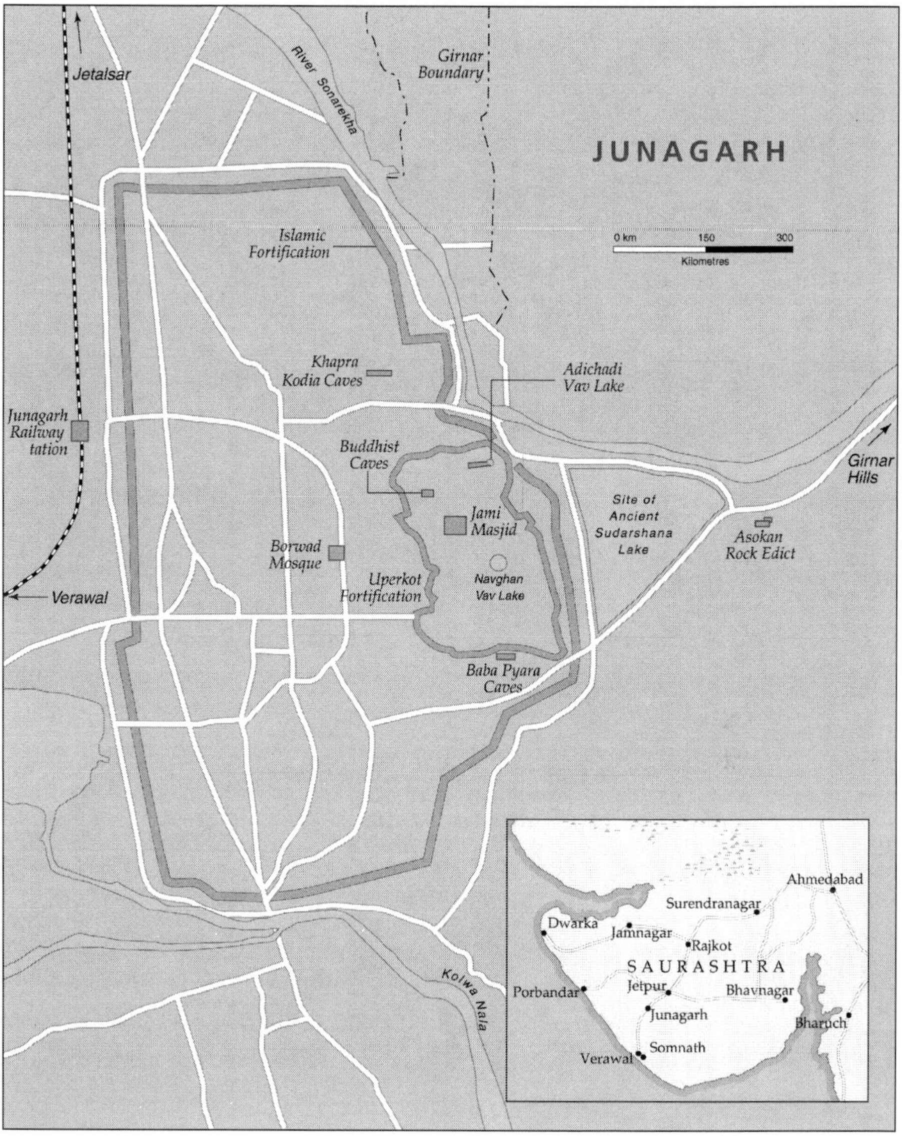

12. Plan of Junagarh.

responsible for the building of two viharas, which were named after them.[56] Reference to fields belonging to Buddhist monks or Sangha occurs in Dhruvasena II's grant.[57]

13. Khapra Kodia cave at Junagarh.

The Vala plates of Dhruvasena I record the grant of the village of Pippalarunkhari and the right to collect its produce to a Buddhist vihara at Vallabhi built by his niece Dudda.[58] Dudda's vihara also received the donation of a village by Guhasena.[59] Dhruvasena I also donated the village Vataprajaka to a vihara at Vallabhi founded by Acarya Bhadanta Buddhadasa.[60] Three copper plates of Dantivarman of the Gujarat branch of the Rastrakuta family dated Saka samvat 789 (latter half of 9th century) refer to the donation of 42 villages after the king had bathed in the river Puravi identified with Purna in the Surat collectorate. These villages were granted to the Buddhist vihara at the sacred pilgrimage centre of Kampilya in the Farukkhabad district in the northwest and were to be enjoyed by a succession of pupils of the Aryasangha. The money was to be used for defraying the worship expenses of perfumes, flowers, frankincense, lamps and ointments and for the repair of the temple.[61] Thus the wealth, ritual and festivities involved in Buddhist worship at this time is abundantly clear.

In contrast to the earlier phase in western India when merchants functioned either in an individual capacity or as a collective, the articulation of lineage identity became important for trading groups from the 8th century onwards. The inscriptions recording their benefactions contain long eulogies or *prasastis*, but very little information on their operations or activities. Another change occurs in the nature of religious affiliation. While the earlier grants invariably record gifts made to Hindu temples, during the 11th–12th centuries patronage to Jain shrines predominates in western India. There is a concomitant recording of detailed family histories of the merchant donors in inscriptions, as well as the writing of biographies.[62] The objective of the *dharmakathas* or religious narratives was the propagation of Jain religious precepts, but the main characters invariably were the merchants, e.g. the *Samaraiccakaha* of Haribhadra Suri and the *Kuvalayamalakaha* of Uddyotana Suri, the latter written in the 8th century CE. Another genre of literature that expands at this time is the legal literature and a good example of this is the *Lekhapaddhati*, an anonymous work, containing model forms of legal and other documents with dates ranging from 755 to 1476. This shift in narrative writing is matched by increased lineage stratification among the Jain preceptors or teachers who exhorted them to a path of righteousness. Several instances of a lineage merging into another and the mobility of the communities further amplify this increasing social complexity.[63] How do these references compare with changes in visual topography along the coasts?

COASTAL FORTS

Forts were important structures that played a major role in the demarcation of space in the Indian Ocean though there are few vestiges that date to the early period. There are nevertheless references in the 1st century CE

Greek text, the *Periplus Maris Erythraei,* to several coastal centres, such as Kalyan, Sopara, Chaul, Bankot, Dabhol, Jaigarh, and Vijayadurg, some of which would no doubt have been fortified.[64] An early site on the west coast was Chandor or Chandrapura on the river Paroda leading to the sea. Archaeological excavations conducted at the site of Chandor (ancient Chandrapura) in South Goa district, have exposed the complete plan of a brick temple complex datable from 4th to 11th century CE (Figure 14). The site was fortified and three phases of fortification have been identified through archaeological work.[65]

One of the characteristic features of maritime trade from the 9th and 10th century onwards was the location of markets in fortified settlements along the Indian Ocean littoral, as also in the interior. Rules governing the payment of taxes and regulating the functioning of the markets were often inscribed on copperplates and provide useful insights into the organization of the trade network. The Quilon or Kollam copperplates of Sthanu Ravi are important in connection with trading rights granted to the Syrian church. A market was located within the precincts of the fortified settlement at the port of Quilon, while the church was situated outside the fortification wall.[66] Similarly, along the Konkan coast, there are references to the fortified market centre of Balipattana. The Kharepatan plates of Rattaraja dated to 1008 CE list out gifts to the temple of Avvesvara built by Rattaraja's father and situated inside the fortifications. In addition the king assigned one gadiyana of gold from every vessel coming from *dvipantara* and a *dharana* of gold from every *vahitra* (ship) coming from Kandalamuliya with the exception of Chemulya (Chaul) and Chandrapura (Chandor). Also, located within the fortifications were settlements of female attendants, oilmen, gardeners, potters, and washermen, as also some land.[67] A record of 1008, containing the earliest epigraphic reference to Balipattana, credits Dhammiraja of the Silahara house of southern Konkan for the foundation of this centre.[68] The inscription in question explicitly mentions the arrival of vessels (*pravahana*) from Candrapura or Chandor (Sindabur of Arab authors, i.e. south of Goa) to Balipattana.

14. Chandor excavations.

While this speaks of the coastal voyages between Balipattana and the area around Goa further south, voyages from the northern sector of Konkan to the same port are mentioned therein as well.[69]

Unfortunately, there is very little that remains of these earlier fortified settlements and a majority of the present forts date from the 13th century onwards, though most of these are at present in a poor state of preservation.[70]

THE TWELFTH TO FOURTEENTH CENTURIES

There were several changes in the second half of the 12th and early 13th century, both in the global context as also along the west coast. The fall of the Abbasid Caliphate in 1258 following attacks by the Mongols adversely affected trade links with India. Ghurid invasions into north India from 1192 to 1206 and the establishment of the Mamluk dynasty in Delhi at the beginning of the 13th century had reverberations for political stability across the Indian subcontinent. Qutbuddin Aibak made the first successful attack on western India in 1197 and mainland Gujarat was annexed to Delhi in 1298.

The 13th century saw a Mongol mission despatched to Quilon and participation of the Malabar coast in maritime networks of the Bay of Bengal. Somewhat later naval fleets were sent by the third Chinese emperor of the Ming dynasty Yong-le (1403–1425) to more than twenty countries in Southeast Asia, as well as to Bengal and the Malabar coast and Aden, popularly known as the voyages of Zheng He. Accounts of these voyages are available in the *Mingshi* (History of the Ming Dynasty), which is considered the most elaborate and complete history of the Ming dynasty.

The Moroccan adventurer Ibn Battuta's account of his travels along the west coast of India in the 14th century provides interesting details for our study and also indicates shifts in coastal centres. After leaving Khambat in Gujarat, Ibn Battuta's four ships made good speed along the Konkan coast bypassing the coastal centres of Chaul, Sandapur or Goa and other busy ports, which lay on little bays or estuaries of rivers flowing from the mountains. The fleet finally put in at Honavar, a town on the north Kanara coast, which was a flourishing centre in the 14th century. Jamal al-Din Muhammad, the ruler of the town, was a Muslim under the vassalage to the Hindu king of the Hoysala kingdom. Ibn Battuta describes him as one of "the best and most powerful rulers" on the coast possessing a fleet of ships and a force of horsemen and infantry so impressive that he could command annual tribute from the ports of Malabar as protection against sea-borne attacks. Further south at Calicut on the Malabar coast, Ibn Battuta saw thirteen Chinese junks wintering. These junks were said to have been built exclusively in the southern Chinese port of Canton, though the owners and big merchants were often Muslims of Indian, Arab or Persian descent.

The kingdom of Vijayanagar (1336–1565) emerged in the aftermath of the expansion of the Delhi Sultanate in the Deccan. The Vijayanagar kings referred to themselves as Lords of the Eastern and Western Oceans and emphasized the importance of maritime trade in their inscriptions.

> A king should improve the harbours of his country and so encourage its commerce that horses, elephants, precious gems, sandalwood, pearls and other articles are freely imported... Make the merchants of distant foreign countries who import elephants and good horses attached to yourself by providing them with villages and decent dwellings in the city, by affording them daily audience, presents allowing decent profits. Then those articles will never go to your enemies.[71]

There is, however, little evidence to suggest that the Vijayanagar kings controlled centres on the Kanara coast, which had traditionally been in the hands of local chiefs, such as the Jain chiefs of Bhatkal.[72] Horses, copper and gold were imported into Bhatkal from West Asia, while the exports included sugar, pepper and textiles. These goods were taxed while in transit through the territory of Vijayanagar kings, but revenues from collections at coastal centres went to the local chiefs. In the 16th century, the Portuguese established their base at Goa and in the 17th century, the coast from Vijayadurg to Goa was marked by Maratha forts.

As the brief survey presented here shows, there is no denying the fact that archaeological sites, shrines and forts form a part of India's maritime heritage and need to be carefully documented and preserved for future generations along with several other architectural features that dot the Indian coastline. In the context of the sea, this is even more important since coastal features along the shore provided visibility and were used as markers by sailing vessels. It was these that defined the sailing world in antiquity and produced a distinctive maritime milieu.

NOTES AND REFERENCES

1. *Mahabharata* VI 12,1; VI 8,19.
2. *Mahabharata* VI 10,8; *Vayu Purana* 45,75; *Visnu Purana* II 3,1.
3. *Epigraphia Indica*, XX: 79.
4. *Indian Archaeology – A Review (IAR 2000-2001)*: 2.

5. S. Nagaraju, *Buddhist Architecture of Western India*, Delhi: Agam Kala Prakashan,1981, pp. 258-81.
6. E. Senart, The Inscriptions in the Caves at Nasik, *Epigraphia Indica*, VIII, New Delhi: Archaeological Survey of India, 1905-6: 59-65.
7. *Ibid.,* no. 22.
8. S. Nagaraju, op. cit., p. 259.
9. Walter Spink, *Ajanta: History and Development*, Volume 2, Leiden: Brill, 2006, pp. 276-77.
10. Walter Spink, *Ajanta: History and Development*, Volume 5, Leiden: Brill, 2007, p. 222.
11. E.B. Cowell (ed.), *The Jataka*, London: Pali Text Society, Vol. 2, 1957, pp. 127 ff.
12. J.J. Jones (tr.), *Mahavastu*, London: Luzac, Vol. 2, 1949-56, pp. 70-92.
13. John C. Holt, *Buddha in the Crown: Avalokitesvara in the Buddhist Traditions of Sri Lanka*, New York: Oxford University Press, 1991, pp. 49-50.
14. Ibid., p. 52.
15. *Mahavamsa* 7.1-3.
16. H. Bechert, The Beginnings of Buddhist Historiography: Mahavamsa and Political Thinking, in B.L. Smith (ed.), *Religion and Legitimation of Power in Sri Lanka*, Chambersberg: Anima Books, 1978, pp. 1-12.
17. John Anderson, *Catalogue and Hand book of the Archaeological Collections of the Indian Museum*, Calcutta: Trustees, 1883: Vol. I, p. 189.
18. Julia Meech-Pekarik, The Flying White Horse: Transmission of the Valahassa Jataka Imagery from India to Japan, *Artibus Asiae*, Vol. 43, No. 1-2, 1981: 111-128. H. Wenzel, A Jataka Tale from the Tibetan, *Journal of the Royal Asiatic Society*, New Series, Volume XX, 1888: 503-510.
19. J.F. Fleet, Sanskrit and Old Canarese Inscriptions, *Indian Antiquary*, VIII, 1879: 13.
20. Ibid.: 11.
21. George Moraes, *The Kadamba Kula: A History of Ancient and Medieval Karnataka*, Bombay: BX Furtado and Sons, 1931, reprinted New Delhi: Asian Educational Services, 1995.
22. V.V. Mirashi, *Inscriptions of Silaharas*, Corpus Inscriptionum Indicarum, VI, New Delhi: Archaeological Survey of India, 1977, pp. 127-30.
23. Ibid., pp. 133-42, no. 23.
24. Ibid., pp. 158-61, no. 31.

25. Jean Deloche, Konkan Warships of the 11th – 15th Centuries as Represented on Memorial Stones, *Bulletin de l'Ecole françaised'Extrême-Orient*, Volume 76, 1987: 165-84.
26. James Hornell, Hero Memorial-stones of Kathiawar, *Antiquity*, Volume, 16 No. 64, 1942: 296-7 [289–300].
27. V.V. Mirashi, *Inscriptions of the Kalachuri-Chedi Era*, Corpus Inscriptionum Indicarum, VI, Ootacamund: Government Epigraphist for India, 1955, pp. 96-102, no. 23.
28. Edward Carl Sachau, *Alberuni's India. An Account of the Religion, Philosophy, Literature, Geography, Chronology, Astronomy, Customs, Laws and Astrology of India about* AD *1030,* Vols. I-II, New Delhi: Munshiram Manoharlal, p. 193.
29. V.K. Jain, *Trade and Traders in Western India*, New Delhi: Munshiram Manoharlal Publishers Pvt. Ltd., 1990, p. 130.
30. George M. Moraes, *The Kadamba Kula: A History of Ancient and Medieval Karnataka*, 1995, p. 171.
31. E. Hultzsch, Paper on the Ganeshgad Plates of Druvasena I, *Epigraphia Indica* III (1894-95): 322ff; Sten Konow, Palitana plates of Dhruvasena I, *Epigraphia Indica* III (1894-95): 108 ff. N.G. Majumdar, A Passage in the Inscription of the Maitrakas of Valabhi, *Indian Antiquary* XLVIII: 207-8.
32. J.F. Fleet, Junagadh Rock Inscription of Skandagupta, Corpus Inscriptionum Indicarum III, (1886): no. 14.
33. L.D. Barnett, Bhamodra Mohota Plate of Dronasimha, *Epigraphia Indica* XVI (1921-22): 17-19. The Navalakhi plates of Siladitya I (year 286 or 605 CE) found in a village about 8-10 miles from Junagarh records the gift of a village to forty-four brahmanas who had moved from Sangapuri (identified with the present Shahapur near Junagarh). H.M. Bhadkamkar, Navalakhi Plates of Siladitya I, *Epigraphia Indica*, XI (1911-12): 174-180. The names of the brahmanas are curious. Some look like family names, while others are names of individual. The name Boppasvami may show that he was very likely a Tailang brahmana (p. 175).
34. The Palitana plates of Sinhaditya (year 255 or 574 CE) refer to several people who were addressed regarding the transfer of land to a brahmana. These included princes (*raja-putra*), palace officers (*raja-sthaniya*), ministers, city officers (*drangika*), headmen (*mahattara*), irregular soldiers, spies, regular soldiers, riders on elephants and horses, etc. E. Hultzsch, Palitana Plates of Simhaditya; the year 255, *Epigraphia Indica* XI (1911-12): 16-20. The same

list is repeated in the E. Hultzsch, Palitana Plates of Dharasena II; Gupta Samvat 252, *Epigraphia Indica* XI (1911-12): 80-85.Palitana plates of Dharasena II (year 252 or 571 CE) which record grants of land in the village of Ekalika.

35. K.J. Virji, *Ancient History of Saurashtra*, Bombay: Konkan Institute of Arts and Sciences, 1952, p. 245.
36. M.R. Kale (ed.), *Dasakumaracarita of Dandin*, Delhi: Motilal Banarsidass, 1986, pp. 164, 332. One of the stories in the text is set in the city (*nagari*) of Vallabhi in Saurashtra where the chief of sea-traders (*navika-pati*) lived. He possessed immense wealth like Kubera.
37. R.N. Mehta and A.M. Thakkar (eds.), *M.S. University Copper Plates of the Time of Toramana,* Vadodara: MS University, 1978.
38. Ibid.
39. D.C. Sircar, Charter of Visnusena samvat 649, *Epigraphia Indica* XXX (1953-54): no. 30, 163-181.
40. Ibid.
41. Norman A. Stillman, The Eleventh Century Merchant House of Ibn 'Awkal (A Geniza Study), *Journal of the Economic and Social History of the Orient*, 16 (1973): 15-88.
42. D.C. Sircar, op. cit., p. 178.
43. The 7.14 hectare site with a 3.2 m thick habitational deposit has provided data for three cultural periods. Period I is Early Harappan (3000-2600 BCE), Period II is Mature Harappan (2500-1900 BCE) and the third period is Early Historic (1st century BCE to 1st century CE). The third period has yielded a range of ceramics such as Red Ware, Red Slipped Ware and Grey Ware together with bangles, beads and terracotta objects, Ashit Boran Paul, A Study of the Material Remains of the Early Historic Period Discovered at Padri of Bhavnagar District, Gujarat in India, *Pratnatattva*, Journal of the Department of Archaeology, Jahangirnagar University, Vol. 6 (June 2000): 53-66.
44. V.S. Shinde, The Earliest Temple of Lajjagauri? The Recent Evidence from Padri in Gujarat, *East and West*, IsMEO, 44 (2-4), 1994: 481-85.
45. These include Kanad and Variav in Surat, Kavi in Bharuch, Pavti Jetpur in Baroda, Tarsang and Bavaka in Panchmahal, Valabhipur and Gagdhali in Bhavnagar, Amreli in Amreli district, Dhanak in Rajkot and Sathal in Ahmedabad. V.H. Sonawane, Some Remarkable Sculptures of Lajjagauri from Gujarat, *Lalit Kala*, Journal of Oriental Art, 23: 27-35.

46. Two New Valabhi Copper Plates, *Journal of the Bombay Branch of the Royal Asiatic Society*, XX: 9-10, which also refer to a temple at the site.
47. Virji, *Ancient History of Saurashtra*, p. 33.
48. G. Buhler, A Valabhi Grant of Siladitya I, Dated 290, *Indian Antiquary* IX: 237.
49. R.D. Banerji, The Bhadreniyaka Grant of Siladitya I, GE 292, *EI* XXI (1931-32): no. 18: 116-19.
50. R.N. Mehta and A.M. Thakkar (eds.), op. cit., p. 23.
51. The legend reads: *maharaja-rudrasena-vihare-bhiksusanghasya*, D. Mitra, *Buddhist Monuments,* Calcutta: Sahitya Sansad, 1980, p. 141. B. Ch. Chhabra, *Findings in Indian Archaeology*, Delhi: Sundeep Prakashan, pp. 181-83; J. Ph. Vogel, Seals of Buddhist Monasteries in Ancient India, *Journal of the Ceylon Branch of the Royal Asiatic Society*, Centenary Volume, New Series, Vol. I (1845-1945): 27-32.
52. R.N. Mehta and S.N. Chowdhary, *Excavation at Devnimori*, Baroda: MS University of Baroda, 1966.
53. M.A. Dhaky and US Moorti, *The Temples in Kumbhariya*, New Delhi: American Institute of Indian Studies, 2001.
54. Buddhist Viharas in Gujarat as recorded in Maitraka inscriptions:
    1. Dudda vihara or vihara mandala near Valabhi (copper plate grant of Dhruvasena I (535 CE). It included Bhataraka vihara, Gohaka vihara, Abhayantrika vihara, Kakka vihara, Buddhadasa vihara, Vimalagupta vihara and Sthiramati vihara.
    2. Yaksa Sura Vihara built by Yaksa Sura, which formed the head of the monasteries for nuns. It included Purna-Bhatta vihara and Ajjita vihara.
    3. Bappapadiya vihara near Valabhi built by acarya bhiksu Sthiramati for monks from foreign countries: nanadesapranatvagatarthyabhik-susanghasya.
    4. Vamsakata vihara built by Siladitya I.
    5. Yodhavaka vihara with water reservoir.
55. D.B. Diskalker, Ten Fragments of Stone Inscriptions and a Clay Seal from Vala, *Annals of the Bhandarkar Oriental Research Institute*, 20 (1) 19838-39: 1-8.
56. A.S. Gadre, Five Vala Copper Plate Grants, *Journal of the University of Bombay*, 3 (1934): 79.
57. *Sangha ksetra, sthavira brahmadeya khetra*, lines 36-9, *JBBRAS*, NS 1: 50-53; *Bavya sthaviraka ksetra* (line 49 in grant of Dharasena IV, *IA* 1, p. 14) and *satka*

.... *Koutumba ksetra* (line 59 in grant of Siladitya III), *Epigraphia Indica* 4, (1896-97): 74.

58. A Grant of King Dhruvasena I of Valabhi, *Indian Antiquary* IV (1875): 104-07.
59. A Grant of King Guhasena of Valabhi, *Indian Antiquary* VII (1878): 66-68. *Indian Antiquary* IV, (1875): 174-176; *Epigraphia Indica* XIII (1915-16): 239.
60. An unpublished grant of king Dhruvasena I, *Journal of the Royal Asiatic Society*, NS Vol. I (1895): 379-84.
61. D.R. Bhandarkar, Plates of Dantivarman of Gujarat, *Epigraphia Indica* VI (1900-01): No. 28.
62. V.K. Jain, *Trade and Traders in Western India*, New Delhi: Munshiram Manoharlal, 1990, chapter I. Another non-canonical Jaina texts significant for this paper is the *Vasudevahimdi* in two parts; the first part dated to the 6th century CE and the second a few centuries later. A.P. Jamkhedkar, *Vasudevahimdi: A Cultural Study*, Delhi: Agam Kala Prakashan, 1984, p. 8.
63. Anita Sharma, Trading Communities, Social Mobility under Religious Patronage: Aspects of Early Medieval Western India from VIII-XVth century, unpublished MPhil dissertation, New Delhi: Jawaharlal Nehru University, 1996.
64. Lionel Casson, *The Periplus Maris Erythraei*, Princeton University Press, 1989, section 53, pp. 83, 297.
65. *Indian Archaeology – A Review 2000-2001*: 19-29.
66. Meera Abraham, *Two Medieval Merchant Guilds of South India*, New Delhi: Manohar Publishers, 1988, p. 110.
67. V.V. Mirashi, *Inscriptions of Silaharas*, p. 185.
68. Ibid.
69. G.M. Moraes, *The Kadamba Kula*, Bombay: B.X. Furtado, 1931; Sindabur of the Arab Authors, *Journal of Indian History* 10, 1931: 191-95.
70. M.S. Naravane, 1995, *Forts of Maharashtra*, New Delhi: APH Publishing Corporation.
71. Rangaswami Sarasvati, Political Maxims of the Emperor Poet Krishna Deva Raya, *Journal of Indian History*, 6, 1925: 69 and 72.
72. Catherine B. Asher and Cynthia Talbot, *India Before Europe*, Cambridge: Cambridge University Press, 2006, pp. 78-80.

3

CONTEXTUALIZING NAGAPATTINAM

Chola Naval Expedition against Sriwijaya

Contextualizing Nagapattinam: Chola Naval Expedition against Sriwijaya

As discussed in the previous chapter, several rulers refer to conquest across the seas in their inscriptions. The best known of these is the Chola king Rajendra I (1012–44) whose inscriptions in the temple at Thanjavur mention expeditions against kingdoms in the Indian Ocean. The beginnings of historical writings on Nagapattinam may be traced to studies by Ramesh Chandra Majumdar on Champa, the Sailendras and K.A. Nilakantha Sastri on the Cholas in the 1930s, which provided a basis for later works devoted to examining overall Indic influences on Southeast Asia, including temple architecture, language and script.[1] The focus shifted to trade especially in the work by Oliver Wolters.[2]

A recent addition to the historiography on the subject focussed specifically on the 11th century naval expedition said to have been despatched against Sriwijaya by the Chola king Rajendra I is the edited volume titled *Nagapattinam to Suvarnadwipa: Reflections on the Chola Naval Expeditions to Southeast Asia*.[3] The papers in the volume suggest that the oft quoted Chola naval expedition is based on a single primary source, viz. the eulogy contained in the inscription of Rajendra I, which is not corroborated by other contemporary sources, especially Chinese sources. Instead, contemporary sources refer to an extensive Indian Ocean trading system extending from the Tamil coast to China and it is this trading system that provided a context to the supposed naval expedition. This brief overview further underlines the point made in the last chapter, i.e. trade as the dominant trend in the writing of early maritime history to the exclusion of discussions on cultural contacts and the continued presence of Buddhist monastic complexes along the east coast of India in the early medieval period.

In this chapter, it is suggested that several aspects of the Bay of Bengal network are inadequately understood, such as for example the location of the Sriwijayan kingdom. Scholars suggest that it comprised two parts, one centred on what is now Kedah in western Malaysia and a second based on Palembang in southern Sumatra. By 1060 CE, following Tamil incursions into the Selat Melaka region, however, the centre of Sriwijayan power was established in the Jambi region. This latter centre, in and around the Muara Jambi area, survived as a major port of trade and an indigenous power base until the Javanese invasion of 1377 CE. In this chapter we would like to draw attention not so much to the expedition/s but to the context within which maritime activity across the Bay of Bengal needs to be studied in the early medieval period with the focus on the site of Nagapattinam on the Tamil coast, which is discussed both in terms of its multi-religious context as also its linkages with other centres along the east coast (Figure 15).

Nagapattinam was an important seaside town located along the east coast of south India. Fifty kilometres to its north was the site of Kaveripumpattinam, located at the point where the river Kaveri enters the Bay of Bengal, which was a flourishing Buddhist establishment from the 2nd century BCE to the 6th century CE (Figure 16). Around the 8th-9th century the centre of activity shifted to Nagapattinam, which has yielded a rich hoard of Buddhist bronzes. Three hundred and fifty Buddhist bronzes were discovered between 1856 and 1930s at Vellipalayam and Nanayakkara street in Nagapattinam. Another forty-two stunning Buddha bronzes and three Buddha artefacts in stone were found in 2004 in nearby Sellur village, Kodavasal taluq, Tiruvarur district, Tamil Nadu. They are all

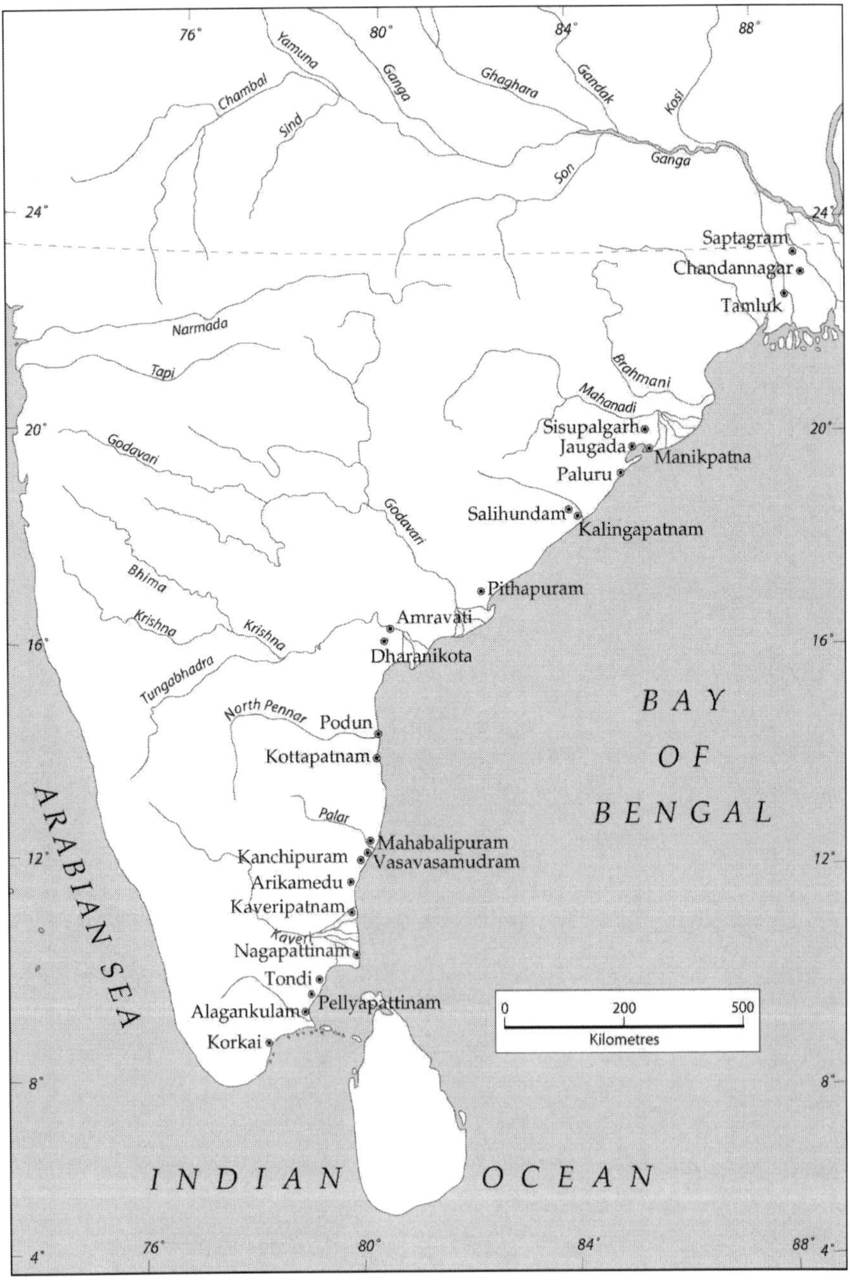

15. Port sites along the East Coast of India.

16. Buddhapada from Kaveripumpattinam now in the site museum.

datable from the 11th to 13th century CE.[4] Nagapattinam was by no means an isolated site. Archaeological data from the Tamil coast indicates the presence of one hundred and twenty-seven contemporary Buddhist sites (Figures 17-18)[5] which complement those that have been located further north along the Andhra coast and underscores the vitality and vibrancy of Buddhism in the early medieval period.

This chapter locates the Buddhist monastic complex at Nagapattinam within the larger context of the East Coast, thereby challenging the theory of the decline of Buddhism in the Indian subcontinent around the 7th–8th century. It thus shifts the focus from studying the period from 8th–9th to 12th and13th centuries largely through the perspective of trade to understanding the archaeology of coastal centres such as at Nagapattinam as maritime cultural landscapes and important centres for religious learning. The objective is to highlight the distinctive features of the Buddhist monastic complex at Nagapattinam and to understand it within the multi-religious milieu of the Tamil coast. This would help emphasize the complexity of the maritime networks rather than studying them within either political framework such as that of the Chola expeditions or merely in terms of trade contacts.

17. Stone Buddha images from Pushpavanam, Nagapattinam district.

18. 11th century Buddha image from Madagaram now in Thanjavur Art Gallery.

The seaside town of Nagapattinam located on the Tamil coast has played an important role in the history of trans-oceanic activity across the Bay of Bengal. The present district of Nagapattinam, which came into being in 1991, is known to have been settled as early as the Neolithic period and provides evidence for continued activity well into the present. It was not only an important port and trading settlement, but was also a major sacred centre, as evident from the 16th century dargah, which continues to be a focus of pilgrimage, as also the 17th century basilica of Our Lady of Good Health at Velankanni, 10 kilometres from Nagapattinam. Thirty-one devotional couplets of the 7th century Tamil saints Appar and Sambandar describe Nagapattinam as a prosperous city with fortification walls and wide roads. Large ships known as *vangam* anchored along the coast, as it was a major centre for onward travel to Sri Lanka and Southeast Asia.[6]

Chinese records of the 1060s and 1070s record the significance of the site for missions said to have been sent to the Imperial Court from the Chola kingdom of south India as well as from the ruler of Sriwijaya located on the island of Sumatra. By the last decades of the 11th century the Chinese court had begun to encourage Chinese traders to venture out to sea. In 852 and 871, the southeast Sumatran port-state of Jambi (formerly at the heart of Sriwijaya's kingdom) is known to have sent its own trade missions to China. Nagapattinam was known for the presence of the Cudamanivihara established in 10th and 11th century by the king of

Sriwijaya. The Chola kings record donations made to the vihara, which continued as a major landmark until the 19th century. These and other references found in Chinese writings and Chola inscriptions further corroborate the maritime links of Nagapattinam with Sri Lanka, Indonesia and China.

It is also important to emphasize the archaeology of the Tamil coast and the wider linkages of the region to centres across the Bay of Bengal. This is important in order to appreciate both continuity and change within the larger networks.

EARLY HISTORIC BEGINNINGS

The beginnings of settlement in Nagapattinam district along the Tamil coast may be traced to the prehistoric Neolithic period as indicated by the find of a stone celt with graffiti at Sembian-Kandiyur near Mayiladuthurai in Nagapattinam district. Iron Age urn burials have also been found in the surroundings of Nagapattinam at Vanjoor and Kilvelur. By the early centuries of the Common Era, Kaveripumpattinam emerged as an important coastal centre on the Tamil coast, which continued into the medieval period. Medieval inscriptions refer to levies on goods coming from across the Ocean being collected at coastal centres. Beyond these, there were two extra-large *nagarams* with administrative, religious, and economic roles: Kanchipuram and Mamallapuram. Kanchipuram had been the political centre of the previous Pallava dynasty and retained a level of importance in the succeeding Chola period, while Mamallapuram expanded from a fishing village in 6th to 10th century to become a major centre on the coast.[7]

The finds of Tamil-Brahmi shards from sites along the Kaveri river and along the east coast from Salihundam in Andhra to Korkai in Tamil Nadu and across the waters at Anuradhapura in Sri Lanka, the west coast of the Malay peninsula and Berenike on the Red Sea coast clearly places the Tamil coast within a larger maritime network extending from Egypt to Southeast Asia.[8] Arikamedu, 4 kilometres south of Pondicherry, is perhaps one of the few historical sites that has been subjected to several seasons of archaeological excavations. Initially excavated for six seasons between 1941 and 1950 separately by J.-M. Casal and R.E.M. Wheeler, the site was excavated again between 1989 and 1992 by a joint University of Pennsylvania and Madras University team.

The more recent excavations have added to our understanding of the site in several significant ways, the most important being in terms of chronology. Wheeler had suggested that the site had been abandoned with the decline of Roman trade in the 2nd century CE, while more recent excavations have provided evidence for the continuation of the site well into the 9th and 10th centuries CE. Wheeler had designated the site as an 'Indo-Roman trading station' in 1946. It is now evident that Arikamedu was one of a series of early historic sites along the Tamil coast extending from Vasavasamudram to Korkai, and perhaps one of the longest surviving coastal settlement. The megalithic antecedents of the region around Arikamedu have been explored and documented. In fact Soutokeny (Suttukeni) is a rich megalithic site located upstream of the Gingee river and is a contemporary to the earliest settlement at Arikamedu. This earliest occupation at Arikamedu was described as a fishing village by Casal after his excavations and fishing continues to be a major occupation in the region. The archaeological record indicates that brick architecture and new ceramic forms were introduced into this megalithic settlement and the site was linked into a larger east coast network as evident from the finds of Rouletted Ware shards.[9] These early connections need to be factored into any discussion of Nagappatinam and transformations and changes from the 9th and 10th century onwards.

CUDAMANIVIHARA AT NAGAPATTINAM

The two sets of Leyden copper plates, the Larger Leyden Plate and Smaller Leyden Plates in Sanskrit and Tamil, refer to the establishment of the Cudamanivihara at Nagapattinam at the initiative of the kings of Sriwijaya. Construction started during the reign of the Chola king Rajaraja I (985–

1016) and was completed under his son and successor Rajendra I (1012–1044). The Smaller Leyden Plates in Tamil refer to nine units of land attached to the Nagapattinam vihara.[10] The larger plates contain a Sanskrit portion, consisting of 111 lines and a Tamil portion, consisting of 332. The Sanskrit text states that in the 21st regnal year, the king gave the village of Annaimangalam to the lofty shrine of Buddha in the Chulamanivarma Vihara, which the ruler of Sriwijaya and Kataha, Mara Vijayottungavarman of Sailendra family with the *makara* crest, had erected in the name of his father in the delightful city of Nagappattana. After Rajaraja had passed away, his son Madhurantaka caused a permanent edict to be made for the village granted by his father. It is mentioned that the height of the vihara towered above Kanaka Giri or Mount Meru.[11] Nagapattinam also finds mention in the 1467 Kalyani inscription of the Burmese king Dhammaceti. Some Burmese monks who were ship-wrecked are said to have visited Nagapattinam and worshipped there.[12]

The Dutch traveller, Wouter Schouten, visited the Tamil coast in the 1660s and described a brick structure at Nagapattinam that he termed the 'Chinese Pagoda'; an account repeated by a Dutch priest François Valentyn in his 1724 publication. The structure was extant until the 19th century. Sir Walter Elliot visited the Chinese Pagoda in 1846 on board the government steamer *Hugh Lindsay*, which travelled down the coast, and described it as a 'four-sided tower of three stories constructed of bricks closely fitted together without cement'.[13] There was a fort in its vicinity and 'about 1⅓ miles NNW from the fort stands the old Black Pagoda, which is one of the most conspicuous objects in approaching this part of the coast'. In spite of local objections, the governor-in-council approved the demolition of the Buddhist monastery on 28 August 1867 by French Jesuits who had been expelled from Pondicherry and wanted to construct a college in its place.

During the demolition of the monastery at Nagapattinam by the Jesuits in 1857 a large number of Buddhist bronze images were recovered (Figures 19-21). In a carefully concealed brick chamber, five bronze images

19. Bronze image of seated Buddha from Nagapattinam.

of the Buddha were found, one of them with a Tamil inscription on the pedestal, which reads: 'Hail Prosperity! The Nayakar (Buddha), who assured the salvation of scholarly Pandits who learnt the Agama (Nikaya).'[14] Three hundred and fifty Buddhist bronzes were discovered between 1856 and the 1930s at Vellipalayam and Nanayakkara street in Nagapattinam. Subsequent finds of Buddha images made in 1910 and 1935 were distributed to several museums, including the museums in Chennai and the British Museum.

The bronzes may be divided into two broad categories: images of the Buddha and votive stupas. In addition to representations of the Buddha, images of Avalokitesvara, Maitreya, Lokesvara, Jambhala, Vasundhara and Tara have also been found, though smaller in number. Some of them carry inscriptions in Tamil on their pedestals dated from 11th to 13th century. Three categories of inscriptions are common: those containing epithets of the Buddha; inscriptions recording setting up of images by monks and nuns; legends consisting of gifts by lay devotees. The longest and perhaps the most interesting is the two-line legend on the pedestal of a 69.2 cms Buddha image now in the John D. Rockfeller III collection. The 2002 decipherment of the inscription reads as follows:

> The image of the Lord Buddha is for festival procession (s) at the temple of the Lord Buddha attached to the *akkacalaipperumpalli* or image house of *Rajendracolapperumpalli*.

20. 16th century Lokesvara image from Vellipalayam Nagapattinam district (ht. with pedestal: 105 cms).

This image of the Lord Buddha has been installed by the venerable Kunakara IV of Cirutavur.
Hail Prosperity! The prefect of artisan manufactories for the merchants of the eighteen countries.[15]

21. Buddhist bronze of Jambhala and Vasudhara from Nagapattinam now in the Government Museum, Chennai (ht. with pedestal: 9 cms).

Thus the Buddha image was invested with attributes of divinity and was involved in several rituals with close parallels to those associated with Siva and Visnu. Two monastic institutions were located at Nagapattinam, viz. the Cudamanivihara and the Rajendracolapperumpalli. The inscriptions from Nagapattinam thus provide evidence of the presence of several monastic orders and gifts by monks and nuns to the Sangha. Pauline Scheurleer suggests that some of the bronze images of the Buddha made in Java in the 9th century used models from Nagapattinam bronzes.[16]

A hoard of forty-five bronzes was found more recently at Sellur village, Kodavasal taluq, Tiruvarur district of Tamil Nadu. The images range in height from 7 to 52 cms and include some extraordinary pieces such as a votive stupa, about 30 cm tall. On the base of the stupa, around the four sides, are tales from the Buddha's life. On one side is Nalagiri, the mad elephant kneeling before the Buddha on hearing his voice, and the Buddha calming it with his hand. On another side is the Buddha preaching his very first sermon, after his Enlightenment, in the Deer Park of Isipatana, now called Sarnath, near Varanasi. Below him is a Dharma Chakra, flanked by two deer and followers with folded hands. Below this panel is a standing Buddha, with an attendant holding a parasol with a tall stem above the Buddha's head. On another side is the Buddha in Maha Parinirvana, that is after his death. On the fourth side is a seated Buddha, with his right hand in "*bhoomi sparsa*" mudra. On top of this base is the circular "*anda*" and above it is the "*harmika*" or the tiered *vimana.* Lift the *anda* and the *harmika* and, lo and behold, there emerges a tiny seated Buddha.[17] Another is a 52 cm image of the seated Buddha with musicians playing various instruments around him.

An analysis of the inscriptions on the bronzes shows that many of the epithets associated with notions of divinity and found in contemporary Saiva and Vaisnava traditions were applied to the Buddha image, indicating considerable inter-religious and inter-cultural communication.[18] Peter Schalk refers to three kinds of Buddhism at Nagapattinam: the first one is evident from bronze pedestal images, which show it to be close to Saivism so that it is difficult to differentiate between the two. The second is documented in the 12th century text the *Viracoliyam* and its commentary, which propagates a devotional form of Buddhism mediated by the sage Agastya. The third form of Buddhism was that of the acaryas or the teachers. Very little of this last form survives, except in the form of stone images from several sites along the Tamil coast.[19] We have earlier referred to the vihara at Nagapattinam, which received gifts from kings of Southeast Asia and China as a part of the linkages between the Tamil coast, Sumatra and China. A second Buddhist circuit is evident between the well-known centre of Nalanda, the Bengal, Andhra and Orissa coasts and the Indonesian archipelago, as evident from the travels of the renowned Buddhist teacher Atisa Dipankara, as will be discussed below.

A Sanskrit inscription engraved on a large copper plate found in Nalanda in 1921 records that the king of the Pala Dynasty, Devapala (ruled

c. 810–847), allocated five villages to support a monastery established there by Maharaja Balaputradeva, lord of Suvarnadvipa (Sumatra).[20] The inscription emphasizes such religious tenets as "*bodhisattvas* well-versed in *tantras*" and the copying of Buddhist texts. The inscription provides important details about the ancestry of Sriwijaya's ruler at the time. It records his claim that his maternal grandfather was King Dharmasetu and his mother was named Tara. His fame is compared to that of the five Pandava brothers of the *Mahabharata.* The inscription goes on to refer to families of Hindu deities including Siva and Parvati, Indra and Paulomi, Visnu and Lakshmi, as well as Buddha, son of Queen Maya as analogous to the parents of Balaputra. It is important to place this interaction between Nalanda and the Indonesian archipelago within the larger context of Buddhist sites along the east coast of India, as also those on the island of Sumatra.

Hiram Woodward has suggested that a distinctive world of Mantrayana and Yogini Tantras pervaded Java and Sumatra, as also large parts of India from the 7th century onwards. "A good argument can be made for treating Indonesia and India as an integral unit well into the 9th century."[21] In this he counters the overview presented in Davidson's study based largely on textual sources and secondary writings.[22] Ronald M. Davidson's synthesis of early medieval Buddhism draws on works of Indian historians, such as Ram Sharan Sharma writing on Feudalism with a focus on socio-economic transformations from the 6th to 13th century.[23] Davidson's thesis is that "esoteric Buddhism is a direct Buddhist response to the feudalization of Indian society in the early medieval period, a response that involves the sacralization of much of that period's social world. Specifically, his book argues that the monk, or yogin, in the esoteric system configures his practice through the metaphor of becoming the overlord of a mandala of vassals, and issues of scripture, language, and community reflect the political and social models employed in the surrounding feudal society."[24]

Important links in Woodward's unit are provided by the sculptural and iconographic programmes of the stupa at Borobudur in central Java and the Tabo monastery in the western Himalayas. Both adopt a sequence of texts and depictions that parallel each other, i.e. the life of the Buddha according to the *Lalitavistara* and Sudhana's pilgrimage as detailed in the *Gandavyuha sutra*. Providing a link between the Western Himalayas, Andhra and Indonesia was the renowned *dhamma* teacher Atisa (982–1054). As discussed by Sarat Chandra Das (1849–1917) based on Tibetan sources, Atisa was born in the village of Vajrayogini of Vikrampur region identified with Dhaka in Bangladesh. At a young age he was ordained as a Buddhist monk and studied with several famous teachers. He is said to have studied with the master Dharmakirti of Suvarnadvipa, identified with Sumatra from 1012 to 1024. He travelled to the Indonesian archipelago on board a merchant ship along with his students. On completion of his studies, he returned to Vikramshila. In 1042 he arrived in Tibet at the invitation of the king of Tibet and is considered the father of Tibetan Buddhism.[25]

How does the Buddhism of Tibet—the much-maligned esoteric Buddhism of the 19th century—relate to that of other sites in the Indian subcontinent? This is an issue that has been discussed in detail elsewhere, especially with reference to the identification in 19th and 20th century writings of peninsular India as the land of the Dravidian temple.[26] Here we return to the main theme of the Buddhist monastic complex at Nagapattinam in the next section.

THE VIHARA AT NAGAPATTINAM AND ITS CULTURAL CONTEXT

The cultural context of Nagapattinam locates it within a multi-religious sacred geography, which preceded and succeeded the establishment of the Buddhist vihara at the site in 1005, rather than a sequential development of Buddhism followed by Hinduism, as often suggested. The Kayarohanaswami temple in Nagapattinam is dedicated to Siva and is said to have 6th century origins, though the present structure is dated to the 11th century (Figures 22-24). Several 11th and 12th century inscriptions engraved on the temple walls provide valuable information. In addition

22. Gopuram of Kayarohanaswami temple at Nagapattinam.

23. Kayarohanaswami temple at Nagapattinam, showing earlier sculptures and inscription embedded in the wall.

to the setting up of the vihara, the king of Sriwijaya gave a set of ornaments and jewels to the silver image of Nakaiyalakar (the handsome lord of Nagapattinam), according to an inscription carved on the wall of the Siva temple thereby corroborating a plural sacred landscape at

Nagapattinam. A second record refers to donations of several types of lamps by the agent of the king of Sriwijaya, while a third mentions donation of gold coins from China for worship of an image of Ardhanarisvara installed on the premises of the temple by the king of Kidar identified with modern Kedah.[27]

Several 7th century Tamil saints, such as Saint Thirunavukkarasar (Appar) are known to have compiled devotional couplets in praise of Nagapattinam and its shrines.[28] Tamil tradition also refers to the semi-legendary saint Shahul Hamid of Nagore, whose 16th century shrine is situated a few kilometres to the north of Nagapattinam.[29] The site had several benefactors all of whom contributed to structural additions to the shrine, including maraikkayar ship-owners, Nayak rulers, as also the Dutch East India Company.[30]

About 120 kilometres inland from Nagapattinam on the Kaveri river is the town of Tiruchirappalli with 7th and 8th century rock-cut shrines and a rock fort. Inscriptions at the highest parts of the fort date from 3rd to 11th century and record names of Jain ascetics. About a kilometre from the fort is the mosque of Abdullah ibn Muhammad, built in the 8th century.[31] This larger cultural landscape thus provides continuity to engagement of both the coastal and inland communities with the sea. It is

24. Pillars of Kayarohanaswami temple at Nagapattinam.

important that this maritime orientation is taken into account when discussing the maritime history of coastal centres.

Besides, the multi-religious sacred landscape as evident from religious architecture is further corroborated by the textual evidence. In a study of the 11th century Tamil-Sanskrit poetic grammar text titled *Viracoliyam*, Anne Monius discusses the wider cultural context of the text, especially its relation to Saiva and Vaisnava devotional literature of the Chola period dated from mid-9th to the mid-13th century CE.[32] The Chola period is marked by "emergence of new Tamil literary styles and genres, mature and confident in their vision of religious communities both Shaiva and Vaishnava .... [which portray] Shaiva and Vaishnava saints, as calm victors in debate over well-meaning but ignorant Buddhist monks."[33] In contrast to this, writings in languages such as Pali of the Theravada monastic tradition depicts south India as a bastion of conservative Buddhist orthopraxy during the Chola period. "At the same time that Cekkilar imagines in literary Tamil the humble conversion to Saivism of the last remnants of Buddhism in the Tamil-speaking region, Buddhist monks writing in Pali increasingly identify themselves or are identified by others as 'Coliya' or 'Damila'".[34]

There is reassertion of the vitality "of a self-sustaining Bay of Bengal commercial network during the 1250–1500 period, which carried over into the next century. This network was inclusive of Pegu (Burma), Ayuddhya (Thailand), Vietnam and Khmer (Cambodia) cultural centres on the Southeast Asian mainland; the Melaka Straits region, inclusive of west Sumatra and the west coast of the Malay Peninsula; Bengal, Andhra and south India's Coromandel coastlines; as well as Sri Lanka."[35] These movements across the ocean and the making of donations for establishing religious centres continue in later periods. How are these wider linkages of Nagapattinam to be assessed?

MARITIME NETWORKS ACROSS THE BAY OF BENGAL

Inscriptions dated from the 9th to the 13th century formed the primary source for these early writings and have continued to be depended upon well into the present. These refer to at least four types of population centres in the far south: the *nagaram* (commercial town, one per area/district), the *brahmadeya* (village gifted to Brahmins, the highest-ranking social caste), the *ur* (village dominated by non-Brahmins) and the *pattana* or centre for overseas exchange. While historians have discussed the nature and role of these centres in trade networks, there has been no discussion on the presence of religious shrines at many of them, such as Kaveripumpattinam, where a Buddhist monastery was excavated by the Archaeological Survey of India and dated to 4th–5th centuries CE. Mamallapuram, as will be discussed in Chapter V, was known for its Hindu temples.

Following in the footsteps of Oliver Wolters,[36] Kenneth R. Hall, on the other hand, underscores the participatory nature of Indian Ocean networks in the ancient period; the agency of local and regional societies; and their reliance on economic and cultural dialogue rather than hegemony and dominance.[37] Hall has suggested that itinerant trade became institutionalized in the 9th to 13th century CE and these trade organizations were also involved with trading activity at coastal centres. At Nagapattinam on the Tamil coast, known as Colakulavallipattinam in the inscriptions of the Chola rulers, for instance, there was no *nagaram*, only *ur* and *sabha* (assemblies) and this was true for other coastal centres also such as Tiruvadandai. An inscription of Rajendra III (1256) from Gandagopalapattinam (Krishnapatnam, Nellore) states that a local *ur* assembly and an itinerant merchant organization controlled the collection of levies associated with boats and ships.[38]

A somewhat different approach was adopted by Tansen Sen in his study of Chinese maritime relations with the Tamil coast from 600 to 1400 CE as stated earlier. Sen suggested that by the 8th century Buddhism started to decline in the Indian subcontinent and this is reflected in transformation in maritime networks across the Bay of Bengal as well. By the 9th century China emerged as a centre of Buddhist learning in its own right with the development of Mount Wutai as a centre of pilgrimage. Relations between

China and India underwent a dramatic change in the 8th century from Buddhist-dominated to commerce-centred exchanges in the 7th to 15th centuries.[39] The Tang and Song dynasties took greater interest in commercial rather than religious exchanges with the regions to China's south and as a result trade networks proliferated.

From the 9th to the mid-14th centuries, several merchant associations dominated economic transactions in peninsular India, such as the Ainurruvar, Manigramam, Nanadesi and the Anjuvannam. Associated with these merchant associations were communities of craftsmen such as weavers, basket-makers, potters, leather-workers and so on. The topographical distribution of the inscriptions is significant and they are clustered in the Dharwad – Bijapur and Mysore localities of Karnataka, while in Tamil Nadu larger numbers are found in Thanjavur, Tiruchirapalli and Madurai districts. Not only did these merchant associations develop powerful economic networks, but also employed private armies. They donated regularly to temples, which were at times named after them, and also contributed to the construction of tanks.[40]

Information about the organization and functioning of the merchant guilds comes from inscriptions recording donations to temples and two types of assembly meetings.[41] One type, namely *pattana-dharmayam* (Kannada) or *pagudi* (Tamil), meaning shared contribution, are those that record decisions linked to contributions made to the temple; and the second refer to the founding of towns where merchants as well as soldiers lived (*erivira-pattinam*). The *pattana-dharmayam* inscriptions appear in Maharashtra and Karnataka in the 12th and 13th century, while they are clustered in Tamil Nadu in the 13th and 14th century. Most of the *erivira-pattinam* or fortified merchant town inscriptions in Tamil Nadu come from the 11th and 12th centuries, suggesting that at this time the importance of soldiers who guarded the merchants increased greatly. Twenty-one different categories of warriors are mentioned in inscriptions and are known to have protected trans-regional mercantile interests. Hero stones known as *viragal* in Kannada and *natukal* in Tamil were erected all over peninsular India for warriors who lost their lives, many of them in the service of merchant guilds. The range of their operations extended well beyond the boundaries of the Indian subcontinent into Southeast Asia.

Several clusters of Tamil inscriptions have been found on the eastern fringes of the Indian Ocean from Burma (Myanmar) to Sumatra. Of the seven mid-9th to late-13th century Tamil or part-Tamil language inscriptions so far found in Southeast Asia, one has been found near Pagan in Burma, two just south of the Isthmus of Kra in the Malay peninsula and four in north and west Java. Perhaps the easternmost record is the bilingual Tamil and Chinese language inscription found associated with remains of one of the two Siva temples at Quanzhou in south China. These inscriptions connect merchants associations operating out of south India with the founding or the endowing of temples or other structures for the use of the resident Indian merchant community.

In the 10th century, local versions of these merchant guilds, termed the *banigrama*, appeared in the north coast ports of both Java and Bali, especially at Julah on the Balinese coast. There are seven Javanese inscriptions dating from 902 to 1053 CE that refer to merchant associations called *banigrama* and to the various tax concessions granted to them. While some foreign merchants may have been included in these groups, these appear largely as indigenous organizations associated with the local economic networks as tax-farmers.[42]

In the final analysis, it is evident that narratives of trans-locality, travel and pilgrimage across the seas lost their centrality with the development of 'scientific' disciplines such as archaeology and the search of national histories. The writing of ancient Indian history from a socio-economic perspective in India in the last six decades emphasized trade and urban centres as the prime movers of social change and the movements of brahmanas as legitimizers of political authority in newly emerging states of the early medieval period. It is important that as maritime history emerges as a discipline in its own right, the focus should shift from sequential developments of Buddhism and Hinduism to researching multi-religious cultural landscapes across the oceans. Studies on sites such as

Nagapattinam become significant, not only as markers of trans-oceanic cultural currents, but also help define local and regional cultural and religious environments.

NOTES AND REFERENCES

1. Geoff Wade, The Pre-Modern East Asian Maritime Realm: An Overview of European Language Studies, in Satish Chandra and Himanshu Prabha Ray (eds.), *The Sea, Identity and History: From the Bay of Bengal to the South China Sea*, New Delhi: Manohar, 2013, pp. 107-15.
2. Oliver W. Wolters, *Early Indonesian Commerce: A Study of the Origins of Srivijaya*, Cornell: Cornell University Press, 1967.
3. Hermann Kulke, K. Kesavapany and Vijay Sakhuja (eds.), *Nagapattinam to Suvarnadwipa: Reflections on the Chola Naval Expeditions to Southeast Asia*, Singapore: Institute of Southeast Asian Studies, 2009.
4. T.S. Subramanian, Stunning Indicators of Nagapattinam's Buddhist Legacy, *The Hindu*, Dec 25, 2011.
5. http://www.pnclink.org/pnc2011/english/ppt/D.%20DAYALAN.pdf accessed on May 2, 2012.
6. Gokul Seshadri, New Perspectives on Nagapattinam, in Hermann Kulke, K. Kesavapany and Vijay Sakhuja (eds.), *Nagapattinam to Suvarnadwipa: Reflections on the Chola Naval Expeditions*, Singapore: Institute of Southeast Asian Studies, 2009, pp. 107-08.
7. R. Champakalakshmi, *Trade, Ideology and Urbanization: South India 300 BC to AD 1300*, New Delhi: Oxford University Press, 1996, p. 114.
8. Tamil-Brahmi shards are dated on the basis of palaeography and stratigraphy to between the 3rd-2nd centuries BCE to 4th century CE. Salihundam in Srikakulam district is the northernmost site along the east coast, which has yielded 69 inscribed shards with inscriptions in Prakrit, the sole exception being a Rouletted Ware fragment with a Tamil inscription reading *nakulán*, a masculine personal name. Other coastal sites where Tamil-Brahmi shards have been found include Vaddamanu, Amaravati, Kanchipuram, Arikamedu, Vallam, Alagankulam and Korkai. A second area of distribution is along the Kaveri river, as well as scattered finds across the sea in Sri Lanka and at Quseir al-Qadim and Berenike on the Red Sea coast of Egypt. Himanshu Prabha Ray, Inscribed Pots, Emerging Identities: The Social Milieu of Trade, in Patrick Olivelle

(ed.), *Between the Empires: Society in India 300 BCE to 400 CE*, New York: Oxford University Press, 2006, pp. 113-43.

9. R.E.M. Wheeler, A. Ghosh and Krishna Deva, Arikamedu: An Indo-Roman Trading Station on the East Coast of India, *Ancient India*, 2, 1946: 17-124. J.-M. Casal and G. Casal, *Site urbain et sites funeraires des environs de Pondichery*, Paris: Presses Universitaires de France, 1956. V. Begley et al. *The Ancient Port of Arikamedu: New Excavations and Researches 1989-1992*, Pondicherry: EFEO, 1996.
10. Peter Schalk (ed.), *Buddhism Among Tamils in Pre-Colonial Tamilakam and Ilam*, Stockholm: Uppsala University, Volume II, 2002, pp. 513-670.
11. Gokul Seshadri, New Perspectives on Nagapattinam, in Hermann Kulke, K. Kesavapany and Vijay Sakhuja (eds.), *Nagapattinam to Suvarnadwipa: Reflections on the Chola Naval Expeditions*, Singapore: Institute of Southeast Asian Studies, 2009, p. 125.
12. Peter Schalk, op. cit., p. 596.
13. Sir Walter Elliot, The Edifice Formerly Known as the Chinese or Jaina Pagoda at Negapatam, *The Indian Antiquary*, Vol. 7, 1878: 224–7.
14. T.N. Ramachandran, *The Nagapattinam and Other Buddhist Bronzes in the Madras Museum*, Madras: Government Press, 1954, pp. 19-21.
15. Peter Schalk, op. cit., p. 595.
16. Marijke J. Klokke and Pauline Lunsingh Scheurleer (eds.), *Ancient Indonesian Sculpture*, Leiden: KITLV Press, 1994, p. 78.
17. http://www.thehindu.com/features/friday-review/history-andculture/stunning-indicators-of-nagapattinams-buddhist-legacy/article2745233.ece accessed on 3rd April 2014.
18. Peter Schalk, op. cit., p. 603.
19. Ibid., p. 517.
20. Hiranand Shastri, The Nalanda Copper Plate of Devapaladeva, *Epigraphia Indica*, 17, 7, 1924, pp. 310-27.
21. Hiram Woodward, Esoteric Buddhism in Southeast Asia in the Light of Recent Scholarship, *Journal of Southeast Asian Studies*, 35, 2, June 2004: 353.
22. Ronald M. Davidson, *Indian Esoteric Buddhism: A Social History of the Tantric Movement*, New York: Columbia University Press, 2002.
23. R.S. Sharma, *Indian Feudalism*, New Delhi: Macmillan, 2006 (updated and revised theory, which first appeared in 1965). B.D. Chattopadhyaya in *The Making of Early Medieval India*, New Delhi: Oxford University Press, 1994,

p. 167 states that the period between the 6th-7th and 12th-13th centuries showed developments vastly different from the society of the earlier period. "State formation was a crucial agent of change in this respect, in the sense that it brought a measure of cohesion among local elements of culture by providing them a focus" (p. 35).

24. Ronald M. Davidson, *Esoteric Buddhism: A Social History of the Tantric Movement*, New York: Columbia University Press, 2002.
25. Ruth Sonam (tr. & ed.), *Atisha's Lamp for the Path*, Ithaca, New York: Snow Lion Publications, 1997, pp. 7-17.
26. Himanshu Prabha Ray, *The Return of the Buddha: Ancient Symbols for a New Nation*, New Delhi: Routledge India, 2013.
27. Gokul Seshadri, New Perspectives on Nagapattinam, in Hermann Kulke, K. Kesavapany and Vijay Sakhuja (eds.), *Nagapattinam to Suvarnadwipa: Reflections on the Chola Naval Expeditions to Southeast Asia*, Singapore: Institute of Southeast Asian Studies, 2009, pp. 121-25.
28. Ibid., pp. 107-11.
29. Sunil S. Amrith, *Crossing the Bay of Bengal: The Furies of Nature and the Fortunes of Migrants*, Harvard University Press, 2013, pp. 88-89.
30. Susan Bayly, *Goddesses and Kings: Muslims and Christians in South Indian Society 1700-1900*, Cambridge University Press, 1989, p. 217.
31. Leslie C. Orr, Gods and Worshippers on South Indian Sacred Ground, in James Heitzman and Wolfgang Schenkluhn (eds.), *The World in the Year 1000*, Lanham: University of America Press, 2004, p. 226.
32. Anne E. Monius, *Imagining a Place for Buddhism: Literary Culture and Religious Community in Tamil-Speaking South India*, Oxford – New York: Oxford University Press, 2001.
33. Ibid., p. 122.
34. Ibid., p. 123.
35. Kenneth R. Hall (ed.), *Structure and Society in Early South India: Essays in Honour of Noboru Karashima*, New Delhi: Oxford University Press, 2001, pp. 24-25.
36. Oliver W. Wolters, *Early Indonesian Commerce: A Study of the Origins of Srivijaya*, Cornell: Cornell University Press, 1967.
37. Kenneth R. Hall, Local and International Trade and Traders in the Straits of Melaka Region 600-1500, *Journal of the Economic and Social History of the Orient*, 2004, Volume 47, 2: 213-260. Kenneth R. Hall, *A History of Early*

Southeast Asia: Maritime Trade and Societal Development, 100-1500, Lanham and Plymouth: Rowman & Littlefield Publishers, 2010, pp. 103-34.

38. Kenneth R. Hall, Trade and Foreign Diplomacy in Early Medieval South India, *JESHO*, 21, 1, 1978: 91.
39. Tansen Sen, *Buddhism, Diplomacy, and Trade: The Realignment of Sino-Indian Relations, 600-1400*, Honolulu: University of Hawaii Press, 2003.
40. Meera Abraham, *Two Medieval Merchant Guilds of South India*, New Delhi: Manohar Publishers, 1988. Noboru Karashima (ed.), *Ancient and Medieval Commercial Activities in the Indian Ocean: Testimony of Inscriptions and Ceramic Sherds*, Tokyo: Taisho University Press, 2002. Hermann Kulke, K. Kesavapany and Vijay Sakhuja (eds.), *Nagapattinam to Suvarnadwipa: Reflections on the Chola Naval Expeditions to Southeast Asia*, Singapore: Institute of Southeast Asian Studies, 2009.
41. Noboru Karashima, South Indian Merchant Guilds in the Indian Ocean and Southeast Asia, in Hermann Kulke, K. Kesavapany and Vijay Sakhuja (eds.), *Nagapattinam to Suvarnadwipa: Reflections on the Chola Naval Expeditions to Southeast Asia*, Singapore: Institute of Southeast Asian Studies, 2009, pp. 135-57.
42. Jan Wisseman Christie, Asian Sea Trade between the Tenth and Thirteenth Centuries and Its Impact on the States of Java and Bali, in Himanshu Prabha Ray (ed.), *Archaeology of Seafaring: The Indian Ocean in the Ancient Period*, ICHR Monograph I, New Delhi: Pragati Publications, 1999, pp. 221-70.

4

THE INDIAN OCEAN NETWORK

An Overview

The Indian Ocean Network: An Overview

"As if I were someone dumb and blind
Whose boat has overturned on a rain-swept night and his heart
is swollen with intolerable suffering and he sinks without hope
into the ocean..." (*Purananuru* 238).[1]

The ocean evoked varied feelings in those who lived on its shores and those who traversed it. These are graphically depicted in early Tamil poems, such as *Purananuru*, an anthology of four hundred poems in Old Tamil. The poems include analogies such as rivers flowing into the ocean, armies like the vast ocean,[2] clouds collecting water from the ocean and so on.[3] Some of these are detailed below:

> People who go to the shore of the sea with its waves still ask
> Those who know where water can be found to quench their thirst
> (*Purananuru* 154, also 204)[4]
>
> May you live long, with your days and your years increasing more
> Than the water of the great ocean dense with waves,
> than the sand in that ocean,
> than the drops of the rain in the trailing,
> Lofty clouds! (*Purananuru* 198).

The Tamil poems are also one of the few literary sources that provide graphic accounts of fishing communities settled along the coast who provided the basic foundation to seafaring ventures in the past. Fishing is described as one of the major activities of the settlement at Muciri or Muziris on the Kerala coast:

> Like Muciri of the sea which roars like a drum, which belongs to the Kuttuvan with the golden garland, who offers toddy as if it were water to those who come to pour there the goods from the mountains and those from the sea, to those who bring ashore in the lagoon boats (*toni*) the gifts of gold brought by the ships (*kalam*), and to those who crowd the port in the turmoil created by the sacks of pepper piled up in the houses, and finally to those who return home having sold the fish and having heaped the paddy on the boat.[5]

These references reflect an engagement with the sea, not only by merchants and trading groups, but also fishing and sailing communities and ship captains who carried cargoes across the waters. In this chapter, I present an overview of textual sources that presented accounts of maritime networks in the Indian Ocean both in the Arabian Sea, as also the Bay of Bengal. The objective is to highlight the deep engagement of the system with the seas.

THE OCEAN IN SANSKRIT NARRATIVE LITERATURE

While archaeology provides evidence for settlements, commodities traded or the water-craft used in maritime travel, literary sources add to that perspective by underscoring ethical and moral values that underwrote economic transactions in society. This is especially valid for tales used to propagate Buddhist and Jain values. The *Divyavadana* is a collection of thirty-eight Buddhist biographical stories. The earliest Avadanas are verse narratives attributed to individual monks and nuns, though the *Divyavadana* may have been compiled as late as the 8th century. It portrays the adventures of wealthy merchants who later became Buddhist monks.[6] The second chapter in the *Divyavadana* narrates the story of *Purna* and celebrates both his business acumen as also his wisdom when dealing with his recalcitrant brothers. This story reached wider audiences through paintings in the rock-cut caves at Ajanta near Aurangabad. It was also repeated in several Indian Buddhist traditions and translated into other languages, such as Chinese in 700 CE and into Tibetan in the 9th century.

The Jain monk Haribhadra Suri lived in the late 8th and early 9th century and wrote in both Sanskrit and Prakrit. He produced both verse and prose largely in illustration of Jain doctrines. Haribhadra's reputation as one of the great Jain poets rests on his composition of the *dharmakatha*, the *Samaraiccakaha*, where the narrative is interspersed with religious instruction. The underlying leitmotif of the work is the idea of retribution and the consequences of transgressing the Jain moral code. Besides its didactic character, the stories provide fascinating glimpses of court life, journeys and sea voyages.

The *Lives of Jain Elders* is an epic poem in Sanskrit written by the Jain scholar monk Hemachandra (1089–1172) towards the latter part of his life. It relates stories of key figures in Jainism and provides lively reading as also insights into the social world of early medieval India. Many of these stories drew on popular narratives to which a Jain moral was attached and the main objective was to edify through entertainment.[7]

The polymath Hemachandra's writings on the wide-ranging themes of dramaturgy, poetics and grammar are fascinating in that they not only provide insights into his incisive intellect, but perhaps what is more relevant for our purposes is that they indicate participation in intellectual rivalry between the courts of the Chalukyas of Gujarat and the Paramaras of central India, especially the 11th century king Bhoja of Dhara. "Bhoja had assembled a magnificent academy of pundits, and with their aid he himself had published encyclopaedic treatises on language and literature and on many other topics as well".[8] In addition to inter-court rivalry, the 12th century was also a period when different themes were being explored and written about. Particularly relevant for this study is his *Yuktikalpataru* or treatise on the art of ship-building, which is perhaps unique in Sanskrit literature. It deals with a range of topics relating to ship-building, such as the two categories of watercraft: those that sailed on the river and those that went out to sea; seasons and periods for ship-building; class of wood best suited for the construction of water-craft; and the nature of jointing to be adopted. The text cautions against the use of iron in joining the planks, as iron would expose them to magnetic rocks in the sea or bring them within a magnetic field and thus risking their craft veering off course.[9] The *Yuktikalpataru* also provides detailed instructions for decorating and furnishing ships and for the construction of cabins. The text thus codifies information already available on various aspects of ship-building and associates this codification with the ruler of central India.

Another genre of writing is represented by plays and poems that often have merchants as heroes. The *Jagaducarita* or Life of Jagadu (in Sanskrit Jagaddeva) is called a *mahakavya* or court epic in the colophon containing seven sargas with 388 verses. Though called a mahakavya, Sarvananda's work has much the same character as the Sanskrit poems of other Jain monks of the 12th and later centuries. It shows that the author had studied and attained a certain degree of proficiency in Sanskrit grammar, poetics and metrics and that he took pains with his composition. Regarding the author, his time and his sources, nothing definite is known. The reference to king Visaladeva of Anahilvad however shows that the work must be later than the middle of the 13th century.[10] These two examples are by no means historical works, but their value lies in projecting a positive image of merchants, which no doubt found favour among their audience.

An almost unique text is the *Lekhapaddhati* or models of fifty documents written in Sanskrit, though in the letters of the later period, the language shifts to Jain Prakrit. The compiler is unknown, but the text contains specimens of drafts of various kinds such as treaties, rules of administration, model drafts of private letters, etc. The dated documents in the *Lekhapaddhati* range from 744–5 CE to 1475–6 CE and it would seem that the earliest version of the surviving manuscripts was copied in the 16th century. That these were not merely model drafts, but were also followed is evident from the close correspondence between D.no. 61

(pp. 169-70) and Rayapala's Nadol inscription of 1191 CE[11] and several other inscriptions of the Chalukyas. While there is agreement between the *Lekhapaddhati* and inscriptions in the case of documentation of land grants, we have no such corroboration for several other practices mentioned in the text, such as the issuing of passes for travel across borders, which being fragile in nature would not have survived. This brief survey presents only a part of the large corpus of literature produced in the subcontinent during this period. In the next section we shift focus and move on to a discussion of the Persian Gulf.

THE PERSIAN GULF

Under the Sasanian Empire (224–651 CE), the political centre shifted to Mesopotamia and the fertile alluvial plains of the region. Siraf, on the Iranian coast of the Persian Gulf emerged as a major centre that continued into the Islamic period. The earliest phase of the city wall and Zoroastrian chamber tombs in the hills behind the city date to the Sasanian period. Siraf provided an outlet to the city of Gur, 90 kilometres south of Shiraz. We first hear of the Sasanian fleet in the Persian Gulf around 326 CE when, according to 9th–10th century Persian historian al-Tabari, Shapur II attacked the Arabian coast after raiders from Bahrain and Hajar plunḍered Rishahr and the coast of Fars. Sasanian merchants are said to have cornered the silk trade with India and Sri Lanka.[12]

Al-Istakhri, a medieval Persian geographer states that the houses in Siraf were built with a wood called Saj brought from India and Zanzibar and that the inhabitants were famed for maritime travel:

> And I have heard that a man from Siraf went for trade to the sea and stayed in the boat for forty years and did not come to land. And when he came to the coast, he did not desire to leave the sea. He sent his workers to conduct trade and make profit and come back to him. And when the ship was in ruins, he moved to another one.[13]

At the beginning of the 9th century Siraf reached its maximum extent covering an area of over 110 hectares between the seashore and the foot of the mountains. This was also the period of intensive building activity coinciding with the construction of the great Friday mosque. Two contemporary geographers, i.e. al-Istakhri and al-Muqaddasi visited the city in the second half of the 10th century and describe its beauty and affluence. Imports included a number of rare and precious Indian goods, such as aloe-wood, amber, camphor, precious gems, ivory, perfumes, drugs, condiments and paper. Ships from Siraf sailed to China and there are references to merchants from Malaya and the Indonesian archipelago acting as intermediaries. Sohar, another coastal centre, was ideally placed in a sheltered bay and became the capital city of Oman. Commodities exported to Oman included perfumes, pharmaceutical goods, teakwood, sandalwood, sapphire, ivory, ebony, pearls, camphor, aloe, iron, lead, silk brocade, glass and pepper.

By the 10th century, Hormuz, an island in the Persian Gulf became the seaport of the province of Kirman, controlling centres on the Arabian littoral of the northern Gulf as well as the Omani coast. Around the 14th century old Hormuz moved its harbour to the island of Jarun opposite the old town. A number of vessels from India and Yemen anchored at New Hormuz, bringing with them all sorts of spices and precious stones and pearls and cloths of silk and of gold and elephants' tusks and many other wares until in the 16th century, Hormuz was conquered by the Portuguese.

EIGHTH TO THIRTEENTH CENTURIES AND THE COMING OF ISLAM

How did the coming of Islam redefine maritime space? Agius argues that with the spread of Islam, Arabic was enriched by borrowings from Aramaic, Persian, Greek, Sanskrit and other Indian languages.[14] The knowledge of the waters had increased considerably and the whole Indian Ocean was referred to as the Green Sea by early Muslim geographers and was divided into seven seas, each possessing distinctive characteristics. The Red Sea was known in Arabic as Bahr al-Hijaz or Bahr al-Qulzum (The Sea of Hijaz or Qulzum) and several toponyms were used for the Persian Gulf. In addition to knowledge of the Indian Ocean that included the entire stretch from East Africa to China, other genres of writing also came into circulation, such as travel accounts of voyages undertaken.

Travel and maritime literature is of special interest to this volume. One of the earliest travel accounts is the 9th century *Akhbar al-Sin wa-l Hind* (News on China and India) though its authorship remains disputed. It is sometimes suggested that these travellers' tales were collected by the merchant Sulayman. Other writings include Ibn Jubayr's (d. 1217–8) *al-Rihla* (The Travel) that describes his travels on Christian ships and his observations on storms and shipwrecks. Similarly interesting is the 14th century work of Ibn Battuta who undertook two long voyages: one of them to the Malabar coast, Maldives and Sri Lanka and then further to Southeast Asia and China. In contrast to the travel accounts of voyages there are also tales of heroism like the *Kitab aja'ib al-Hind* or the Book of Marvels by Buzurg b. Shahriyar al-Ramhurmuzi (d. 1009), a sea-captain from Ramhurmuz. A feature of this work is that countries were grouped according to the trade commodities that they were known for. Thus the south Arabian coast was called land of incense; India was land of pepper; Sumatra and Java were lands of gold; and Moluccas were known as the Spice Islands. Some of these maritime stories appear to be similar to the Seven Voyages of Sinbad the Sailor. A navigational treatise by Ibn Majid of 1500 CE presents a synthesis of earlier Persian manuals on navigation and encapsulates knowledge of nautical theory and practice that came down to the Arabs through Sanskrit and Persian.[15]

Islam was an Arabian religion with Arabic as the language of the Holy Book, the Quran, and also as the language of administration. Islam, however, spread through several ethnic and language groups such as Persians, Indians, East Africans and Malays. The common factor was the Islamic community or the *umma* to which every Muslim belonged. As mentioned earlier Agius cautions against equating religious and ethnic identity as Arabic sources do not make this distinction and label as Muslim all non-Arab foreigners who converted to Islam irrespective of their ethnic background. There are nevertheless exceptions. For example, the historian and geographer al-Mas'udi (d. 345/956–7) writing in the 10th century states that the Sirafis and Omanis were the leading seafarers of the time, thereby highlighting regional coastal identities. It should also be remembered that before and after the coming of Islam, many Arabians were Christians, Jews and pagan and continued to be so. Secondly, even though Persians adopted Islam, they continued to speak Persian and not Arabic.[16]

The use of a distinctive terminology to differentiate between a variety of coastal stations continues in Arabic sources, which refer to *andar* (Sanskrit *bhandara* or storehouse), *daryabar* (a sea port), *furda* (small port town), *iskila* (commercial centre), *kalla* (harbour) and *marfa'* or *murfa'* or anchorage.[17] In addition to terminology, Arabic sources also provide insights into collection of customs duties at coastal centres, especially important in the 13th century being Aden at the mouth of the Red Sea, where merchants from Egypt, Persia and India had settled. Foreign merchants reported to the *wakil al-tujjar*. Imports included ambergris, fine linen, shields, tiger skins, as well as Abyssinian slaves and eunuchs. The city was surrounded by watch towers and small forts, which were used to keep track of incoming vessels, first information of which was conveyed to the governor of the town. Ibn Jubayr in 578/1183 refers to a similar practice at Alexandria and Ludovico di Varthema in the 16th century states that in the case of cargo ships, officials boarded the vessel and made preliminary enquiries about the origin of the ship, its merchandise and the nature of commercial goods on board. After inspection the quantum of duty was calculated and the officials removed the masts, sails, rudder and anchors from the ship to ensure compliance with the rules. These were returned only when the duty had been paid. There are references to a duty of one-tenth of the goods being levied by the Sultan of Oman in 317/929. When Ibn Battuta arrived in Malabar in 743/1342 the Sultan demanded a tax on each passing ship.[18] It is significant that the only harbour installation that finds mention is the lighthouse, which consisted of wooden posts driven into the seabed to assist navigators in approaching the coast. Lanterns with lights enclosed in glass were often placed on these posts.

In addition to coastal centres in the Persian Gulf, Ibn Battuta refers to several centres on the western Indian coast, such as Khambat in Gujarat, which was a rich town whose population consisted of foreign merchants who built fine mansions and magnificent mosques. Further south, Sindabur or Goa was an important trade centre to where horses, perfumes and Chinese pottery were brought. Another important centre was Mangalore—a large and busy harbour where 4000 Muslims lived alongside Jews and others. South of Mangalore was Calicut, which was visited by merchants from China, Sumatra, Sri Lanka, Persia and Yemen, as also those from Gujarat. Timber trade activity centred around Calicut and several workshops were found for ship-building and repair.[19] Thus it is evident that in the 6th to 13th century maritime trade was a profitable though risky business and that in spite of taxes levied by coastal rulers, merchants garnered huge returns. In this section the discussion has largely focussed on the Persian Gulf. We now move to consider the extent of participation across the Bay of Bengal to Southeast Asia and China.

SOUTHEAST ASIA AND THE MARITIME NETWORK

In maritime Southeast Asia, the earliest Sanskrit inscriptions are inscribed on seven *yupa* or stone pillars located in the Kutei region of East Kalimantan on the east coast of Borneo, dated palaeographically to the 5th century CE. These record the performance of a sacrifice by king Mulavarman at the sacred place of Vaprakesvara and the setting up of the sacrificial post by the brahmins. A large number of donations were made on this occasion and these included twenty thousand cows, bulls, ghee, sesame seeds and lamps. The genealogy of Mulavarman is recorded and he is described as the grandson of Kundunga, whose son, Asvavarman was the founder of the polity. Mulavarman is compared to the epic hero Yudisthira and is said to have defeated his enemies and made them pay tax.

There has been no systematic survey or archaeological excavation on the island of Borneo, though surface finds indicate the presence of remains contemporary to the *yupa* inscriptions, such as ceramics and bronzes. Later period pottery includes Chinese stoneware of the 9th to 14th centuries. Amongst other significant finds from the site are bronze and gold images of the Buddha, a four-armed gold Visnu and a gold turtle.

Another region that provides evidence for early participation in trade is the region of Sunda on the western end of Java. This is evident from five 5th century inscriptions in Sanskrit, archaeological data on settlements and the early polity of Purnavarman. Three of these inscriptions present a marked contrast not only to those from Kutei, but also to those from the Indian subcontinent. Unlike the *yupa* pillars from Kutei, these records are engraved on boulders and have for their subject matter the footprints of the king and his elephant.

In contrast, a cluster of 5th century inscriptions of unequivocal Buddhist affiliation has been found in Kedah on the west coast of the Malay peninsula. This includes engraving of the Buddhist formula on stone – a feature that does not occur among contemporary records from the Indian subcontinent, though the formula is found on terracotta sealings. Three of these inscriptions are made of local stone and bear similar illustrations of Buddhist stupas. Texts very similar to these inscriptions have been found on the island of Borneo and on the coast of Brunei.[20] The most interesting of these inscriptions in Sanskrit is that which refers to the setting up of the stone by the mariner Buddhagupta, resident of Raktamrttika, identified with Rajbadidanga, on the successful completion of his voyage (Figure 25).[21]

The 9th century marks a turning point and several major coastal sites in peninsular Malaysia date to this period, such as Ko Kho Kao near Takuapa, Laem Pho near Chaiya and Kampong Sungai Mas in south Kedah known for large collections of Chinese as well as West Asia ceramics. Other characteristic features of these sites are the brick architectural remains that survive and have been unearthed in archaeological excavations as well as stone statuary, both Hindu and Buddhist.[22] The founding of Sriwijaya in 670 CE in Sumatra is often described as a momentous

25. Buddhagupta's inscription now in the Indian Museum.

event in that it led to the consolidation of the first Southeast Asian maritime polity, whose influence extended to the Malay peninsula as also to Java and west Kalimantan. Inscriptions date to the 680s and are in Old Malay with Sanskrit lexical inputs, while centres of manufacturing, commercial, religious and political activity have been identified in the archaeological record on the banks of the Musi river.[23]

Thus trade has often been credited with introducing social change in Southeast Asia and here it is generally argued that carriers of this maritime trade were members of Southeast Asian trading communities. In his pioneering study of Indonesian trade and exchange based largely on Chinese textual accounts, Wolters argued for the entrepreneurship of early coastal polities in western Southeast Asia, which thrived on commerce with India in the first five centuries CE and only later with direct exchange with China.[24]

By the 9th century the major states on the islands of Java and Bali, especially the central Javanese state of Mataram, had developed complex economic infrastructures and had integrated diversifying agricultural systems into a web of regional and long-distance trade networks. Sanskrit language inscriptions from Buddhist sites refer to religious teachers travelling to the region from Gujarat, Sri Lanka and Gaur in Bengal. Mataram also produced maritime Southeast Asia's first standardised indigenous coinage based on gold and billon (silver-copper alloy) divided into weight-value units integrating local and Indian systems. By the 10th century, coins based on the same system of weights and values were beginning to be minted across the maritime region from Sumatra to Bali and to the Philipine island of Luzon.[25]

As discussed in chapter III, several clusters of Tamil inscriptions have been found on the eastern fringes of the Indian Ocean from Burma to Sumatra. These inscriptions connect merchants' associations operating out of South India with the founding or the endowing of temples or other structures for the use of the resident Indian merchant community. Inscriptions dating from 840 to 1305 CE from Java are especially significant for this discussion as these list foreigners involved in trade and tax farming on the island.

All of these inscriptions that survive in their original form are, in fact, *sima* charters connected with communities located away from the coast. The settlements that received these charters, like the settlements that supported *kabanyagan* merchant enclaves, formed important links between the domestic marketing network and the ports downstream. This group of charters stands apart—by virtue of the detail that they provide—from the larger number of inscriptions that merely contain vague references in tax collecting lists to *juru kling* (head of the Indian/foreign community) – and later occasionally the *juru barata* and *juru cina* (heads of the Indian Ocean? And Chinese communities?)[26]

By the second half of the 9th century, foreign seafaring merchants are mentioned in inscriptions as operating from Javanese ports. During the 10th and 11th centuries their importance to the local court increased as evident from the Kamalagyan inscription from the Brantas delta dated 1037 CE, which records the construction of dykes in order to return the flow of the Kali Pepe river to its original course from which it had shifted as a result of silting. The inscription refers to the damaging effect that this had on both the local farming and religious communities, as well as on "the *parahu*-owners and commanders who collect merchandise at [the port of] Hujung Galung, including ship-captains [*puhawang*] and seafaring merchants [*banyaga*] from other lands [*dwipantara*]".[27]

The term 'kling' was widely adopted in Indonesia as a blanket-term covering all South Asians and in some cases all foreigners. The earliest inscription to contain such a list dates to 883 CE and is from Yogyakarta in central Java. The list includes foreign members of the tax farmer group from Champa, lower Burma and Cambodia or Kmira, as well as Kling, Pandikira, Aryya and Singhala from South Asia. These groups continue to find mention in four 11th century inscriptions issued by the rulers of Mataram in central Java, though an addition appears, that of the Drawida, soon to be replaced by the Colika and Karnataka. After the middle of the 11th century there was a hiatus in inscriptions containing lists of foreign tax farmers and these reappear in 13th and 14th centuries when an important addition is that of China, though Kmir (Khmer) and Champa retain their position.[28] The Javanese text *Nagarakertagama* completed in 1365 CE mentions merchants from Jambudvipa (India), especially from Karnataka and Bengal, from China and various parts of Southeast Asia.

One of the enigmatic issues of Khmer history is that there is no evidence of monetised transactions from 802 CE to the latter part of the 13th century, when inscriptions refer to taxes being collected in kind and exchanges based on barter. In the 13th century there are references to Chinese cash, hemp cloth, gold and silver. A similar situation prevailed in Champa where there is no evidence of local coinage, though 9th and 10th century inscriptions occasionally refer to *pana,* possibly signifying a gold or silver coin. It is only during the 12th and 13th centuries that gold and scented wood served as a measure of value.[29]

There are occasional references to merchants or *vanik* in 10th and 11th century inscriptions from Angkor and to merchant quarters, but the question relates to the presence of monetised exchange. In 8th century inscriptions from Cambodia, land value was often expressed in terms of silver or cloth, but this changed subsequently and it is only in the 10th and 11th century that inscriptions record the actual price paid for land. In place of the simple payment of silver and cloth, these inscriptions append long lists of objects given up in exchange for land, such as cattle, paddy, spittoons, copper, elephants and slaves, though their valuational component is not clearly defined.[30] Another interesting practice was to gift goods to a religious complex before using them for the purchase of land.

CHINESE PILGRIMS TO THE SUBCONTINENT

Another network that needs to be taken into account is that with China. As recorded in the written history of the Han (*Qian Hanshu*) under the reign of Emperor Wudi (140–87 BCE), the emperor sent a mission to the kingdom of Huangzhi, which contemporary writers generally agree was located on the shores of the Indian Ocean very likely in India.[31] More often quoted are records left by Chinese pilgrims who travelled to India and visited Buddhist sites. The pilgrim Faxian arrived overland in India in 399 CE and returned by sea to China in 413–4 CE from Sri Lanka, heading towards the northwest tip of Sumatra. The ship was wrecked on the way and perhaps landed in the Andamans. The next phase took Faxian to the northwest of Borneo where he arrived in 414 after 90 days at sea. The pilgrim remained in Borneo for five months and then left for China in mid-414 heading towards Canton.

A second Chinese pilgrim to visit India in the 7th century was Xuanzang (Figure 26), though he travelled by the overland route, and while his writings are of not much relevance to maritime archaeology, they formed the basis of archaeological exploration and survey by Alexander Cunningham (1814–1893), the first Director-General of the Archaeological Survey of India who brought Buddhism to the forefront and established its study as a legitimate branch in the second quarter of the 19th century.

A point that Cunningham did not take into account was the audience of Xuanzang's writings. It is suggested that the Chinese pilgrim's narrative of his pilgrimage to India was written specifically for the eyes of the Chinese emperor Taizong of the Tang dynasty (618–907) and hence Xuanzang highlighted aspects that would satisfy the curiosity of the emperor and also indicate his personal contacts and knowledge of foreign political leaders. Peiyi Wu argues that Xuanzang's narrative includes "almost everything except his pilgrimage."[32] Nevertheless Xuanzang's writings seem to have had the desired effect at the royal court and official Chinese sources record the arrival of an embassy from the ruler of Kanauj in central India in 641 AD and credit Xuanzang with initiating contacts between the Chinese empire and king Harsha of Kanauj.[33]

26. Xuanzang Memorial at Nalanda.

Two years later, Chinese sources record the visit of another high-level mission from the Tang court to Kanauj (which arrived in 644 CE) where they attended a Buddhist ceremony organised by the king and also in 645 visited the Mahabodhi monastery at Bodhgaya and placed an inscription under the Bodhi tree. The mission also included an artist Song Fazhi who made a painting of the Boddhisattva Maitreya under the Bodhi tree that he later used as a blueprint for a sculpture at the Jing'ai monastery in Luoyang.[34] This was followed by a fourth mission under the Tang dynasty led by Wang Xuance, which carried a robe for presentation to the head of the Mahabodhi monastery on behalf of emperor Gaozong. The mission also included a Sogdian monk and was well received. A grand reception was held for the Chinese and in addition they were showered with gifts, including pearls, ivory, relics of the Buddha and impressions of the Buddha.[35] Wang Xuance also seems to have paid four thousand bolts of silk to purchase a small parietal bone of the Buddha from Kapisha in north-western India. As indicated by the exchange of letters between Xuanzang and monks Jnanaprabha and Prajndeva of the Mahabodhi monastery, communication continued between the Buddhist monks. Other missions went from the south and Chinese histories record that the first mission to China from *Chu-lien* (Chola king) travelled by sea and reached their country in 1015 CE.[36]

In addition to the land routes into the subcontinent, there is ample evidence for the presence of sea routes across the Bay of Bengal. The most interesting information about circum-peninsular navigation of the Malay Peninsula is contained in Yijing's accounts of the voyage of the Chinese pilgrims who travelled to India and returned during the second half of the 7th century CE. Yijing provides an account of his journey from Canton in October-November with the northeast monsoon and his arrival in Palembang on Sumatra a month later. He stayed there for six months, and then went to Jambi near Palembang some time around May. He stayed there for another two months and then re-embarked in order to take advantage of the winds of the southwest monsoon to reach Kedah (Jiecha) on the west coast of the Malay Peninsula. He did not leave this region for India until the beginning of the following year when the north-east monsoon was well-established. He reached the Nicobar islands in ten days and fifteen days later arrived at Tamralipti in Bengal. This was clearly the most direct route to the holy places of historic Buddhism.[37]

Twelve years later, Yijing returned by the same route travelling on the winds of the north-east monsoon to reach Kedah, but this trip required two months, when the outward journey had taken only twenty-five days. Sailing against the winds was a well-tried technique but it took much longer than sailing with the winds. One of the voyages recounted by Yijing lasted only the time of one monsoon – the pilgrim Wujing left China "in the period of the east winds," i.e. in October-November and arrived in Sriwijaya at the end of a month. After stopping at Jambi he took another month reaching Jiecha and from there he left for Negapatam on the Tamil coast with the same winds before they began to wane towards the end of March. As late as the 17th century the ships of the French diplomatic missions to Siam still had the same concern: they must not miss the 'season' as it took seven months on an average to sail from Brest and reach the estuary of the Chao Phraya.[38]

Pilgrimage continued as a prime motive for travellers from China and in 1021 CE the monk Yunshu worshipped at the site of Bodh Gaya. In addition to the accounts of Chinese monks, five stone tablets with 10th–11th century Chinese inscriptions were found at Bodhgaya and two of the names that have been identified include those of Chi-I and Ho-yun, the former in the company of some other priests.[39] It is significant that Chinese visitors to Bodhgaya included not just monks, but also members of the naval fleets sent by the third emperor of the Ming dynasty, Yong-le (1403–1425), to more than twenty countries in Southeast Asia, as well as to Bengal and the Malabar coast and Aden, popularly known as the voyages of Zheng He. Accounts of these voyages are available in the *Mingshi* (History of the Ming Dynasty), which is considered the most elaborate and complete history of the Ming dynasty.[40] It is based on the *Ming Shi-lu*, each of the *shi-lu* comprising an account of one emperor's reign compiled after that emperor's death on the basis of a number of sources created during the reign.[41] What is relevant for this chapter is the description of visits undertaken to Bengal, *Zhao-na-pu-er* or Jaunpur in 1412 located to the west of Bengal, and to Dili or Delhi. The accounts also mention that Hou Xian, the lesser eunuch, stopped at *Jin-gang bao zuo*, the Vajrasana at Bodh Gaya on his way to or from Jaunpur and offered gifts to the elders there.[42]

CHINESE CERAMICS IN INDIAN OCEAN TRADE

Chinese ceramics have a wide distribution in the Indian Ocean region as mentioned earlier and two of the most popular wares are the Yue ware dated 8th–12th centuries CE and Longquan ware present at sites of 13th–14th century CE, though scholars continue to debate unities of time and space as encompassed by the use of these two terms. One group of scholars suggest that Yue ware includes any ceramics made within the territory of the ancient Yue polity, while others restrict the use of the term to green glazed wares made between the Han period (206 BCE–220 CE) and the 11th century in the metropolitan areas of the Yue and Wuyue kingdoms.[43] The two wares were much in demand on account of their vibrant colours, durability and delicacy, though rival potters in other provinces quickly picked up techniques to imitate them, especially kilns in southern China. It has been frequently suggested that the highest quality Yue vessels were made for a small elite, while ordinary good quality Yue and Longquan wares seem to have been exported.[44]

In the 9th-10th centuries, Yue wares are commonly found at sites in Southeast Asia, extending from the Philippines to Palembang and Muara Jambi on Sumatra, Jakarta Bay and Borobudur, as well as Bujang valley on the west coast of Malaysia. It is suggested that with the exception of central Java, other sites in coastal Southeast Asia represent transit points, rather than end-users or local distribution points of foreign ceramics. The primary markets at this time seem to have been located in South Asia and West Asia, though this pattern changed in the 13th and 14th centuries, when inland sites in Southeast Asia emerged as major consumers of imported ceramics.[45]

A similar pattern is repeated in Thailand where large quantities of Yue wares occur only at 9th–10th century coastal sites and at least thirteen of these are known. In contrast, very few Yue wares appear at settlement sites or burial sites. On the other hand, Longquan wares of the 12th to 14th centuries have been found at 32 sites, many of them being coastal sites and nine of these also contained Yue wares. A large number of sherds of Longquan wares have been collected from underwater shipwrecks and waterways joining the coast and inland settlements. Thus local people emerge as major consumers of these ceramics, which were not only used in households, but also appear as burial goods. It is significant that in Buddhist monastic centres Longquan wares served as containers for votive tablets, as well as for relics enshrined in stupas. Yue and Longquan sherds were also found at local kiln sites or at sites near kilns and green glazed wares are known to have been produced at the Buri Ram kilns in north-east Thailand from at least the 8th century onwards. This raises the question of the relationship between the Chinese and Thai glazed wares long before the supposed formal import of technology in Thailand. It has been traditionally suggested that the Chinese Emperor gave permission to a Thai envoy to take Chinese potters to Thailand only at the end of the 13th century.[46]

In Sumatra, the earliest Yue and Yue-type wares were confined to the southern parts of the island, such as Lampung, south Sumatra and Jambi, while Longquan wares were found all over the island at 13th–14th century sites. As in Thailand, imported ceramics were not only for domestic use, but were also employed for ritual purposes and were recovered in close proximity to a Saiva shrine at Kota Cina in northeast Sumatra.[47]

The data from Sri Lanka corroborates the pattern from Southeast Asia. 8th to 14th century Chinese ceramics have been found at eleven archaeological sites, both coastal such as Mantai on the north-western coast near Mannar and Galle harbour on the south-western coast, as also at inland centres, associated with monastic complexes like Anuradhapura, Abhayagiri vihara, Polonaruwa, Sigiriya, etc. But perhaps the most significant is Mantai, which yielded a rich assemblage of 2,288 sherds with a predominance of sherds of storage jars, though the yield of Islamic wares was larger with a total of 3,304 sherds. The Chinese wares include Dusun jars, Changsha, Yue and Yue related wares as also Tang ceramics. As compared to Mantai, finds from other sites were small.[48]

From the 8th and 9th century onwards, maritime space expanded to include East Asia and Chinese wares were distributed through the Indian Ocean networks.[49] Excavations at Fustat in Egypt have yielded Chinese ceramics dating from 9th through the 15th century, with the largest concentration from the 10th to 14th century.[50] As the following example indicates, however, these need to be used with caution for demarcating the extent and nature of the network. The excavations at Siraf in the Persian Gulf yielded a Chinese stoneware fragment bearing two Arabic names Yusuf and Mansur or Maymun, incised before glazing the vessel, belonging to a jar probably sent by a merchant resident in China.[51]

A search for Chinese ceramics along the Indian coasts has yielded mainly post-11th century ceramics, a majority belonging to the 13th and 14th centuries along the Tamil and Malabar coasts.[52] The evidence from the Persian Gulf, however, presents a different picture. The earliest Chinese ceramics in the Persian Gulf have been found at Siraf (period II) and most of them were fragments of stoneware jars, mainly of the typical olive green variety of the Tang period together with sherds of blue-glazed Sasanian-Islamic jars. Chinese imports, however, represent less than one per cent of the total amount of excavated ceramics from the site and only one-third of these are from luxury porcelain or Celadon pieces, while the majority two-thirds come from stoneware jars. In contrast to the limited quantities dated to the 9th–10th century, imports increased in the 13th–14th century and in his 1969 survey in southern Iran, A. Williamson picked up about 10,000 Chinese sherds from coastal sites, but no more than ninety from inland centres.[53]

Relevant to this discussion are the voyages of Zheng He, who is regarded within the Chinese tradition as a Ming envoy sent abroad at the head of naval armadas by the Yong-le Emperor (1403–1425) on seven occasions to develop relations of peace and friendship with rulers in the

Indian Ocean region. During these voyages Zheng He engaged in trade and brought many of the foreign rulers back to China to offer tribute to the imperial court. It should not, however, be forgotten that the primary motivation of these voyages was military expansion.

The voyages sent by the Yong-le Emperor were different from earlier ones in that they were commanded by eunuchs. "It is obvious that these fleets were crewed by a wide range of peoples. Many of the eunuch commanders were Muslims, the navigators were often non-Chinese, and it is possible that descendants of Fujian Arabs were also included in the crew".[54] The primary motivation was, however, clear: that of establishing staging posts at centres such as Malacca in the Malay Peninsula and of subduing the local rulers by their might and strength. The accounts of these voyages are replete with accounts of violence and attacks on the local forces of Java, Burma, Sri Lanka and Sumatra and can at best be termed "gun-boat diplomacy". It is significant that the 13th and 14th centuries CE provide evidence for the increased presence of Chinese wares in the Indian Ocean region as discussed above, thereby reinforcing the need to discuss archaeological data within the emerging political complexity in the Indian Ocean region, especially with reference to Southeast Asia.

THE THIRTEENTH CENTURY

There were several changes in the second half of the 12th and early 13th century, both in the global context as also along the west coast. The fall of the Abbasid Caliphate in 1258 following attacks by the Mongols adversely affected trade links with India. Ghurid invasions into north India from 1192 to 1206 and the establishment of the Mamluk dynasty in Delhi at the beginning of the 13th century had reverberations for political stability across the Indian subcontinent. Qutbuddin Aibak made the first successful attack on western India in 1197 and mainland Gujarat was annexed to Delhi in 1298. The dynasty of the Goa Kadambas came to an end after the invasion of Malik Kafur, the general of Alauddin Khilji (1296–1316) of Delhi.

In Chapter 2 we discussed attacks from the sea on coastal centres in Gujarat. The earliest writer to mention Kanbayat or Khambat was Mas'udi who wrote about 943 CE followed by Istakhri in 951 CE. Idrisi (1154 CE) also mentions it as a port with considerable trade and adds that it was fortified to defend it from attacks by sea emanating from the Isle of Kish/Qays in the Persian Gulf (Dames, 1989: 139). Both al-Yaqut (d. 1228) and Ibn al-Mujawir (d. 1291) mention that the ruler of Qays owned large galleys and warships which were a threat to vessels trading with Yemen and Egypt.[55]

There are no doubt references to attacks by the ruler of Qays on other centres in the region leading to the suggestion that Qays and Dahlak, an island group located in the Red Sea, may be termed predatory city-states.[56] Madmun b. Japeth writes to Ben Yiju about an attack on Aden by the ruler of Qays. Fifteen enemy ships and five hundred men arrived in Aden and waited in ambush for incoming ships at the *mukalla 'adan* (Aden's station for ships), which appears to have been the routine anchorage for oceangoing ships in Aden's harbour.[57] Madmun relates that the enemy did not enter the town, but the presence of the strong force in the anchorage and the two month long blockade caused great panic.[58] However, in spite of this force, the island of Qays was conquered by Hormuz in 1229 CE.[59]

Were these naval attacks part of a larger policy or only indicate random attempts at control of maritime trade? The data to answer these questions is somewhat limited, though the case of Yemen in the 13th century provides significant insights. Eric Vallet has suggested that the Rasulid Sultanate of Yemen developed an oceanic policy in an attempt to establish its supremacy in the western Indian Ocean at a time when the three major powers in the region, i.e. Mamluks in Egypt and Syria, Mongols in Persia and the Turkish Delhi Sultanate had no direct access to the Indian Ocean. This is based on a unique collection of administrative and fiscal reports written between 1290 and 1294 for Sultan al-Muzaffar of Yemen. These documents show that the Rasulid Sultan and his administration owned ships that carried goods and men between Aden and the Egyptian port of 'Aydhab. All goods had to be unloaded in Aden and reloaded on boats bound for Egypt and Rasulid ships had priority on this route and offered protection to the ships of Qays and also those from India or al-Hindi. Was Yemeni policy only intended for control of trade? Here the documents contain lists of annual grants sent by the Sultan to Muslim judges and preachers in Gujarat, Konkan Malabar and Coromandel. Given that many of these territories were outside the control of the Delhi Sultanate, it is evident that the grants to Muslim religious leaders had a significant political dimension.[60] Thus it is necessary to include within the ambit of trade and maritime contacts the religious and political dimensions of these contacts as well. It is these issues that have been dealt with in this book as we have discussed maritime cultural landscapes from a holistic point of view rather than merely through trade activity.

NOTES AND REFERENCES

1. George L. Hart and Hank Heifetz, *Purananuru* (translated & edited): 125, New York: Columbia University Press, 1999, p. 148.
2. Ibid., p. 189.
3. Ibid., p. 130..
4. Ibid., pp. 97, 129.
5. F. De Romanis, Rome and the Notia of India, F. De Romanis and A. Tchernia (eds.), *Crossings: Early Mediterranean Contacts with India*, New Delhi: Manohar, 1997, p. 95.
6. Joel Tatelman, *The Heavenly Exploits: Buddhist Biographies from the Divyavadana*, The Clay Sanskrit Library, New York University Press, 2005.
7. R.C.C. Fynes, *The Lives of the Jain Elders*, Oxford – New York: Oxford University Press, 1998.
8. Gary A. Tubb, Hemacandra and Sanskrit Poetics, in John E. Cort (ed.), *Open Boundaries: Jain Communities and Cultures in Indian History*, Albany: State University of New York Press, 1998, p. 54.
9. R.K. Mookerji, *A History of Indian Shipping and Maritime Activities from the Earliest Times*, Bombay – Calcutta – London – New York: Longman's Green and Company, 1912, p. 21.

10. G. Bühler, translated, *The Jagaducarita of Sarvananda: A Historical Romance from Gujarat*, Akademie der Wissenschaft in Wien, Vienna, 1892.
11. *Epigraphia Indica* XI, pp. 38-39.
12. David Whitehouse, Siraf: A Sasanian Port, *Antiquity* XLV, 1971: 262-67.
13. Touraj Daryaee, The Persian Gulf Trade in Late Antiquity, *Journal of World History*, Volume 14, no. 1, March, 2003: 3.
14. Dionisius A. Agius, *Classic Ships of Islam: From Mesopotamia to the Indian Ocean*, Leiden – Boston: Brill, 2008, p. 15.
15. Ibid., pp. 28-29.
16. Ibid., pp. 7-11.
17. Ibid., p. 174.
18. Ibid., pp. 227-28.
19. Ibid., p. 86.
20. J.W. Christie, State Formation in Early Maritime Southeast Asia: A Consideration of the Theories and the Data, *Bijdragen tot de Taal-, Land- en Volkenkunde*, 151, 2, 1995: 256.
21. B. Ch. Chhabra, *Expansion of the Indo-Aryan Culture during Pallava Rule*, Delhi: Munshiram Manoharlal, 1965, pp. 23-24.
22. Michel Jacq-Hergoualc'h, *The Malay Peninsula: Crossroads of the Maritime Silk Road (100 BC – 1300 AD)*, Leiden: Brill, 2002, pp. 134-60.
23. Pierre-Yves Manguin, The Archaeology of Early Maritime Polities of Southeast Asia, in Ian Glover and Peter Bellwood (eds.), *Southeast Asia: From Prehistory to History*, London–New York: Routledge Curzon, 2004, pp. 305-08.
24. O.W. Wolters, *Early Indonesian Commerce: A Study of the Origins of Sri Vijaya*, Ithaca: Cornell University Press, 1967.
25. Christie, 1999, pp. 222-23.
26. Ibid., p. 246.
27. Ibid., p. 245.
28. Jan Wisseman Christie, Javanese Markets and the Asian Sea Trade Boom of the Tenth to Thirteenth Centuries AD, *Journal of the Economic and Social History of the Orient*, 41, 3, 1998: 369.
29. Robert S. Wicks, *Money, Markets, and Trade in Early Southeast Asia*, Ithaca: Cornell University Studies on Southeast Asia, 1992, p. 183.
30. Ibid., p. 217.
31. Paul Wheatley, *The Golden Khersonese*, Westport: Greenwood Press, 1973 (first published 1961), pp. 8-13.

32. Peiyi Wu, An Ambivalent Pilgrim to T'ai Shan in the Seventeenth Century, Susan Naquin and Chun-fang Yü (eds.), *Pilgrims and Sacred Sites in China*, Berkeley: University of California Press, 1992, p. 67.
33. Tansen Sen, In Search of Longevity and Good Karma, *Journal of World History*, Volume 12, no. 1, 2001: 1-28, p. 6.
34. Ibid., p. 9.
35. Ibid., p. 20.
36. K.A.N. Sastri, *The Colas*, Madras, 1955, p. 219.
37. Michel Jacq-Hergoualc'h, *The Malay Peninsula: Crossroads of the Maritime Silk Road (100 BC – 1300 AD)*, Leiden: Brill, 2002, pp. 53-54.
38. Ibid., p. 55.
39. *Journal of the Royal Asiatic Society*, NS xiii: 552-572.
40. Haraprasad Ray, *Trade and Diplomacy in India-China Relations: A Study of Bengal during the Fifteenth Century*, New Delhi: Radiant Publishers, 1993, p. 7.
41. Geoff Wade (tr.), *Southeast Asia in the Ming Shi-lu*, an open access resource, Singapore: Asia Research Institute and the Singapore E-Press, National University of Singapore, 2005.
42. Haraprasad Ray, *Trade and Diplomacy in India-China Relations: A Study of Bengal during the Fifteenth Century*, New Delhi: Radiant Publishers, 1993, p. 78.
43. Chuimei Ho, Yue-type and Longquan-type Green Glazed Wares made outside Zhejiang Province, in Chuimei Ho (ed.), *New Light on Chinese Yue and Longquan Wares*, The University of Hong Kong, 1994, pp. 103-19.
44. Ibid., p. 111.
45. Chuimei Ho, Problems in the Study of Zhejiang Green Glazed Wares with Special Reference to Ko Kho Khao and Laem Pho-Payang, Southern Thailand, in Chuimei Ho (ed.), *New Light on Chinese Yue and Longquan Wares*, The University of Hong Kong, 1994, pp. 187-212.
46. Amara Srisuchat, Discovering Chinese Yue and Longquan Green Glazed Wares and Reconsidering Their Socio-Economic Roles in the Development of Ancient Communities in Thailand, in Chuimei Ho (ed.), *New Light on Chinese Yue and Longquan Wares*, The University of Hong Kong, 1994, pp. 213-28.
47. E. Edwards McKinnon, Yue and Longquan Wares in Sumatra, in Chuimei Ho (ed.), *New Light on Chinese Yue and Longquan Wares*, The University of Hong Kong, 1994, pp. 284-98.

48. Martha Prickett-Fernando, Middlemen and End-Users: The Finds of Yue and Longquan Celadons in Sri Lanka, in Chuimei Ho (ed.), *New Light on Chinese Yue and Longquan Wares*, The University of Hong Kong, 1994, pp. 299-321.
49. A. Rougelle, Medieval Trade Networks in the Western Indian Ocean, in H.P. Ray and J.-F. Salles (eds.), *Tradition and Archaeology: Early Maritime Contacts in the Indian Ocean*, New Delhi: Manohar, 1996, pp. 159-80.
50. Katherine Strange Burke and Donald Whitcomb, Quseir al-Qadim in the Thirteenth Century, *Ars Orientalis*, 34, 2004: 92.
51. M. Tampoe, *Maritime Trade between China and the West*, Oxford: BAR International Series 555, 1989.
52. Noboru Karashima (ed.), *In Search of Chinese Ceramic-sherds in South India and Sri Lanka*, Taisho University Press, 2004.
53. A. Rougelle, op. cit., pp. 159-80.
54. Geoff Wade, *The Zheng He Voyages: A Reassessment*, Asia Research Institute Working Paper Series, 31, 2004.
55. Dionisius A. Agius, *Classic Ships of Islam: From Mesopotamia to the Indian Ocean*, Leiden – Boston: Brill, 2008, pp. 80-81.
56. Roxani Eleni Margeriti, Mercantile Networks, Port Cities, and "Pirate" States: Conflict and Competition in the Indian Ocean World of Trade before the Sixteenth Century, *Journal of the Economic and Social History of the Orient*, 51, 2008: 543-577.
57. S.D. Goitein, Two Eyewitness Reports on an Expedition of the King of Kish against Aden, *Bulletin of the School of Oriental and African Studies*, 16, 1954: 247-57.
58. Roxani Eleni Margeriti, *Aden and the Indian Ocean Trade*, The University of North Carolina, Chapel Hill, 2007: 78-9.
59. Dionisius A. Agius, op. cit., p. 81.
60. Eric Vallet, Yemeni 'Oceanic Policy' at the end of the 13th century, in Rob Carter and St John Simpson (eds.), *Proceedings of the Seminar for Arabian Studies,* Volume 36, Papers from the Thirty-ninth Meeting of the Seminar for Arabian Studies, held in London in July 2005, 2008.

5

NARRATIVES OF TRAVEL AND SHIP-WRECK

Maritime Orientation of Coastal Shrines

Narratives of Travel and Ship-wreck: Maritime Orientation of Coastal Shrines

Chapters 2 and 3 examined conceptualization of maritime space in royal inscriptions and attempts by the polity to control the seas. This was followed in Chapter 4 by a survey of textual accounts that reflect wider perceptions of the society and the diverse communities towards the waters. In this chapter the focus is on deeper concerns regarding dangers of sea travel. I use narratives of sea travel as an entry point to discuss monastic complexes in the Indian subcontinent and extending across the Indian Ocean to emphasise both trans-locality of Buddhist sites and inter-connectedness of religious shrines. In Chapter 2 transformation in the religious landscape in early medieval Gujarat was discussed while Chapter 3 highlighted the multi-religious landscape of the site of Nagapattinam on the Tamil coast. In the last section of this chapter we return to the theme of pilgrimage and the use of coastal routes to travel on pilgrimage to temples is taken up.

Pioneering work on portrayals of ships and seafaring activity was done by Dieter Schlingloff who painstakingly documented references in literary sources and their representation at monastic centres in the Indian subcontinent.[1] In this chapter, the discussion moves beyond a listing of sites to situate the monastic centres within their specific social domains –

why are depictions of shipwreck limited to only a few sites? Are these representations specific to coastal centres? How is the representation of the Avalokitesvara as a Saviour of travellers in time of trouble to be understood? Why does it occur largely in the western Deccan caves? It is some of these questions that this paper aims to answer. The chapter starts with a description of the location of early Buddhist sites in Gujarat and peninsular India in order to emphasise their maritime orientation. Was this orientation merely a matter of coincidence or does it indicate interaction between monastic sites and the coastal lay community? What was the nature of this interaction? Was it merely for obtaining patronage from merchants and other travellers? Was it aimed at pilgrims who came by sea? Or else was it a manifestation of Buddhist cosmology?

COASTAL ORIENTATION OF EARLY BUDDHIST SITES

The inscriptions of Asoka, written mainly in the Brahmi script in the eastern dialect of Prakrit (though those in Kharosthi are also known, as also in Greek and Aramaic), have generally been classified into Rock Edicts (Major and Minor), cave inscriptions, and pillar edicts. The Minor Rock Edicts (MRE) are said to form the earliest group of Asokan inscriptions, followed by the Major Rock Edicts. The Pillar Edicts were the last to be promulgated, but no example of these has so far been found in the peninsula.[2] MRE 1 was meant to be inscribed (*likhita*) on rocks at clearly defined places. We find the so-called MRE 2 only in the South where it appears five times alongside MRE 1. MRE 2 never speaks of *likhita*, but only of *anapayati* or *nivesayati,* i.e. it uses terms relating to oral instruction, indicating perhaps that these were read aloud and explained.[3]

An alternative scheme of categorising Asokan edicts would be to study the inscriptions in their regional and local contexts. Thus the cluster in peninsular India would form a unit and would contrast with those located along the coast, such as at Sopara on the west coast, Dhauli and Jaugada in Orissa and perhaps Amaravati in Andhra, though the authenticity of the latter has been questioned, as it is of granite and not the usual sandstone. The coastal orientation of many of the edicts and the differential development of centres along the coasts, as compared to those located in the inland region has been discussed elsewhere and need not be repeated here.[4] It is nevertheless evident that an active engagement with seafaring activity led to longevity and increased prosperity of Buddhist centres in coastal regions, e.g. Kanheri, Amaravati, Ratnagiri, etc.

Maritime voyages in the early centuries of the Common Era were regarded as profitable ventures and Buddhist literature describes a variety of social groups who were involved.[5] In addition to merchants there are references to princes who travelled across the seas to make money.[6] The prosperity and status of these mariners is evident from the donations made by them to the Buddhist monastic establishments and recorded in the inscriptions of the Early Historic period. It was also at this time that maritime activity between South and Southeast Asia intensified, leading not only to increased commercial activity between the two, but also the spread of the religions of the subcontinent, especially Buddhism and Hinduism.

The peninsular part of Gujarat is referred to as Saurashtra and forms a rocky tableland with an altitude of 300 to 600 metres, fringed by coastal plains. It is known for its black cotton soil, making it a fertile tract for agriculture and is dissected by various rivers that flow in all directions. Gujarat has a total coastline of 1600 kilometres with the Gulf of Kachchh and the Gulf of Khambat providing major inlets. The Saurashtra coast is marked by sandy beaches, which extend from Dwarka to Diu and the distinction between the coast and the interior is not as marked as elsewhere in peninsular India. The Girnar hills, which contain the site of Junagarh, are important for pilgrimage to the Buddhists, Hindus and the Jainas. The hills are marked by five peaks and are the site of three reservoirs. The rounded boulder on which the Asokan edicts are inscribed is situated at the entrance to the valley near the edge of what was once Sudarsana lake.[7] Also carved within the hills are a series of caves: the Khapra Kodia,

Baba Pyara and the caves at Uperkot. The late Professor R.N. Mehta explored the Junagarh area and located an earthen bund which acted as a dam across the Suvarnarekha river. It seems to represent the dam of the lake Sudarsana, mentioned in the Junagarh inscription of Rudradaman and Skandagupta.[8] Junagarh was linked to the coast through sites such as Prabhas Patan or Somnath located at the mouth of the Hiram river. In the Vankia hills at Sana, 25 kilometres from Una in Amreli district, sixty-two rock shelters were excavated at different levels, including a caitya cave and water cisterns.[9]

In the coastal regions of Gujarat, Buddhist caves were excavated from 2nd century BCE to the 6th century CE. Rock-cut caves are known from Kateshwar and five from Siyot in Lakhpat taluka in the extreme north-west of Kachchh, as also bronze images of the Buddha have been found datable from 4th to 7th century CE. Other coastal sites in south Gujarat include Talaja in Bhavnagar district with thirty rock-cut caves and Kadia Dungar near Bharuch.

Starting from modest beginnings in the form of apsidal *caityas* dated to the 4th-3rd centuries BCE, more than a thousand Buddhist caves were excavated in the hills of the Western Ghats and its offshoots at about fifty centres in the western Deccan. Broadly, these sites are located overlooking creeks and coastal settlements and at passes along overland routes. Of these, nineteen centres are significant in terms of providing inscriptional data and have yielded a total of more than two hundred inscriptions.[10] As compared to this exuberance of rock-cut architecture, a majority of the monastic complexes in the Andhra region are structural and are concentrated along the coast with a scatter along the inland route in the Telengana area. Nearly 140 sites are listed in the region and the distribution along the coast from Srikakulam in the north to Ramatirtham and Nandalur in the south is quite striking. Of these Buddhist centres, thirty sites have yielded stone inscriptions.

A 3rd century CE Prakrit inscription from Nagarjunakonda in Andhra refers to the fraternities of monks at Tosali, Palur and Puspagiri, identified as major Buddhist centres in Odisha.[11] Recent archaeological research has brought to light several Buddhist sites in coastal Odisha, though the major expansion occurs from 5th to 13th centuries CE, when more than one hundred Buddhist sites are known in the region (Figure 27). Several sites have earlier beginnings, one of these being Langudi, on a low hill running from north to south, located in the plains of the Mahanadi Delta about ninety kilometres from Bhubaneswar in the Jajpur district. The river Kelua, a tributary of the Brahmani, the second largest river system in Odisha, meanders across the northeast and eastern parts of the Langudi Hill. Thirty-four rock-cut stupas on the northern spur of the hill have been dated to 2nd–3rd century CE, though most of the sculpture is dated from 7th to 9th century CE. Archaeological excavations at Lalitagiri have provided evidence for a 2nd–1st century BCE stupa, an apsidal shrine built over the remains of an earlier structure, inscriptions in Kushana-Brahmi, Gupta and post-Gupta script, as also a Gupta coin. Relics in gold foil were found

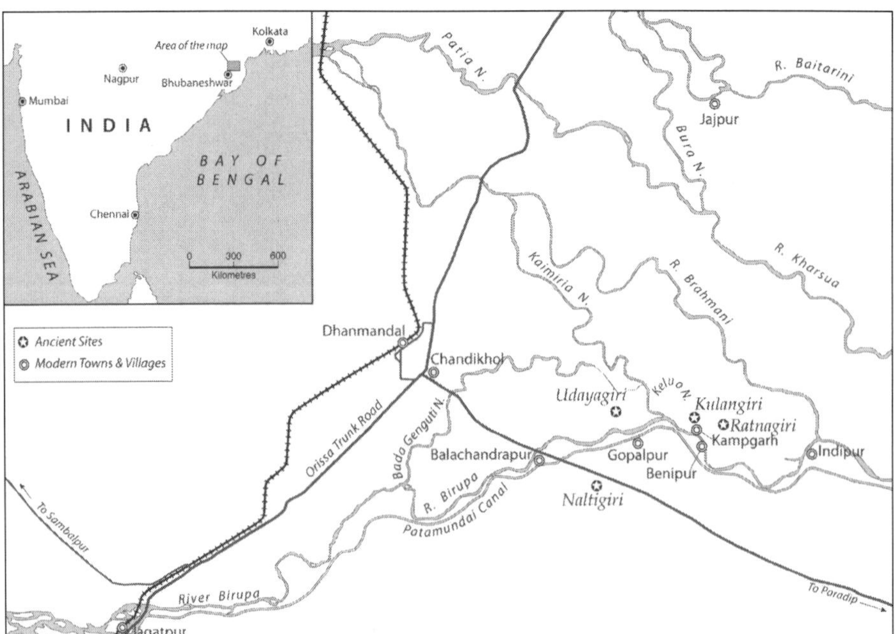

27. Location of coastal Buddhist sites in Odisha.

at the site.[12] A 2nd century CE Brahmi inscription from the pavement of the apsidal shrine records the completion of a seat by several lay devotees and a nun. Also found from the site were dull Red Ware sherds with inscriptions dated to 1st century BCE.[13]

Thus the maritime orientation of a large number of Buddhist sites in Gujarat and peninsular India is striking. This is further reinforced by the presence of the largest and longest-lasting centres along the coast, such as Kanheri on the west coast; Amaravati in Andhra; and Ratnagiri in Odisha. How is the coastal location to be explained? How was maritime space conceptualized? As was suggested in Chapter 2, royal patronage of Buddhist cave sites such as Nasik and Ajanta is clearly reflected in the sculptural programme and the inscribing of royal records. Patronage at the coastal sites of Amaravati, Kanheri and Ratnagiri was varied, though representations of the Avalokitesvara as saviour are represented prominently at the last two sites.

AVALOKITESVARA / TARA:
SAVIOUR OF MARINERS AND TRAVELLERS IN DISTRESS

> *If one happens to fall into the dreadful ocean, the abode of Nagas, marine monsters and demons, he has but to think of Avalokitesvara, and he shall never sink down in the king of waters.... (Saddharmapundarika Sutra,* 24, 6).

The Avalokitesvara represents the earliest appellation of the Boddhisattva known to us from extant Buddhist literature, such as the *Sukhavativyuha*, which was translated into Chinese between 148 and 170 CE and the *Amitayurdhyanasutra* dated before 424 CE. The Chinese pilgrim Faxian records in accounts of his voyages that he prayed to the Boddhisattva Avalokitesvara in times of danger during the sea voyage. This aspect of the Boddhisattva also entered China and became one of the most popular manifestations of the Avalokitesvara, as is evident from 10th century Dunhuang.[14] As compared to the large number of icons of the Bodhisattva Avalokitesvara found across almost all parts of Asia, the religious literature dedicated to him is relatively limited, the exception being the *Saddharmapundarika Sutra*, where a whole chapter is devoted to him. He assumes any form or body necessary to deliver his devotees to salvation.[15]

The emergence of the cult of the Bodhisattva Avalokitesvara as a saviour of mariners and travellers in distress is generally associated with the *Saddharmapundarika Sutra* (chapter 24), though an enumeration of dangers of travel is to be found in earlier texts as well such as the *Anguttara Nikaya* (Kessivagga 119-20; Vol. II: 121) and the *Divyavadana* (p. 92: 25-8).

How does one explain the clustering of representations of Avalokitesvara in the western Deccan caves? The icon of Avalokitesvara as protector of the faithful is a type that occurs widely in the caves of western India. Several renditions were made in the western Deccan and over twelve painted and/or sculpted versions are known from Ajanta (caves 2, 4, 6, 10A, 11, 17, 20, 26),[16] four from Kanheri (caves 2, 41, 66 and 90), one from Aurangabad (cave 7), one from Pitalkhora (cave 3) and two from Ellora,[17] though nowhere is the composition so elaborate and the treatment so elegant as in cave 90 at Kanheri. The image in cave 90 is unique in that it depicts Avalokitesvara as protector against ten perils (rather than the usual eight) and includes numerous subsidiary figures. In this litany, Avalokitesvara offers the devotee promise of salvation from the various perils depicted at the sides of the composition including attack by elephants, lions, robbers and similar disasters.[18]

Based on his study of pictorial representations of the litany of Avalokitesvara at Ajanta, Schlingloff does not prioritise any particular text that was followed by the artists. "On the contrary, they developed their own relatively flexible iconographic tradition in which neither the number nor the subject of the perils, to say nothing of a prescribed sequence, were generally considered compulsory."[19] In contrast, Gregory Schopen attempts to identify Mahayana Sutras that may have formed the basis for the painting tradition at Ajanta and suggests after examination of a painting of the Avalokitesvara in cave 10 that as the *Gandavyuha sutra* contains a similar enumeration of perils, it would have been taken recourse to at Ajanta.[20] On an esoteric level, the dangers may be interpreted as obstacles to salvation. Spink suggests that the large number of Avalokitesvara representations from Ajanta indicate physical dangers rather than spiritual salvation.[21] Schlingloff argues against this position and states that "Buddhist artworks financed by laymen and executed by lay artists were primarily intended to help and guide the monks in their path to salvation."[22] Before we address the issue of choice of specific themes at monastic sites, a discussion of the placement of paintings and images may not be out of place.

Walter Spink has suggested that the bulk of the work at Ajanta dates from 462 to 480 CE during the reign of Harisena of the Vakataka dynasty, though there was an early phase, as evident from caves 9, 10, 12, which were excavated in the first phase dated from 1st century BCE to the 1st–2nd centuries CE.[23] Work at cave 2 at Ajanta was started in the mid- 460s, though the elaborate work was done on it after 475. Cave 4 the largest vihara at the site, was started in the early 460; cave 11 is another inaugural Vakataka vihara; and in cave 26, work continued until 478.[24] The impressive litany of Avalokitesvara in cave 4 was, according to Spink, carved early in 479 CE and the scene of the Bodhisattva as Saviour continued to be popular at Ajanta. The eight dangers depicted are shipwreck, fetters and chains, attack by a robber, fire, wild animals such as lions, snakes, elephants and witchcraft. This popularity is indeed striking, as the other iconic images are either of the Buddha or the stupa.[25] In addition scenes of sea travel and ship-wreck are depicted, such as the voyage of prince Kalyanakarin in cave 1; the painting of the Purnavadana in cave 2; and Simhala legend showing ships carrying an army of elephants and cavalry to Sri Lanka in cave 17.[26]

Clearly, sea-travel is depicted prominently and the popularity of Avalokitesvara as saviour from ship-wreck at sites such as Ajanta indicates an engagement with the concept not only in its Mahayana manifestation, but also with its political ramifications of Simhala-vijaya, as also the commercial voyages of prince Kalyanakarin. This multi-layered meaning of the caves and their paintings is further confirmed by the ninety-seven inscriptions that record donations by the ruling elite and rich benefactors in the viharas with shrines, such as caves 1, 2, 4, 11, 17 and 20, as also the *caitya* cave 26. In addition, cave 2 has verses or labels from Aryasura's *Jatakamala*. The patrons of the caves at Ajanta included the wealthy *viharasvamin* or owner of vihara 4, i.e. Mathura and Upendragupta whose records survive in caves 17 and 20. An inscription (no. 63) recording the religious gift of an *upasaka* or lay devotee accompanies the much faded *astamahabhaya* Avalokitesvara scene in cave 11, while a second epigraph in the cave refers to *upasaka* Mitradharma. The *caitya* cave 26 was the gift of the monk Buddhagupta who was born of a noble family, but became a monk at an early age.[27] How does this compare with data from Kanheri, where the Bodhisattva is shown saving the worshipper from eight great perils namely shipwreck, conflagration, wild elephant, lion, serpent, robber, captivity and demon?

Kanheri was the largest religious centre along the west coast of India with one hundred and four caves located in the fertile basin of the Ulhas river. Most of the caves at Kanheri are located in small clusters between 60 and 90 metres above the surrounding plain and ancient inscriptions provide the name of the site as Kanhasela.[28] The site dates from the 1st to the 11th century CE and thus is longer lasting than the caves at Ajanta. Almost every cell contained a *podhi* where rainwater from the top of the hill was collected and at least ten of the inscriptions record donations of cisterns, tanks and water bodies.

The inscriptions from the site do not refer to the Bodhisattva Avalokitesvara, though, as mentioned earlier, the site contains the most elaborate scene of the litany of the Avalokitesvara in cave 90. The litany scene depicts the Bodhisattva saving the devotee from ten dangers and Tara is shown as his companion, both in cave 90 and in cave 3. There are three Pahlavi inscriptions in cave 90 that record visits of Parsis to the site in the 11th century.[29] A unique eleven-headed image of the Avalokitesvara dated to the 6th century is carved in cave 41, in a niche to the entrance of the cave. An iconographic description of the eleven-headed Avalokitesvara occurs in *Avalokitesvara Ekadasamukhadharani* translated into Chinese in 561–77 CE. A representation of this theme on a Chinese stele dates to 691 CE and suggests the prevalence of this concept in China in the 7th century.[30] The cave is an astylar hall with a shrine at the back depicting an image of the seated Buddha. A 2nd century inscription on a detached rock opposite cave 41 at Kanheri refers to the construction of a tank by setthi Punaka. The stone slab measures 1.10 x 1.25 metres and is located close to an ancient stonewall across a rain-water stream emerging from the nearby catchment area at the foot of the hill. In the broken wall a conduit excavated in the rock and measuring 1.7 x 1.75 x 1 metre has been located. This perhaps provides the earliest evidence for the damming of water and construction of a tank.[31]

Cave 2 actually consists of six separate excavations in the rock face, which is much destroyed now. Caves 2c and 2e are flat roofed rectangular *caityas* with stupas at the end and are dated to the early stages of rock-cutting at the site. In front of cave 2, a stone casket was found containing an earthen pot with shell and carnelian beads, coins, terracotta objects, a copper lotus and pottery.[32] Three inscriptions are carved on the back wall of the hall designated 2f and record gifts from residents of nearby sites such as Nasik and a goldsmith from Kalyan.[33] Nor are these the only inscriptions that provide evidence of visits of devotees to Kanheri from different parts of the coastal regions. A six-line inscription in cave 11 dated to 12th September 854 CE records the visit of a devout worshipper of the Buddha from Gauda or Bengal and a permanent endowment made by him of one hundred dramas for the construction of a meditation room and clothing for monks residing at the *mahavihara* at Krsnagiri.[34] The link with eastern India is further corroborated by the finds of a wooden image of a seated Tara in front of cave 31 at Kanheri. The image bears a striking resemblance to the Pala figures of Tara from Nalanda.[35] Thus Kanheri continued to be linked to several other sites through coastal networks, as also to several inland centres.

Cave 7 at Aurangabad is the most elaborate and famous for its sculptural embellishments. On plan it includes a central shrine with a circumambulatory passage and an outer corridor running all around. The front wall of the veranda has an elaborate representation of the litany of Avalokitesvara and Bodhisattvas on both sides to the entrance to the shrine. The litany of Avalokitesvara is particularly more intricate depiction of the theme (fire, theft, demon, elephant, lion, shipwreck, snake, monkey), as compared to similar examples from Ajanta and Ellora. The other important sculptural panels are of Tara, the principal consort of Avalokitesvara, depicted to the left of the central shrine door and a group of six female musicians on the left wall of the main shrine. The main figure at the centre is in a dancing attitude, with the five others playing different musical instruments.

Geri Malandra has shown that the twelve Buddhist caves at Ellora present new features and are thus a visual record of the development of Esoteric Buddhism starting from simple forms in cave 6 (around 600 CE) to a more complex iconography in cave 12 (730 CE). Ellora shares the groupings of Bodhisattvas surrounding a Buddha with sites in Odisha such as Ratnagiri, Udaigiri and Lalitagiri, though there are significant differences as well. The evidence from the rock-cut caves at Ellora retains the context of the sculptures, which have been preserved *in situ* and is also a significant indicator of Ellora's relationship with other sites in the Buddhist world.[36] The image of the Avalokitesvara was important at Ellora and while he is shown as *dvarapala* and shrine attendant to the Buddha, sculptural panels and a small shrine are also devoted to him.[37] The litany of Avalokitesvara is sculpted between caves 3 and 4 at Ellora and is dated mid-6th to mid-8th century CE. It is significant that though the cult of the Avalokitesvara continued in Karnataka until the 11th century, there were changes in the notion of the saviour elsewhere in peninsular India.

Around the same time, in the rock cut sanctuaries at Ellora, the function of the Avalokitesvara as the saviour from the eight perils is delegated to Tara in cave 9. This theme occurs prominently in the monastic establishment at Ratnagiri in Odisha. It was in Odisha that the major expansion of Buddhism took place in the 5th to 13th century period and stupendous monastic complexes were constructed in the three hill ranges of Jajpur district, the Alti or Nalti, Assia and Mahavinayaka. Local tradition refers to the region being close to the sea in the past.

Ratnagiri is a 25 metre high isolated hill of khondalite formation of the Assia range bounded on three sides by the rivers Brahmani, the Kimiria and the Birupa. In the vicinity of Ratnagiri, the extensive Buddhist site of Udayagiri is located in the easternmost part of the Assia hills in a horse-shoe formation, while Naltigiri or Lalitagiri is not very far on the south bank of the Birupa. The three monastic complexes form a triangle; the distance between Ratnagiri and Udayagiri is 5.5 kilometres as the crow flies and 3.5 kilometres between Udayagiri and Lalitagiri. The latter two hills are much broader and higher than Ratnagiri.[38]

As late as the 1950s, Ratnagiri was marked by two compact mounds: one circular and conical, which yielded the stupa; and the other quadrangular, with several Buddhist sculptures scattered on the surface of the mounds. The site was located in close proximity to the major centre of Jajpur and was surrounded by navigable rivers, productive plains and khondalite bearing hills. The excavations yielded a large impressive stupa surrounded by a number of smaller stupas and two quadrangular monasteries. Several slabs found during excavations were inscribed with texts such as the *Pratityasamutpada sutra* or the *dharanis*.

Of all the three major sites in the Assia hills, the stupa at Ratnagiri is indeed striking. The precincts of Stupa I were crowded with smaller stupas of varying dimensions and forms and comprised both structural stupas of brick and stone, as well as portable stone stupas. It is interesting that there were several levels of stupas and sometimes stupas were built on top of earlier ones, the largest number of dedications being built between the 9th and 13th centuries CE. Many of the stone portable stupas had niches for enshrining deities such as Buddha, Tara, Lokesvara, Manjusri and sometimes deities from the Vajrayana pantheon. Some of the smaller stupas yielded *saririka* relics in the form of charred bones, though hardly any attention was paid to reliquaries, which were generally plain earthen vases or stone blocks with sockets.[39]

Two standing images of *astamahabhaya* Tara were found from the surface at Ratnagiri. In 1927–8, R.P. Chanda, an official of the Indian Museum, Calcutta, visited Ratnagiri and other sites in Odisha to collect Buddhist sculptures for the museum. He found a number of sculptures near the Mahakala temple on the hill at Ratnagiri, including the *astamahabhaya* Tara image, which is now in the Patna Museum (Figure 28).[40] The standing image is dated to the 11th century on the basis of a fragmentary inscription and graphically portrays the *jalarnava-bhaya* or fear of drowning in a sinking boat.[41] A second image now in the site museum at Ratnagiri, dated to the end of the 8th century CE, shows Tara flanked by scenes of the eight perils depicted in two vertical rows of four panels each.[42] A third 11th–12th century seated image is fixed to the outer compound wall on the outskirts of Shergarh district in Balasore district.

28. Astamahabhaya Tara from Ratnagiri now in the Patna Museum.

A striking feature of Buddhism in Odisha is the lack of narrative sculptures, one of the few exceptions being the *astamahapratiharya* sculpture, now in the Raghunatha temple at

Solampur.[43] Tara was a popular deity in Odisha, especially at Ratnagiri, where she is found sculpted in 99 niches of monolithic stupas. She is represented both in her seated *lalitasana* form as also in various other types described in the *Sadhanamala*. The 11th century manuscript of *Astasahasrika Prajnaparamita* in the Cambridge University Library (MSS no. Add 1643) illustrates Buddhist images and shrines from different parts of India and four of the illustrations relate to Odisha. It is not surprising that three of these refer to images of Tara, perhaps from Banpur, while the fourth refers to the monastic complex at Kuruma, near Konarak in Puri district.[44] From the 7th to 12th centuries, Tara is shown as the saviour from a variety of dangers including shipwreck in sculpture as also in epigraphs. She is invoked in several inscriptions, such as the Nalanda record of Vipula Srimitra dated to the first half of the 12th century, as also the Kalasan inscription from Java. Nevertheless, the Avalokitesvara as Saviour from shipwreck form does not seem to have wide prevalence in Southeast Asia.

Patronised as Kanheri was by merchants and wealthy trading groups, the sculptural programme at the site was in contrast to that from Ajanta, which was sponsored by the ruling elite or, as Spink argues, was 'an elitist undertaking'. The shift to Tara as saviour at Ellora and Ratnagiri is often attributed to new developments, such as Esoteric Buddhism, but these new developments do not explain the continued importance of Avalokitesvara at Kanheri, nor the fact that the veneration of Tara does not take place at other contemporary sites in coastal Odisha such as Lalitagiri and Udayagiri. The Saviour at several sites in Angkor in Cambodia, on the other hand, seems to have been depicted as a winged horse or Balaha as discussed in the second chapter.

SUPPARAKA JATAKA

Once upon a time, a king named Bharu reigned in the kingdom of Bharu. There was a seaport named Bharukaccha or the marsh of Bharu. At that time the Bodhisattva was born into the family of a master mariner there;

> amiable he was, and of complexion a golden brown. They gave him the name of Supparaka-kumara. He grew up with great distinction; and even when he was no more than sixteen years old, he had gained a complete mastery over the art of seamanship. Afterwards when his father died he became the head of the mariners and plied the mariner's calling: wise he was, and full of intelligence; with him on board, no ship came ever to harm.[45]

The Pali *Jataka* is a collection of narratives adapted to Buddhist teachings and while only the verses are regarded as canonical, the prose commentary also draws on older material. By the 2nd century BCE many of the Jataka stories find representation on Buddhist monuments in central India. More importantly, these narratives inform us of a world of coastal settlements, sailing and the dangers at sea and also indicate a symbiotic relationship between religious institutions and seafaring communities. Several issues emerge, such as the nature of the settlement at Bharukaccha or Sopara on the west coast of India, the wisdom and learning associated with the profession of a mariner and, more significantly for this chapter, the relationship between religious monuments along the coast and maritime activity. One of the Buddhist monuments important for this chapter is that of Borobudur in central Java.

Construction at Borobudur probably began around 760 CE and was completed by about 830 CE. Two inscriptions found in the region may be relevant. The first dated 824 CE refers to the construction of a religious edifice by king Samaratungga and the second of 842 CE mentions queen Sri Kahulunan who allocated revenue from a village to support the sanctuary.[46] Borobudur is a unique Javanese monument consisting of a series of terraces of decreasing size that rise above the Kedu plains. Exquisitely carved with 1460 stone panels, Borobudur contains more than 500 life-sized Buddha images set around the monument. In the middle of each of the four sides, a long, straight stairway leads from the ground to the uppermost terrace, a climb of nearly 26 metres. The most striking are the sculpted galleries which illustrate five Buddhist scriptures, some of them highly abstract. Of all the texts, one that occupies four hundred and sixty panels is the story of prince Sudhana and his quest for knowledge, as inscribed in the *Gandavyuha*.

The *Gandavyuha*, part of the *Avatamsakasutra*, is an important text for the study of pilgrimage in early Buddhism. It was translated from Sanskrit into Chinese in the 4th century and was popular both in China and Japan, but in Java not only is there divergence between image and text, but it also acquires representation very different from anywhere else in the Buddhist world. The somewhat slender narrative provided by the text of the *Gandavyuha* has been profusely sculpted on the 8th century Buddhist monument at Borobudur in central Java, though there are a number of variations between the sculpted panels and the textual data, and there is "no clear correlation between the iconography and location of the narrative scenes and the corresponding passages in the text."[47]

In addition to the *Gandavyuha* there are several Jataka stories represented on the monument. In the lower register of the walls of the first gallery at Borobudur, a series of four panels illustrate the life of the Bodhisattva as a sea captain and how he and his sailors had been shipwrecked on the island inhabited by female ogres. Sea travel is prominently represented in the narratives of Maitrakanyaka; Supparaka Jataka, where the Bodhisattva is born as a navigator who saves the ship from a storm and a monster; and the Kacchapavadana, where a giant turtle saves shipwrecked merchants on his back.[48] Besides, the monument at Borobudur is well known for detailed depictions of more than ten watercraft, many of them were sea-going vessels.

> Inasmuch as the Buddhist faith was preferred at Nagor Pathom before it was adopted in any other of the cities of Suvarnabhumi, the earliest *caitya* erected there was from its first foundation called Phra Pathom Cetiya.[49]

King Mongkut (1804–1868) set up this inscription at Nagor Pathom or Nakorn Pathon declaring that Buddhist religion was introduced into the city at the time of king Asoka. He reached this conclusion based on the shape of the stupa, which resembled those said to have been constructed by Asoka in the Indian subcontinent, as also the fact that brick was used rather than stone. Secondly, Nakorn Pathom has yielded a large number of stone fashioned in the shape of a wheel.[50]

Two stucco reliefs from Chulapathon chedi at Nakorn Pathon need to be brought into the discussion here (Figure 29). One of these shows two merchants seated on a tortoise, the Bodhisattva incarnate who saved the merchants. This theme identified as Kachhapa Jataka is also found at Borobudur. The second stucco panel shows a ship carrying two merchants identified as a representation of Supparaka Jataka, which occurs both in the Pali Jataka collection (no. 479), as also in Aryasura's *Jatakamala*. These reliefs were brought to light during excavations by the Thai Fine Arts Department in 1968. As the present chedi had covered the earlier one, Pierre Dupont's 1939–40 excavations had failed to unearth them. It would seem that the chedi was renovated and expanded three times in the past.

29. Stucco from Nakorn Pathon showing Supparaka Jataka.

How are these depictions to be explained in the context of the monument at Nakorn Pathon, especially as there is no evidence for them from other stupa sites? Are these representations linked to the association of the site with the landing of Buddhist monks sent by Asoka and the setting up of the earliest stupa in Thailand?

Nandana Chutiwongs[51] suggests that Bodhisattva images began to be made locally in Thailand in the latter half of the 7th century, both for independent worship, as also as acolytes of the Buddha. The known provenances of small bronze images of the deity include U Thong in Suphanburi, Ku Bua in Ratchaburi, Si Thep in Phetchaburi, Muang Fa-daed in Kalasin and an unspecified site in Prachinaburi, which shows a twelve-armed standing image, but so far no images have been recorded from Nakorn Pathon.[52] Two silver plaques are however known from Chedi Chu'la Pathom in Nakorn Pathon, which show the Buddha accompanied by attendant figures wearing princely ornaments.[53] The Bodhisattva is often represented as an acolyte of the Buddha as evident from a relief on the rock wall of Thamorat cave in the province of Phetchabun and from several votive tablets showing the descent from Trayastrimsa heaven riding on the mythical creature referred to as Banaspati or scenes of the first sermon.[54]

It is evident from the discussion above that no general explanation can work for all the Buddhist sites. Instead, while a notion of the Saviour and its depiction on monastic structures reflects an active engagement of the patrons and sponsors of Buddhist monastic architecture with the sea, it also underscores the unique context of each monastic site that needs to be studied. More importantly, it is the interaction between the sites and the linkages provided by travel, search for knowledge and pilgrimage that bound the coastal sites closely with the community. These connections have often been studied in linear terms, but as discussed elsewhere, it is important that the diverse nature and plural fabric of these early maritime linkages across the Bay of Bengal are recognized.[55]

COASTAL TEMPLES AND PILGRIMAGE

Monastic and temple-centred religious institutions formed an important intermediate group between the state and the family. The temples and monasteries were not merely centres of devotion and worship, but were also principal institutions in medieval India for establishing laws and enforcing them on their members. A large number of inscriptions from early medieval India document complex arrangements for the use of temple resources, whether these were lands or else revenues from shops and markets. In the larger temples, we find mention of several classes of temple employees such as administrators, treasurers, accountants, temple women, cooks, sweepers, artisans, watchmen, etc. Resources for temple rituals and for the large number of employees were generated through surplus agricultural production on temple lands and from donations in cash and kind from trading groups. The inscriptions also provide a record of legal transactions conducted and, in addition to the temple archives on income and expenditure, form a valuable source of information on the legal jurisdiction of the temple. A good example of this is the study of the early 17th century archives of a temple in Kerala.[56]

In Chapter 2, the site of Chandor (ancient Chandrapura) in district South Goa was discussed, where archaeological excavations have exposed the complete plan of a brick temple complex datable from 4th to 11th century CE. Nor is this the only early coastal temple site, as is evident from the extant group of rock-cut temples on the Tamil coast dated from the second half of the 6th century onward and credited to the Pallava dynasty.[57] A characteristic feature of these early temples referred to as *mandapas* in inscriptions was their association with large water-bodies, either irrigation tanks or river-banks (*tirtha*). Perhaps the best known of all the temples of the period is the Shore Temple complex at Mamallapuram or Mahabalipuram in Kanchipuram district, 60 kms south of the modern city of Chennai, built in the early 8th century CE. It is evident from recent archaeological work at the site that the three extant temples were a part of a larger complex, many of which have since been submerged. At the southern edge of Mahabalipuram is a group of five free-standing temples also known as *rathas*. Four of them were carved out of a single long granite boulder.

On the Kerala coast, temple architecture dates from 9th century onward. Early rock-cut caves are known from southern parts of Kerala especially the present districts of Kollam, Thrissur and Thiruvananthapuram and have been dated to the 8th century. Most of these are single cell shrines enshrining a Siva-*linga*, but at least one cave dedicated to Visnu is also known. As with other parts of the coast, the Malabar region also presents a multi-religious milieu. Images of the Buddha here date to the 7th and 8th century and Buddhism is known to have continued at least until the middle of the 11th century CE. In contrast, the Jain monuments of Kerala include both rock shelters and structural temples, though very few of the latter have survived. Thus the association of religious shrines along the coast with a range of communities who traversed the seas is evident.

NOTES AND REFERENCES

1. Dieter Schlingloff, *Studies in Ajanta Paintings*, Delhi: Ajanta Publications, 1988, chapter 22.
2. R. Salomon, *Indian Epigraphy*, New York: Oxford University Press, 1998, p. 136.
3. Harry Falk, *Asokan Sites and Artefacts*, Mainz am Rhein: Verlag Philipp von Zabern, 2006, p. 57.
4. Himanshu Prabha Ray, Inscribed Pots, Emerging Identities: The Social Milieu of Trade, in Patrick Olivelle (ed.), *Between the Empires: Society in India 300 BCE to 400 CE*, New York: Oxford University Press, 2006, pp. 113-43.
5. *Jatakas*, Book I, no. 4; Book X, nos. 439, 442; Book XI, no. 463; Book XVI, no. 528.
6. *Jatakas*, Book XXI, no. 539.
7. K.V. Soundara Rajan, *Junagadh*, New Delhi: Archaeological Survey of India, 1985, p. 12.
8. *Indian Archaeology – A Review (IAR) 1967-68*: 13.

9. K. Krishnan, Rukshana Nanji and Atusha Irani, *Revisiting Buddhist Gujarat*, Government of Gujarat, 2010, p. 97.
10. Himanshu Prabha Ray, *Monastery and Guild: Commerce under the Satavahanas*, New Delhi: Oxford University Press, 1986.
11. *Epigraphia Indica* XX: 23.
12. B. Bandyopadhyay, *Udayagiri – 2*, New Delhi: Archaeological Survey of India, 2007, pp. 9-10.
13. *Indian Archaeology – A Review 1987-88*: 88.
14. Nandana Chutiwongs, *The Iconography of Avalokitesvara in Mainland Southeast Asia*, New Delhi: IGNCA and Aryan Books International, 2002, p. xxxv.
15. John C. Holt, *Buddha in the Crown: Avalokitesvara in the Buddhist Traditions of Sri Lanka*, New York: Oxford University Press, 1991, pp. 30-37.
16. Walter M. Spink, *Ajanta: History and Development*, Volume III, *The Arrival of the Uninvited*, Leiden: Brill, 2005, p. 5.
17. M.E. Leese, *Ellora* and the Development of the Litany Scene in Western India,in R. Parimoo et al. (eds.), *Ellora Caves, Sculptures and Architecture*, Delhi: Books and Books, 1988, pp. 164-79.
18. Susan L. Huntington, *The Art of Ancient India: Buddhist, Hindu, Jaina*, New York – Tokyo: Weatherhill, 1993, pp. 264-65.
19. Dieter Schlingloff, op. cit., chapter 18: 177.
20. G. Schopen, *Figments and Fragments of Mahayana Buddhism*, Honolulu: University of Hawaii, 2005, p. 293.
21. Walter M. Spink, op. cit., pp. 6-7.
22. Dieter Schlingloff, op. cit., p. 177.
23. Walter M. Spink, *Ajanta: History and Development*, Volume V, *Cave by Cave*, Leiden: Brill, 2007, p. 15; also Volume 4: *Painting, Sculpture, Architecture*, Brill, 2009, pp. 1- 4.
24. Ibid., Volume V: chapter 3.
25. Spink, *The Arrival of the Uninvited*, pp. 6-7.
26. Dieter Schlingloff, op. cit., chapter 22.
27. Richard S. Cohen, Problems in the Writing of Ajanta's History: The Epigraphic Evidence, *Indo-Iranian Journal*, 40, 1997, pp. 125-48.
28. Nagaraju, *Buddhist Architecture*, p. 190.
29. Shobhana Gokhale, *Kanheri Inscriptions*, Pune: Deccan College Post Graduate and Research Institute, 1991, p. 142.

30. Nandana Chutiwongs, op. cit., p. 37.
31. Shobhana Gokhale, op. cit., p. 84.
32. D. Mitra, *Buddhist Monuments*, Calcutta: Sahitya Samsad, 1980, p. 168.
33. Nagaraju, op. cit., pp. 192-93.
34. Shobhana Gokhale, op. cit., pp. 70-71.
35. H.D. Sankalia, A Unique Wooden Idol of the Buddhist Goddess Tara from Kanheri Caves, *Journal of the Asiatic Society of Bombay*, Volumes 56-59, 1981-84: 296-9.
36. Geri H. Malandra, *Unfolding a Mandala: The Buddhist Cave Temples at Ellora*, Albany: State University of New York Press, 1993, pp. xvii-ix.
37. Ibid., p. 99.
38. D. Mitra, *Ratnagiri (1958-61)*, Memoirs of the Archaeological Survey of India, no. 80, New Delhi: Archaeological Survey of India, 1981, Vol. 1, p. 7.
39. Ibid., Vol. 1, pp. 25-28.
40. Ibid., Vol. 1, p. 11.
41. Ibid., Vol. 2, p. 428.
42. Ibid., Vol. 2, pp. 444-45.
43. T.E. Donaldson, *Iconography of the Buddhist Sculpture of Orissa*, New Delhi: Indira Gandhi National Centre for the Arts and Abhinav Publications, 2001, p. 94.
44. Ibid., p. 25.
45. *The Jataka*, Book XI, no. 463.
46. John Miksic, *Borobudur: Golden Tales of the Buddhas*, Berkeley – Singapore: Periplus editions, 1990, p. 23.
47. J. Fontein, *The Pilgrimage of Sudhana: A Study of Gandavyuha Illustrations in China, Japan and Java*, The Hague: Mouton, 1967, p. 125.
48. A.J. Bernet Kempers, *Ageless Borobudur*, Wassenaar: Servire, 1976, pp. 110-19.
49. HRH Prince Damrong Rajanubhab (translated by J. Crosby), Siamese History Prior to the Founding of Ayuddhaya, *Journal of the Siam Society*, XIII, 1919: 11.
50. *Journal of the Siam Society*, XIII, 1919: 1-66.
51. Nandana Chutiwongs, op. cit., p. 152.
52. Ibid., p. 156.
53. Ibid., p. 187.
54. Ibid., pp. 158-59.

55. Himanshu Prabha Ray, The Shrine in Early Hinduism: The Changing Sacred Landscape, *The Journal of Hindu Studies*, 2009, 2: 76-96; Himanshu Prabha Ray, Multi-religious Maritime Linkages across the Bay of Bengal, in Nicolas Revire and Stephen Murphy (eds.), *Before Siam: Essays in Art and Archaeology*, Bangkok: River Books & The Siam Society, 2014, pp. 132-51.
56. Donald R. Davis Jr. *The Boundaries of Hindu Law: Tradition, Custom and Politics in Medieval Kerala*, Torino: CESMEO, 2004.
57. K.R. Srinivasan, *Cave Temples of the Pallavas*, New Delhi: Archaeological Survey of India, 1964.

6

MULTIPLE PARTNERS ACROSS THE INDIAN OCEAN

Multiple Partners across the Indian Ocean

> And by the lowest count India, China and the Arabian peninsula remove 100 million sesterces from our empire each year – that is what our luxuries and our women cost us (Pliny, *Natural History*, 12.84).

How is this statement by Pliny the Elder, who held senior positions in the Roman Empire, to be read? Is this a reflection of the money-drain that the East is often accused of by the West, in this case the Roman Empire? Or else is this moral rectitude on the part of Pliny to caution against the implications of luxury consumption by a very small group of the wealthy Roman elite? However one reads it, it is clearly not a statement based on statistical analysis of the Roman economy, but reflects political compulsions vis-à-vis foreign trade. Rather than discussing the functioning of the Roman economy, in this section the focus is on practical texts that provide insights into the working of maritime networks in the western Indian Ocean. This overview is meant to underscore the multiple partners and groups involved in trans-oceanic trade, the changes that took place over time starting from the beginning of the Common Era to the 14th century CE.

The nature of global interconnectedness no doubt changed over time and the contemporary phase of globalization is marked by an intensification of multiple forms of global interconnectedness. Nevertheless, there are lessons to be learnt from the rapid traversing of ideas, attitudes and values across national borders in South Asia in earlier periods. This sharing of ideas led to an interconnectedness and interaction between peoples of diverse cultures and ways of life and provided dynamism to local groups and societies. The emphasis was on plurality of culture and celebration of difference as several groups coexisted and shared maritime space.

In this chapter the diverse ethnic nature of trading groups will be discussed as evident from texts written at different periods and in varied languages. The choice of texts is naturally limited to those that deal specifically with the theme of sailing and trading in the western Indian Ocean, in order to highlight the varied experiences and expectations from maritime trade among communities settled along the western Indian Ocean littoral and engaged in trade with the west coast of India. Within this corpus, writings in Greek and Arabic are prominently represented. India entered Greek imagination through the campaigns of Alexander into north-western parts of the Indian subcontinent in the 4th century BCE (327–325 BCE) and took on a variety of interests ranging from the geographical compendia of Strabo (64/63 BCE–21 CE) and Claudius Ptolemy (90–168 CE); to the *Natural History* of Pliny the Elder (23/24–79 CE) and the practical *Periplus of the Erythraean Sea*.[1] In contrast to early writings in Greek is the 6th century CE *Christian Topography* of Cosmas Indicopleustes, which combined theological and geographical discussions. Sri Lanka and India figure in the eleventh book where the discussion shifts to topography and natural history. In contrast to all these writings, the *Periplus* limits itself to the coastline and focuses on commercial travel in the region.

THE *PERIPLUS OF THE ERYTHRAEAN SEA*: INDIA IN GREEK AND ROMAN IMAGINATION

A text that is unique not only in the corpus of Greek writings, but also within the domain of historical literature on the Indian Ocean is the 1st century CE *Periplus of the Erythraean Sea* by an anonymous writer possibly based in Egypt. It provides an unembellished listing of commodities traded at different centres along the coasts of the western Indian Ocean both eastward from the Red Sea into India, as well as southward along the east African coast (Figure 30). It is thus a practical rather than a literary text, but crucial to an understanding of the trade networks. No doubt sailors and merchants had traversed the sea lanes between the Makran and Gujarat coasts to centres in the Persian Gulf as early as the 3rd millennium BCE. These sea lanes had expanded by the early centuries of the Common Era and connected not just large parts of the western Indian Ocean, but eastward into the Bay of Bengal as well. Many of the commodities already known in the Mediterranean region had been imported over long distances, but in the early centuries of the Common Era came through more direct routes. A good example of this is pepper. Shipwrecks from the Bronze Age show that pepper was being imported into the Mediterranean as early as the 2nd millennium BCE, but texts in the

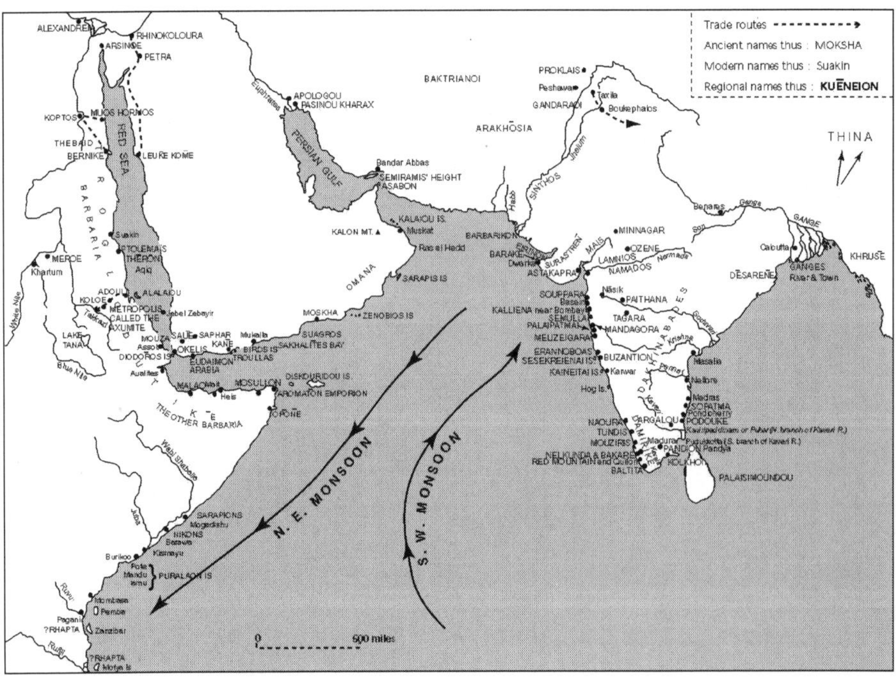

30. Map based on the *Periplus Maris Erythraei*.

1st century CE refer to many more varieties of pepper, such as black pepper, long pepper and white pepper and diverse and varied uses, including in desserts.[2]

A few issues emerge from a careful reading of the *Periplus*. One is the mix in terms of low-cost and high value luxury commodities that traders carried in their travels to India. The second is the need to carefully estimate the varied requirements at coastal centres and to adjust the cargo accordingly, and finally is the issue of payments and the role of currency as a medium of exchange. Let us start with the first issue of trade being a mix of low-cost and high-value commodities.

A comparative analysis of commodities traded along the east African, Arabian and Indian coasts shows that the west coast of India provided the largest variety of goods. While east Africa yielded ivory, tortoise shell, frankincense, myrrh and various grades of cassis, the products of the Arabian coast were restricted to frankincense, myrrh and aloe. On the island of Socotra at the mouth of the Red Sea, grain, rice, cotton cloth and female slaves could be picked up.[3] In contrast, the Indian coast provided spices, medicinal and aromatic plants, gems, textiles, both cotton and silk, dyes such as indigo, grain, rice, sesame oil, ghee, ivory, pearls and tortoise shell.[4]

India has traditionally been one of the major producers of cotton fabrics in the Indian Ocean region. The paintings at Ajanta provide details of patterned textiles and especially noteworthy are the costumes worn by women. For example, a *cauri*-bearer or attendant walking in front of a raja's horse in a procession wears a full-sleeved tunic in which the figures of *hamsa* or geese are woven or printed (cave I). In a representation of the Campeya Jataka in cave II, a lady is dressed in a long tunic decorated with an assortment of small flowers. Patterned textiles also appear in the representations of pillows, curtains and cushions. Royal attendants (cave I) are often shown wearing tunics on which complex patterns are worked. An attendant depicted in cave I wears a tunic with a pattern in bands consisting of rosettes, circles within compartments and chevrons, while another seated on the ground wears a tunic of silver brocade with floral designs in dark brown.[5]

Indigo is perhaps the oldest organic dye used in the Indian Ocean region. The Greek sources refer to its origin in India and the *Periplus* catalogues it as an item of export from Barbarikon at the mouth of the Indus river (section 39). The term used for it in South Asia is *nila*, a term that spread eastwards into Southeast Asia with the adoption of Indian textiles, especially for ceremonial purposes. Ethnographic studies indicate that though the indigo plant grows wild in several regions of the subcontinent, producing good dye requires diligent cultivation and an even more laborious process is involved in the production of a hard and durable lump of concentrated indigo pigment. The charter of Visnusena dated to 592 CE from Lohata in the Gujarat – Kathiawar region mentions a tax on the pressing of the indigo dye.[6] It is significant that in the Geniza papers discussed in a later section, indigo figures as one of the items of trade from India westward to Egypt handled by the business house of Ibn 'Awkal in the period from 980 to 1030.[7]

It is owing to the importance of trade with the Indian coast that the *Periplus* provides graphic descriptions of entry into the different harbours and landfalls at several centres. For example, entry into the Indus river known for its seven mouths, narrow and full of shallows, is indicated by changes in the colour of the water and the sea-snakes that emerge from the depths. The Rann of Kachchh is described with bodies of water with shoals and shallow eddies, as a result of which the land is scarcely visible and vessels run the risk of being grounded. The Gulf of Barygaza or the present Gulf of Khambat is described as being too narrow and difficult for vessels coming from the sea to negotiate and the mouth of the river [Narmada] on which Barygaza is located is hard to find, because the land is low and the structures are not clearly visible (section 43). These graphic accounts resonate with descriptions of the west coast in later texts and the problems associated with navigating this stretch.

Coastal centres along the west coast of India could be divided into two spheres: those on the north-west coast comprising of Barbarikon and Barygaza; and the south-western ports of Muziris and Nelkynda. It is significant that the *Periplus* also makes a distinction between Barbarikon and Barygaza, while it slots the two centres further south in a single category. Barbarikon was merely a mooring or landing place and all goods were taken up the river to the king at the metropolis (section 39). In contrast, Barygaza was not only a landing place for cargoes but also a market centre. It imported both raw materials such as glass, copper, tin and lead and a range of more expensive goods like fine wine, precious silverware, expensive clothing, etc. and not only provided an outlet for Chinese cloth but also for a variety of cotton textiles, silk yarn, long pepper and other items brought from centres in the vicinity. The two centres on the Malabar coast were quite similar and were major exporters of pepper, pearls, gems, ivory and tortoise shell, while the items of import were less diverse and high end as compared to those going to Barygaza (section 56).

How were these commodities traded: through barter or against a commonly accepted currency? In contrast to the general practice of barter, the import of coins was relatively rare and is mentioned only in a few instances. Zoskales, who was proficient in reading and writing Greek, is referred to as the ruler of the African coast of the Red Sea and a little Roman money is said to have been imported in the region "for the resident foreigners" (section 6). Further southeast, towards the mouth of the Gulf of Aden, was the settlement of Malao that offered a market for "Roman money, in limited quantity" (section 8). Similarly, Muza, though without a harbour, provided an outlet for considerable amounts of money (section 24), while at Kane on the coast of Yemen, embossed silverware and large quantities of money were imported for the king (section 28).

Along the Indian coast three regions are mentioned as providing a market for Roman money and these three are the same as those discussed above, i.e. Barbarikon (section 39), Barygaza or Bharuch (section 49) and

Muziris and Nelkynda on the Malabar coast (section 56). The *Periplus* refers to the import of Roman coins at two centres in some detail: at Bharuch, where Roman gold and silver "commands an exchange at some profit against the local currency" (section 49); and along the Malabar coast which offers a market for "a great amount of money" (section 56). The text also refers to other coins in circulation in Barygaza, such as old drachmas stamped with inscriptions in Greek lettering and the coins of Apollodotus and Menander, who were kings after Alexander (section 47). While the reference to import of Roman coins along the Malabar coast may explain the concentration of these coins in the district of Coimbatore, their occurrence around Bharuch has been somewhat scanty.

Andhra or the Krishna valley is one region on which the *Periplus* has not much to say, though it does mention a route across the Deccan connecting Bharuch with the east coast via Paithan and Ter. However, as compared to the western Deccan or the area around Bharuch, the finds of Roman coins in the eastern Deccan corresponding largely with the present state of Andhra Pradesh have been more numerous and are scattered in the districts of Bijapur, Cuddapah, Guntur, Krishna, Nalgonda and Visakhapatnam, with the Akkenapalle hoard comprising of 1531 silver coins being the largest. In addition, a hoard from Nasthulpur, Karimnagar district, yielded thirty-nine Roman and eight silver punch-marked coins, the former belonging to Augustus and Nero, while fifty-seven gold coins were discovered during a survey of Nagavarapupadu village in Khamam district. Roman coins have also been found in the excavations at Nagarjunakonda, Kudavelli, Peddabankur and Dhulikakatta, together with imitations in lead gilded for use as pendants. Thus it is evident that rather than being symbols of trade or reflections of trading patterns, Roman coins were received and integrated very differently in various parts of the subcontinent, as also the Indian Ocean littoral (Figure 31).

The inscriptions from peninsular India do not mention Roman coins, though there are several recorded examples of money transactions, but the coin referred to in the inscription cannot always be identified. A

31. Clay bullae made in imitation of Roman coins found in India.

Nasik inscription mentions that Usavadata bought a field for 4,000 *kahapanas* and donated it for procuring food for those dwelling in the Buddhist monastic establishment at Nasik. Similarly, a majority of the donations at the Buddhist site of Kanheri near Mumbai were in the form of perpetual endowments of money ranging from 200 to 16,000 *kahapanas*. Another inscription of Usavadata mentions a payment of cloth money of twelve *kahapanas* each to the monks. Most of the perpetual endowments were in the form of investments with guilds or the Sangha and only the interest was to be paid and utilized. Thus 2,000 *kahapanas* were invested in a guild of weavers at Govardhana at an interest rate of one *pratika* (monthly) for the hundred and 1,000 in another weavers' guild at three-quarters of a *padika* (monthly) for the hundred. An inscription at Junnar records investment with the guild of bamboo workers at one and three quarters a month and with a guild of braziers at a quarter.

Perhaps the closest one can get to identifying the presence of Roman coins in epigraphs are the 3rd century Iksvaku records from Nagarjunakonda, which record donations of *dinaris*, stated to be a derivative of the Roman *denarius*. The purpose of the record was the creation of a perpetual endowment by depositing one hundred dinaris in four different guilds, seventy dinari in one of them and ten dinari in each of the others. Other inscriptions from the site refer to *dinari-mashaka*.[8]

Does the text indicate the ethnic identity of traders who traversed the sea lanes of the western Indian Ocean? While discussing Muza or Mocha on the Yemen coast of the Red Sea, the text refers to Arabs—ship-owners or charterers and sailors—who "trade across the water and with Barygaza, using their own outfits" (section 21). Muza is termed a "port of trade" even though it is without a harbour. Another important harbour and storehouse at the entrance to the Red Sea was the island of Socotra, which was settled by Arabs and Indians and even some Greeks, who sail out of there to trade (section 30). Merchants from Barygaza or Bharuch customarily traded with Oman and centres in the Persian Gulf and brought in supplies of copper and logs of teak and ebony. The Malabar coast owed its prosperity to Greek shipping and also to traffic from Ariake or Gujarat (section 54). On the east coast, the *Periplus* refers to Poduke identified with Arikamedu near Pondicherry where local boats mix with those that sail down from the region of the Ganga and from across the Bay of Bengal. Clearly, there was a variety of watercraft engaged with maritime trade and involved participation from several groups and communities. It would be worth examining the nature of coastal settlements and landing places.

COASTAL CENTRES AND HARBOURS

The extent to which ships sailed directly between the Red Sea and India or vice versa is a moot point. A second issue relates to the definition of the term 'port,' which is often used rather loosely to indicate a coastal centre and is often not differentiated from landing places, beach and inlet market places, tidal harbours at which cargoes were exchanged or coastal centres where customs duties were levied.

The *Periplus* uses the term '*limen*' six times and '*hormos*' thirteen times, often interchangeably, and in this it follows the practice of the Greek papyri from Egypt. The most frequently used is the term '*emporion*,' which occurs fifty times and refers to places for mooring that also offered facilities for buying and selling.[9] Prominent examples of the first two in Ptolemy are Leukos Limen on the Red Sea coast, Moscha Limen (Khor Rori) on the south Arabian coast, which was a collection point for frankincense, and Myos Hormos on the Red Sea coast, which we shall discuss later, while many of the Indian coastal sites are termed '*emporion*'.

The *Periplus* describes at least three coastal centres as '*emporion nomimon*' translated by Casson as a "legally limited port of trade" where all trade had to pass through the king's representatives.[10] In the context of Kalyan on the west coast of India, it indicates a change of status. Earlier, all goods were sent there, but with a change in political control, hindrances were being placed in the movements of goods to the centre (section 52). The one coastal centre that appears prominently in the *Periplus* and is mentioned twenty-eight times is Barygaza at the mouth of the Narmada. It was a major market centre and also provided access to a large hinterland, which produced a variety of goods and commodities.

In contrast, the *Arthasastra* makes a distinction between local trade transacted in fortified cities of the interior, identified as *nagara*, from that originating at distant places and exchanged at the *pattana*, located either on sea coasts or on river banks of the interior.[11] The two had different organisation of trade and different administrative structures, with itinerant merchants' organisations being active at coastal centres. The concept of *pattinam* is further refined in Tamil epigraphy. At Nagapattinam on the Tamil coast, for instance, there was no *nagaram*, only *ur* and *sabha* assemblies and this was true for other coastal centres also such as Tiruvadandai. An inscription of Rajendra III (1256) from Gandagopalapattinam (Krishnapatnam, Nellore) states that a local *ur* assembly and an itinerant merchant organization controlled the collection of levies associated with boats and ships.[12]

SOCOTRA AND THE SOUTH ARABIAN COAST

Recent research has brought to light nearly eight thousand inscriptions in the south Arabian alphabet carved on rock and dated from the 1st millennium BCE to 6th century CE. These have been divided into four thematic groups, viz., prescriptive texts including decrees relating to socio-economic issues; religious texts, property claims and commemorative texts.[13] The Nabateans in modern Jordan had been involved in trade with the Eastern Mediterranean, transhipping aromatics and incense from modern Yemen and Oman to Gaza in Judea long before the *Periplus*. The *Periplus* refers to three coastal centres of the south Arabian coast, viz. Muza (sections 20-24), which was termed *emporion nomimon* and describes a long list of commodities bought and sold there; Okelis is described as a 'watering station' (section 25) and the first place for those sailing on; and finally the seashore village (*kome*) of Eudaimon Arabia (section 26).

The preferred centre for exchange on the south Arabian coast was Qana, situated below the cliff at Husn al-Ghurab, 300 kilometres east of Aden close to the modern village of Bi'r 'Ali. The period between the early 2nd century and 5th century was probably the heyday of the Bi'r 'Ali settlement and it expanded to more than 5 hectares at that time. A huge temple probably dedicated to Sayin was built at this time to the south-west of the settlement. On the north-western outskirts of the city a building used as a synagogue was erected. In the 6th–7th century the ancient town of Qana occupied the north-western part of the settlement only and the settlement was abandoned around 7th century CE.[14] Amphora fragments of the Aqaba kilns from the upper (BA-III) period at Qana show strong trade links between Late Qana and the regions of southern Palestine or south-west Jordan.

The walled ancient settlement of Sumhurram, located about 45 kilometres east of Salalah on the coast of Dhofar, was visited in the 19th century, but archaeological work has been undertaken at the site first by an American team in the 1950s and then by the University of Pisa from 1996 onwards. A series of radiocarbon dates from the site and analysis of pottery sequences and numismatic material indicate that the city was founded at the beginning of the 3rd century BCE and continued until the 5th century CE. There is a graffito of a boat on the plaster of the city wall near the gate representing a whale fishing scene. Thus, recent excavations at Sumhurram have underscored its importance in the kingdom of Hadramawt and the centres on the south Arabian coast within western Indian Ocean sailing networks well into the 7th century CE.[15] This recent evidence highlights the significant participation of centres along the south

Arabian coast in maritime networks – though no doubt centres of political authority had meanwhile changed, as is evident from the writings of Cosmas.

Socotra is a small archipelago of four islands about 250 kilometres east of the Horn of Africa off the coasts of Yemen and Somalia in the western Indian Ocean. The largest island in the group is also called Socotra (Figure 32). The 132 kilometre-long island is often described as the most isolated place on Earth, though this account does not agree with its central location in the maritime networks of the early centuries of the Common Era, evident from archaeological excavations conducted over the years. The excavations at Socotra need to be viewed in the context of the marine resources of the island. One of the earliest descriptions of the island is to be found in the *Periplus Maris Erythraei* (sec.30) which refers to it as Dioscurides. Several varieties of tortoise shell found on the island are referred to, and are said to be in demand by shippers from Arabia and the west coast of India who exchanged big cargoes of tortoise shell for rice, grain, cotton cloth and female slaves. The other resource referred to is cinnabar, which is collected as an exudation from the *Dragon's* trees.

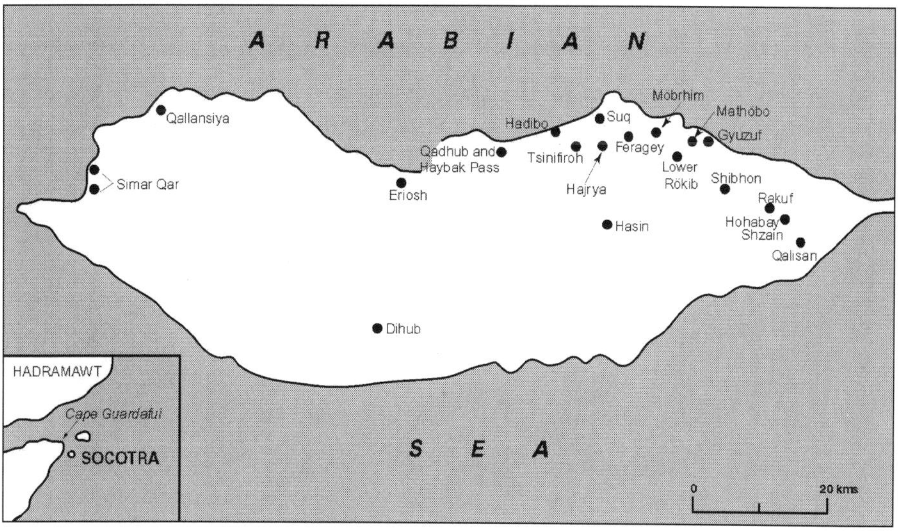

32. Map of the island of Socotra.

One of the oldest known archaeological sites on the island of Socotra has been located in the vicinity of the modern village of Rakuf in the eastern part of the island. Remains of a workshop used for the manufacture of flint tools were found here. Close to the site was a small cemetery, comprising ten dolmen-shaped grave structures having burial chambers of stone cists unique on the island. These burials had scant grave furniture and as a result the excavators found it difficult to provide a precise date. The graves were very different from those found in other parts of the island, but structurally similar ones have been found in south Arabia and in the Persian Gulf and Oman.[16] On the basis of analogies with these remains, the burials on Socotra have been dated from the second half of the 1st millennium BCE - a date which corresponds well with the evidence from Greek sources regarding beginnings of trade contacts with the island. It also indicates colonisation of the island by local communities with close links to the south Arabian coast.

Contemporary to these burials is the graffiti found on limestone outcrops on the eastern coast of the island at Eriosh. The graffiti includes drawings of outlines of feet, purely geometric shapes and animal and human forms. There are attempts at imitating a script but no identifiable South Arabian inscription could be found. Another type of stone structure found extensively on the island of Socotra is what has been described as 'boundary walls', though the function of these is not quite clear. It would seem that they demarcated plots of land growing incense trees such as aloe and cinnabar. In many cases, in the vicinity of these walls were found stone structures and cemeteries.

One of the most interesting discoveries was that of a settlement along the northern littoral of the island two kilometres south of the modern village of Suq. An analysis of the archaeological data from the site indicates two phases of settlement: an earlier phase dated to the early centuries of the Common Era; and a second phase from around the 10th–13th centuries CE. The archaeological data also suggest similarities with the Arabian Peninsula and Persian Gulf.

In the early centuries CE, Hoq cave on the northern face of the island of Socotra was known in a wide region by merchants travelling between Africa, India, the Middle East and Far East. Explorations in the 2000 metre-deep cave in 2001 led to the discovery of 200 graffiti, drawings and small offerings dated to the late 2nd to 4th century CE. Of these, 192 are in the Brahmi script, 1 in Kharosthi, 1 in Bactrian, 3 in Greek, 1 in Palmyrene Aramaic and 20-odd in Axumite or ancient Ethiopian. The graffiti and inscriptions are not engraved randomly in the cave; instead they occur in clusters at specific sites, most likely representing a deliberate choice of location. In the graffiti written in the Brahmi script at site 14, for example, individuals adopt several terms to identify themselves, such as sea-captains, yavana, a term that is frequently also used in the epigraphs of the western Deccan caves, or by their place of residence such as Barygaza or Bharuch on the west coast of India.[17]

These overwhelming cases of self-representation of individuals/groups from the Indian subcontinent may be compared with contemporary epigraphs on the west coast of India,[18] both with reference to content and locations and add a hitherto under-researched perspective to maritime activity in the western Indian Ocean, which has largely centred on discussions of pottery and identifications of coastal centres mentioned in early Greek writing.[19] This network underwent changes in the middle of the 1st millennium CE as discussed in the next section.

THE NESTORIAN CHRISTIANS AND THE PERSIANS

Cosmas was probably of Greek descent born in Alexandria and had travelled in the western Indian Ocean for commercial activity. On his return to Alexandria he gave up secular life and entered the Nestorian Church. The Nestorian Church became an important institution not only in Alexandria, but more significantly in the region of the Persian Gulf by the 5th century CE. There is evidence for the reorganisation of the Nestorian Church in the region after the 7th century and growth and expansion at sites such as on the island of Failaka in Kuwait, Sir Bani Yas in the UAE and Kharg

Island in Iran. The Church continued to maintain its presence until the end of the 9th century.

The *Christian Topography* of Cosmas survives in three manuscripts, one dated to the 9th and the other two to the 11th century CE. Cosmas refers to his travels to the three gulfs: the Roman, the Arabian and the Persian identified with the Mediterranean, the Red Sea and the Persian Gulf. The text differs from the *Periplus* in many ways and unlike the *Periplus* incorporates miniatures of animals, such as the rhinoceros, the ox-deer, the giraffe, the musk deer, the unicorn and the hippopotamus. In addition are representations of the plant that produces pepper and the tree that bears the large Indian nut known as the coconut. The focus of the text shifts from the west coast of India to Sri Lanka. In Book XI, Cosmas refers to a harbour in the southern part of the island visited by ships from all parts of India, Persia and Ethiopia and which also sends its own water vessels to these regions. The text also shows familiarity with Christian missionary activity in the region and mentions a church of Persian Christians in Sri Lanka and a Presbyter appointed from Persia. What makes the text significant is that Cosmas himself was a trader and his representation of animals underlines their importance in public display and luxury consumption.[20]

He refers to a series of coastal centres on the west coast of India:

> The most notable places of trade in India are these: Sindu (Diul-Sind at the mouth of the Indus), Orrhotha (Saurashtra), Calliana (Kalyan), Sibor (Simylla of Ptolemy identified with Chaul), and then the five marts of Male (Malabar coast) which export pepper: Parti, Mangarouth (Mangalore), Salopatana, Nalopatana, Poudopatana.[21]

There are details of commodities in demand at these ports, such as pepper on the Malabar coast, cloth, sesame-logs and copper exported from Kalyan and musk and castor at Sindu. The Indus river is stated to form the frontier between India and Persia.

The text then narrates a story of two merchants, one a Greek and the other a Persian, who were brought into the presence of the king of Sri

Lanka by the customs house officers. The two debated the greatness of their respective monarchs and finally the Greek suggested that the Sri Lankan king examine the coins from his sovereign, Constantine the great who minted aurei in gold, with the silver currency of the Persians, to judge the relative wealth of the two rulers. No doubt the Sri Lankan king was impressed with the gold coins and honoured the Greek trader with gifts. This story occurs in other contexts as well, highlighting the prevalent notion that the minting of gold coins was an indicator of the wealth and prosperity of the Roman Empire and of Constantinople that succeeded it.[22]

Cosmas has however been largely disregarded by later writers on account of his views on the shape of the earth, which he described as a square, though as has been shown above there is much in the text that provides valuable insights into the maritime world of the 6th century CE. It is evident that from the 4th to 7th centuries the focus of maritime activity shifted further south along the Red Sea coast to Adulis. Adulis with the two harbours of Diodorus island and Oriene is located at a spot where the Red Sea winds are less ferocious. At present the site is located 7 kms from the coast – though there is evidence that it was connected with the sea by a silted channel of the River Haddas. Cosmas refers to the town in the Aksumite period and contains a sketch map showing Adulis a little way from the coast, clearly connected with Aksum. There are also indications of the presence of a church at the site. This brief survey has shown the diverse communities who participated in maritime trade from the beginning of the Common Era to the 6th–7th centuries CE.

QUSEIR AL-QADIM: EXCAVATING THE SHAYKH'S HOUSE

As with Greek writings discussed above, data from both Quseir al-Qadim on the Red Sea and Geniza documents from Cairo show that other kinds of associations and partnerships were being forged outside of the family. It is important to stress that the amount of goods and money required to fill and equip a ship was beyond the reach of most individuals and even if one individual could have done it, the risks were considerable. It was safer to send smaller loads in many ships sailing for different destinations and this is a practice that continued to be adopted. Taking interest on loans was another thorny issue within both Jewish and Muslim law, as was Sabbath desecration among the Jews. It is suggested that a partnership between a Jew and a non-Jew was a simple solution for overcoming religious sanctions, where it was stipulated in the contract that the Gentile receive all profits earned on the Sabbath.[23]

The evidence from Quseir al-Qadim, a coastal centre on the Red Sea coast of Egypt, is perhaps unique in the Indian Ocean world as unlike the Cairo Geniza in Judeo-Arabic in the Hebrew alphabet and other contemporary documents, it can be located within an archaeological context and material remains from the excavations at Quseir al-Qadim of the Shaykh's house help provide a cultural milieu to the texts. A survey of the more than five hundred paper fragments written in the Arabic script recovered during excavations at Quseir al-Qadim in the central area of the town confirms that the majority were addressed to or written on behalf of a certain Shaykh Abu Mufarrij, and his son Shaykh Ibrahim, and to a lesser extent other people associated in the family business in the first half of the 13th century. Inside the house, several hundred paper fragments, mainly personal and business correspondence written in Arabic, were found along with other small objects. These documents have been studied and translated by Li Guo and this discussion is largely based on his work. The general pattern was for the letter to be written on the recto, while the verso contained the address of the recipient.[24]

Shaykh Abu Mufarrij was the owner of a prosperous transit warehouse in the Red Sea port of Quseir. His elder son Ibrahim worked as a merchant and broker rising to the rank of *rayyis* or trade head and also a *khatib* or one who gave the sermon at the local mosque. Thus it is evident that the Shaykh and his son were merchants who did not travel themselves, but sent shipments through others. The overlapping responsibilities of being a trade head and a *khatib* in the local mosque underscores the close relationship between economic and religious activities. Pilgrims to Mecca via the Egyptian Red Sea southern route formed an important category of clients. Two kinds of pilgrims are featured in the documents. One consisted of individuals who had gone on the pilgrimage journey to Mecca and had business dealings back home in Quseir with Abu Mufarrij (himself a *hajji*) as well as other members of his family. The other kind of pilgrims are those who for the most part spoke in a collective voice, as groups, and were perhaps customers of a substantial portion of the grain trade that took place at the warehouse.[25]

One of the few complete letters requesting supplies written from a ship stuck in Yemen would suggest "some kind of regular transport of correspondence, supplies, merchandise, and even cash through a kind of maritime shuttle service between Quseir and Yemen".[26] The coastal centre of al-Qasr al-Yamani, where the ship was stuck cannot be identified, but it was most likely on the Yemeni side of the Red Sea and the ship was travelling along the Yemeni coast for Hijaz.

> We are in a cold spell whose severity none knows save God. O God! O God! O my father!
>
> 4. Pay for us the [cost of the] cloak by all means, for the weather has been deadly and extremely
> 5. cold. Forward its cost in the amount requested. O God! O God!
> 6. O my lord! Supply us with two water bags at any rate. O God! O God!
> 7. We have been in al-Qasr al-Yamani for three days. And as long as this
> 8. wind continues [to blow], we are unable to travel-O God! O God!
> 9. if you could [find] for us some baked food, please purchase it for us and send it along [to us]. O God! O God![27]

The invocational repetition of *allaha allaha* is frequently found in private letters as a rhetorical device to emphasize the urgency of the matter. Did the warehouse of Shaykh Abu Mufarrij also function as a caravanserai? Given the multiple capacities in which Shaykh Abu Mufarrij and Ibrahim worked, ranging from merchant, agent and manager to tax-farmer, trade head and market inspector in addition to the social services the warehouse provided, such as funeral arrangements, medical care and magic practices, the answer should perhaps be positive. The frequent mention of agents and merchants 'arriving' and 'staying' in the house also suggests that the warehouse might have provided lodgings for travelling merchants and their employees – a major function of the *dar al-wakala* along the major trade routes all over the Islamic Near East.[28] It would also seem that Shaykh Abu Mufarrij's warehouse functioned as a government agency in charge of grain distribution on the Red Sea and Indian Ocean trade routes, especially for the pilgrims to Mecca. There is mention of *al-nafaqa* (funds, expense), which was granted or allotted by the sultan or the court to military expeditions or organized long-distance caravans, such as the annual pilgrimage to Mecca.[29] It is evident from the discussion here that the Arabic documents from Quseir supplement not only the archaeological data from the coastal site, but also that available from the Geniza papers of the India trade.

THE CAIRO GENIZA AND INDIA TRADE

The Judeo-Arabic texts recovered from the Geniza chamber of the Ben Ezra synagogue in Fustat – Old Cairo – provide fascinating insights into the maritime world of the Indian Ocean. The recently translated 459 documents (comprising 523 shelf marks of the India Letters from the Cairo Geniza dated from 1080 to 1160 CE) are crucial to this discussion (Figure 33).[30] Documents in the Cairo Geniza may be categorized into letters, documents of legal character and memos accompanying shipments, such as accounts and wage payments of a brass factory in western India.

The second category of documents or deeds of 'partnership according to Muslim law' drawn up before a merchant embarked on a journey are of particular relevance to this chapter. Invariably a merchant did business not only for himself, but also for others or acted as an agent for one or several investors. On his return, the merchant was required to make a statement to the local rabbinical or Muslim court and the partners would write out a release indicating that the deed had been concluded to their satisfaction. It should be stressed that whenever possible, merchants preferred sending goods rather than gold, and silk is at times mentioned as a means of payment.[31]

Several prominent Jewish business families are represented in the documents (Figure 34). Joseph b. David Lebdi of Tripoli undertook a voyage from 1094/5 to 1097 CE, which started at al-Mahdiyya, Tunisia and was destined for Nahrwara (Anahilavada) in Gujarat, the country of lac, textiles, steel and beads. The Cairo Geniza contains several records pertaining to the lawsuits relating to the family with customers in Egypt and Tunisia whose goods he had carried with him on his journeys, which lasted from November 1097 through to August 1098. Once the lawsuit was settled, Joseph Lebdi undertook a second voyage in 1099–1101. Lebdi also had dealings with Hasan b. Bundar, representative of merchants in Aden. His son was Madmun b. Hasan b. Bundar, a shipowner and representative of merchants in Aden and Nagid or Prince of the land of Yemen.

33. Letter from Khalaf b. Isaac to Ben Yiju regarding ship-wrecked goods.

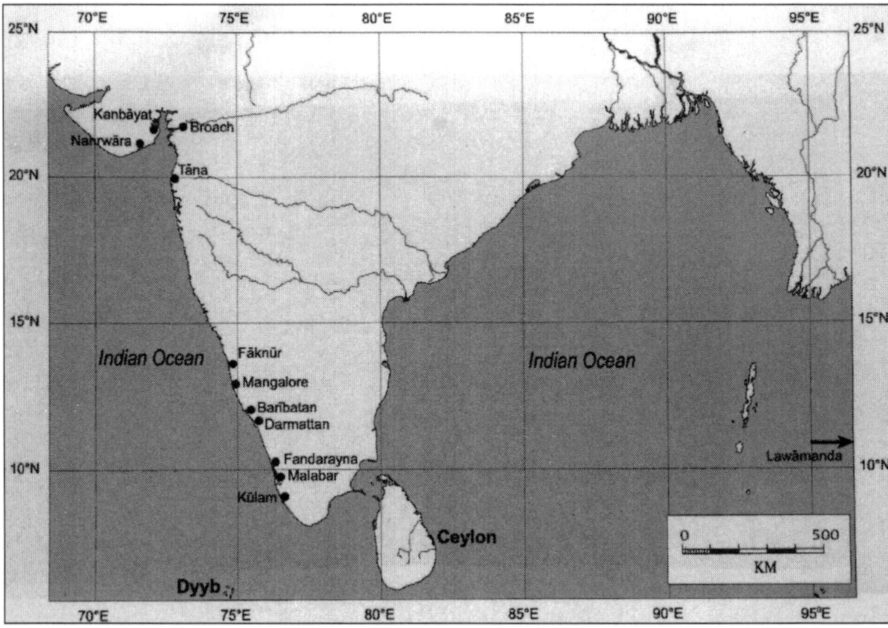

34. Indian localities mentioned in the Geniza letters.

Madmun b. Hasan b. Bundar represented foreign merchants in local lawsuits in Aden, supervised the sale and purchase of goods for overseas traders, took care of customs payments, stored the goods of his clients in a large warehouse, which also served as a clearing house for transactions and a post office, and functioned as a banker. Madmun had a close business association with Bilal b. Jarir, the Muslim governor of Aden and also worked in close cooperation with other Jewish merchants in Aden, some of whom were his relatives.[32]

In contrast to the Lebdi family who travelled to India, Abraham Bin Yiju was resident largely at Mangalore on the south Kanara coast of India. Most of the documents relating to Bin Yiju indicate that his permanent residence in India was at Mangalore (Manjarur). However, he also despatched shipments to Aden from Fandarayna (Pantalayini) where he must have lived for some time and also from Dahbattan (Valarapattanam) and engaged in business in Faknur. On one occasion we are told that his family was in Jurbatan – all cities on the Malabar coast.[33]

The travels of Joseph Lebdi, one of the prominent merchants who appears in the Geniza papers, are indicative of maritime voyages of 11th–12th century. Lebdi left Fustat for India around June 1099 and returned after an absence of one year and ten months.[34] One of the reasons for further complication in the case of Joseph Lebdi was his avoidance of landing at Aden both on the way out to India and on the way back. Instead, he preferred to land at Mirbat on the southeastern tip of the Arabian peninsula and at Dahlak on the west coast of the Red Sea.

Lebdi arrived at 'Aydhab with 80 bales of lac packed in Nahrwara, Gujarat, and 50 bales of pepper. The overseas venture was in partnership with two other merchants Abu Nasr and Farah and was for an amount of 800 dinars. On arrival while Lebdi returned to Fustat, after receiving 'governmental prescripts' allowing foreigners and non-Muslims safe passage, he left his two partners at 'Aydhab to send the lac in instalments to Fustat. Unfortunately the two men were murdered, which led to complicated lawsuits.[35] Thus, letters of the India trade provide information on several aspects of trade in the Indian Ocean, especially those dealing with various aspects of partnerships. But perhaps the most significant partnership was between the shipper and the trader, as we discuss in the next section.

SHIPPING AND OWNERSHIP OF WATERCRAFT

This section is based on the premise that fishing and sailing communities formed the foundation of maritime activity in the Indian Ocean and provided a continuum to seafaring throughout history, though no doubt their fortunes fluctuated over time. These communities adopted numerous occupations associated with the sea: fishing and harvesting other marine resources, salt making, sailing, trade, shipbuilding and piracy. A common feature of the sewn boats of the Indian Ocean was the use of coir-rope for stitching. As coconut palm plantations were restricted to certain parts of the Indian Ocean littoral, coir-rope would have been one of the commodities in demand along the boat-building settlements of the coast. Thus, the building of the *dhow* or traditional watercraft involved trade and transportation of wood for planking and coconut coir for stitching from different regions of the Indian Ocean, thereby creating and sustaining networks of interaction.

Maritime travel in the ancient period involved a variety of watercraft. Cargo carriers formed the foundation of trading ventures. Merchants and traders in some cases certainly owned ships and watercraft, but they neither manned nor sailed these, as discussed in this and the earlier chapter. More often, goods and cargoes were entrusted to the captain of the vessel, who was then responsible for their sale and profit. Thus maritime activity involved diverse groups from the owners of watercraft to those who commanded these, and still others who sailed them.

Roxani Margeriti in her study of Aden, based on the published and unpublished records of the Cairo Geniza, has concluded that the terminology used in them is ambiguous and it is not easy to distinguish ship owners from captains and other crewmen.[36] She also draws attention to differences in ownership of shipping craft and the role of officials of the State in the Mediterranean as opposed to those in the Indian Ocean. In contrast to practice in the Mediterranean, in the Indian Ocean, while government officials did own ships, the Geniza papers suggest that merchants dominated this business.[37] This ambiguity in terminology and the need to distinguish modern practices from those in the medieval period is further corroborated by a careful reading of the India letters, as evident in Friedman's statement:

> The ambiguity in terminology in our sources, especially in connection with the *nakhuda*, which certainly was used in more than one sense, and the difficulty in equating medieval terms with modern concepts present a major obstacle in any attempt to define the word with precision. Some *nakhuda*s were clearly ship owners; others evidently served as captains or may have filled other functions on the ship.[38]

The number of crew members depended on the size of the ship. *Nakhuda* was a Persian term from *naw* meaning 'boat/ship' and *khuda* meaning master, though its meaning varied over time. The *nakhuda* was the general supervisor in charge of the ship and trade and his responsibility included the safe delivery of passengers and goods. The term was also used for a ship owner.[39] Al-Mas'udi (d. 345/956–7) replaced the Persian term for one in Arabic, viz. Rabb al-markab or 'master of the ship'. In the Geniza collection there are at least seventy-five instances of *nakhuda*, but the term is not used in texts relating to Mediterranean shipping, which use the term '*rayyis*'.[40]

The partnership between the *nakhuda* and local communities is best exemplified by the Somnath-Veraval inscription of 1264 CE consisting of two slabs of stone inscribed with a Sanskrit epigraph and two months later an Arabic record. Located at Somnath-pattana on the Gujarat coast, the inscription records endowments for the maintenance of a mosque (*dharmasthana* in Sanskrit) and for providing it other services by *Nakhuda* Nur al-Daula wa-l-Din Firuz, son of Khoja *Nakhuda* Abu Ibrahim of Hurmuja-desa or Hormuz at the mouth of the Persian Gulf together with the local community leaders (*thakura* in Sanskrit).

At that time the king or *raja* of the coastline (*velakula*) of Hormuja was Amir sri Rukana Dina, Sultan Rukn al-Din. The Sanskrit version of the inscription provides a detailed description of the land acquired as a part of the endowment. This land was located in the vicinity of the city and at least four local residents are listed as providing the land for the endowment. In addition, Nur al-Din acquired and donated the products of an oil mill and two shops or marketplaces (*hattas*). The surplus, if any, from these was to be sent to the holy places of Mecca and Medina (*mashamadina-dharmasthana*). This transaction was witnessed by all the *jamathas* or groups of Somanath who were also responsible for the upkeep of the property. The groups named are: *Nakhuda- navika*; *gamchikas* or oil men along with their preacher; *chunakaras* or whitewashers; and also *mushalamanas* or Muslims of the town.[41]

It is important that the Arabic version of the inscription is much shorter in length and is only 28 lines as compared to the Sanskrit record of 43 lines. While it agrees in several significant details with the Sanskrit version, it lists the *imam* and the *mu'azzin* of the mosque as beneficiaries. The Arabic version credits Abu Ibrahim ibn Muhammad al-'Iraqi, the father of Nur al-Din Firuz, with the foundation of the mosque and one of the titles that it attached to Nur al-Din Firuz is that of *malik muluk al-tujjar* or leader of business-leaders. The Arabic text does not contain details of the land transfer, nor does it mention that the surplus was to be sent to Mecca and Medina and concludes by quoting from the Quran against tampering with the endowment.

Alka Patel suggests that while public inscriptions engraved in Sanskrit were part of the administrative procedure of the subcontinent, this was not valid for the central Islamic lands, where paper documents were the norm and foundation inscriptions containing basic information about the founder were monumentalized in ornate epigraphs on buildings. In keeping with the legal requirements of Islamic law the mosque was definable as a *waqf* or charitable endowment and trustees and beneficiaries had to be appointed. The Arabic version is thus crucial to an understanding of the establishment of the institution of *waqf* in western India.[42]

Two other surviving bilingual records from Gujarat indicate the integration of diverse communities in the medieval social world of merchants and traders. A Persian-Sanskrit inscription of 1304 CE documents the donation of Sampa village in central Gujarat to the congregational mosque of Khambat at the head of the Gulf of Khambat. A second Persian-Sanskrit epigraph is dated 1323 CE and documents the construction of a stepwell by Hajji Isma'il 'Uthman Shirazi along with land for its maintenance.[43] The Somnath-Veraval inscription has either been discussed as a symbol of harmony between the Muslim and Jain communities in Gujarat or as an indicator of aggression in the Indian Ocean in the pre-Portuguese period.[44] Its location inside a mosque at the sacred site of Somnath has wider implications for the diverse nature of seafaring activity in the Indian Ocean ranging from religious travel and pilgrimage to trade and cargo carrying, as also for the overlapping coastal and trans-oceanic networks, as discussed in this chapter.

NOTES AND REFERENCES

1. Grant Parker, *The Making of Roman India*, Cambridge University Press, 2008.
2. Ibid., pp. 151-53.
3. Lionel Casson, *The Periplus Maris Erythraei*, Princeton University Press, 1989, sections 31.
4. Ibid., sections 39 – 63.
5. Moti Chandra, *Costumes, Textiles, Cosmetics and Coiffure in Ancient and Medieval India*, New Delhi: Oriental Publishers, 1973, p. 93.
6. *Epigraphia Indica*, 30: 172.
7. Norman A. Stillman, The Eleventh Century Merchant House of Ibn 'Awkal (A Geniza Study), *Journal of the Economic and Social History of the Orient*, 16, 1973: 15-88.
8. D.C. Sircar, More Inscriptions from Nagarjunakonda, *Epigraphia Indica*, Vol. XXV, 1963-1964: 1-7.
9. Lionel Casson, op. cit., pp. 271-77.
10. Ibid., pp. 63, 274ff.
11. The term *pattana* derives from *pattana* or market town. The *Arthasastra* (II.6.3) refers to *pattana* as a coastal settlement where traders have to pay a part of their goods as duty (II.28.40) and it occurs in Tamil as *pattinam* in the same meaning.
12. Kenneth R. Hall, Trade and Foreign Diplomacy in Early Medieval South India, *Journal of the Economic and Social History of the Orient*, 21, 1, 1978: 75-98, p. 91.
13. K.A. Kitchen, *Documentation for Ancient Arabia*, Parts I & II, Liverpool: Liverpool University Press, 1994 & 2000.
14. Alexander Sedov, The Port of Qana' and the Incense Trade, in David Peacock and David Williams (eds.), *Food for the Gods: New Light on the Ancient Incense Trade*, Oxford: Oxbow Books, 2007, pp. 92-94.
15. Alessandra Avanzini, Sumhurram: A Hadrami Port in the Indian Ocean, in Eivind Heldaas Seland (ed.), *The Indian Ocean in the Ancient Period*, Oxford: BAR International Series 1593, 2007, pp. 23-31.
16. V.V. Naumkin and A.V. Sedov, Socotra, *Topoi*, 3, 2,1993, pp. 581-82.
17. Ingo Strauch, *Foreign Sailors on Socotra: The Inscriptions and Drawings from the Cave Hoq*, Bremen: Hempen Verlag, 2012.

18. Himanshu Prabha Ray, *Monastery and Guild: Commerce under the Satavahanas*, New Delhi: Oxford University Press, 1986.
19. Eivind Heldaas Seland, Archaeology of Trade in the Western Indian Ocean, 300 BC–AD 700, *Journal of Archaeological Research*, published online, 2nd April 2014.
20. Grant Parker, op. cit., p. 142.
21. J.W. McCrindle, *The Christian Topography of Cosmas, an Egyptian Monk*, London: Hakluyt Society, 1897: Book XI, 367.
22. Ibid., pp. 368-69.
23. Goitein and Friedman, 2008, p. 133.
24. Li, Guo, *Commerce, Culture and Community in a Red Sea Port in the Thirteenth Century,* Leiden – Boston: Brill, 2004.
25. Li, 2004, pp. 27-28.
26. Li, 1999, p. 181.
27. Li, 1999, p. 183.
28. Li, 2004, p. 97.
29. Li, 1999, p. 186.
30. S.D. Goitein and Mordechai Akiva Friedman, *India Traders of the Middle Ages*, Leiden – Boston: Brill, 2008.
31. Ibid., p. 20.
32. Ibid., p. 37.
33. Ibid., p. 57.
34. Ibid., p. 237.
35. Ibid., pp. 241-47.
36. Roxani Eleni Margariti, *Aden and the Indian Ocean Trade*, Chapel Hill: University of North Carolina Press, 2007, pp. 223-24.
37. Ibid., pp. 21-22.
38. Goitein and Friedman, 2008, p. 138.
39. Agius, 2008, pp. 178-79.
40. Goitein and Friedman, 2008, p. 125.
41. Alka Patel, Transcending Religion, in Grant Parker and Carla Sinopoli (eds.), *Ancient India in Its Wider Context*, Ann Arbor: The University of Michigan Press, 2008, pp. 143-64.
42. Ibid., pp. 143-64.
43. Ibid., p. 158.
44. Roxani Eleni Margariti, Mercantile Networks, Port Cities, and "Pirate" States: Conflict and Competition in the Indian Ocean World before the Sixteenth Century, *Journal of the Economic and Social History of the Orient*, 51, 2008: 543-77.

7

FROM GLOBAL TO LOCAL

Early Medieval Gujarat and Konkan Coast

From Global to Local: Early Medieval Gujarat and Konkan Coast

The previous chapter reviewed historical literature and texts on trade partnerships across the Indian Ocean and emphasized the overlap between trans-oceanic and coastal networks. Here the focus shifts to the region of Gujarat (Figure 35) to underscore two aspects of maritime history that are fundamental to this study: the need to balance global trans-oceanic systems with distinctive regional and local networks; and to shift the emphasis from trade and political control to adoption of a holistic approach highlighting the social and cultural milieu of maritime interconnectedness. The East Coast maritime network was discussed in Chapter 3 within the intertwined strands of political ambitions of the Chola rulers, economic activity under the trading guilds and the multi-religious milieu within which the Buddhist vihara of Nagapattinam is to be located. In this chapter, I highlight major centres in western India that participated in Indian Ocean networks and investigate the extent to which they replicated developments along the East Coast of India.

The West Coast differed from the East Coast in a variety of ways, as is evident from the archaeological records. For example, in the early centuries of the Common Era, the East Coast provides data for inter-connectedness as indicated by the distribution of Rouletted Ware from sites on the Bengal coast to those in Sri Lanka. The wider linkages connected the East Coast

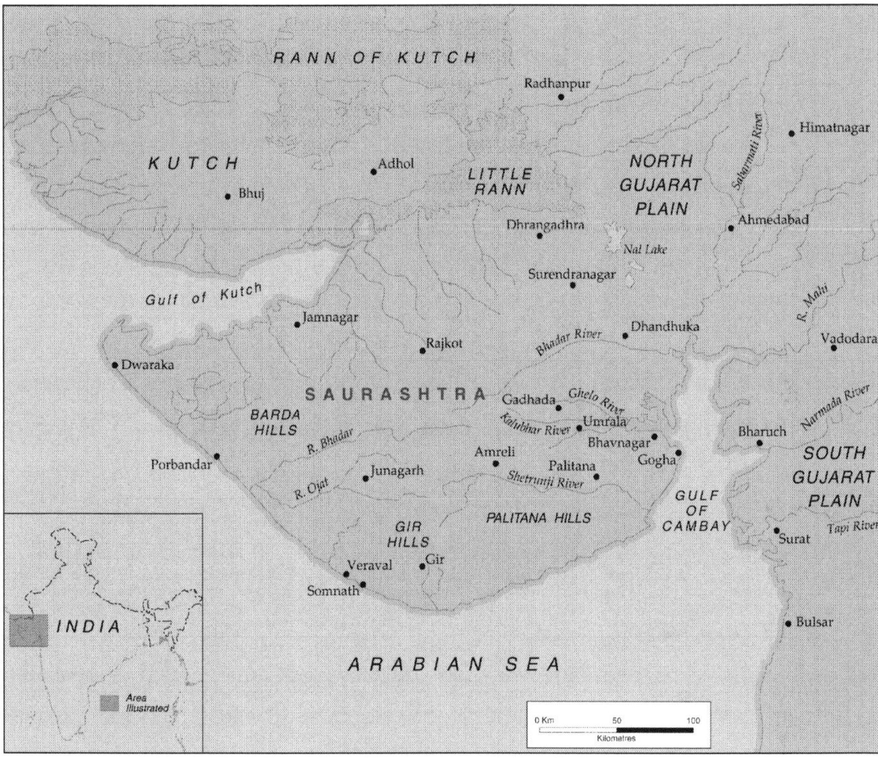

35. Distribution of sites in Gujarat mentioned in the text.

to centres in Indonesia and Vietnam, as also those on the Red Sea, such as the site of Berenike. In contrast, two spheres of influence are indicated on the West Coast: one along the Gujarat and Konkan coasts; and the other further south along the Kanara and Malabar coasts. Do these differences in maritime activity along the two coasts continue in the early medieval period? This is an issue that is discussed in this Chapter, as we examine engagement between various communities and the sea in Gujarat and the Konkan coast.

There is another interesting difference between the Tamil and Gujarat coasts of India, which relates to the availability of fishing grounds and the nature of watercraft used. For example, a rich variety of fish is available close to the southeast coast of India and fishermen do not have to venture out into the sea. As a result fishing nets and other devices show tremendous variety, but the craft used are surprisingly simple and are no more than rafts made of logs tied together. These however are well suited to the local requirements since the wash through raft also keeps the catch fresh. In contrast, the fishing grounds are further afield off the Gujarat coast and fishing becomes profitable only when combined with cargo carrying. Hence the boats are larger and fitted to sustain fishermen over longer distances.[1] To what extent did this fundamental difference in availability of fishing grounds impact the cultural milieu?

The earliest reference to territorial identity in western India occurs in the *Arthasastra*.[2] While defining two types of *sangha* or oligarchic organization, the *Arthasastra* (11.1.4) places Surastra in the first category together with Kamboja as living by commerce and vocation of arms. The author of the text Kautilya identifies members of this type of *sangha* as engaged in cattle rearing or trades in peace time, but taking to arms when necessary.

The archaeological data would, however, indicate that in the 4th–3rd centuries BCE, a much smaller unit within Surastra or Saurashtra, i.e. the area around Junagarh, formed the core area of economic and political activity in the region. At least five coin hoards containing more than 4,800 silver coins have been recovered from Junagarh district. These are essentially small coins of about one gram, each produced from a single die and some re-stamped coins of the Magadha *janapada*.[3] This distinctive territorial identity by no means translated into isolation from other parts of the subcontinent as is evident from the epigraphic data preserved on the hill at Girnar, about 1.5 kilometres to the east of the town of Junagarh. Inscribed on the hill are records of two of the major dynasties of the north, viz. the Mauryas (317 to 186 BCE) and the Guptas (dated in the reign of king Skandagupta 455–467 CE), while the third, engraved on the western side belongs to the Ksatrapa ruler Rudradaman (2nd century CE).

Archaeological exploration in Gujarat has provided evidence for twenty-two early historic sites located in a linear pattern along the river and a multi-tier settlement hierarchy. The site of Hathab was the largest site, located close to the sea with an area of over 40 hectares, while the largest number of sites, i.e. eleven fall in the category of 3-12 hectares. It is significant that while thirteen sites were located in the black cotton soil zone, six were situated close to the coast. The site of Padri, situated 3-4 kilometres inland, was known for extraction of salt.[4] Amreli is an important archaeological site located upstream of the survey area on the Thebi, a tributary of the Shetrunji, and excavations conducted here yielded continuous occupation of the site from the 1st century BCE to the 8th century CE.[5] Similarly, the site of Vallabhi first occurs in inscriptions from the 6th century onwards, though archaeological excavations at the site date the earliest settlement located on a small island between the two arms of the Ghelo river to the 1st–2nd centuries CE. The settlement gradually expanded in a linear pattern along the river.[6] This complex settlement pattern is further supported by information from inscriptions. While the 2nd century CE inscription of Rudradaman refers to the three-fold division of town, market and rural space (*nagara-nigama-janapada*), Maitraka epigraphs (493–776 CE) mention a diverse variety of territorial sub-units (*palli*, *padraka*, *grama*, *dranga*, *bhukti*, *bhumi*, *patta*, *petha*, *visaya* and so on).[7]

In Chapter 2 we discussed the emergence of Vallabhi as a port city from the 5th to 8th century CE and its links with the ruling dynasty of the Maitrakas. The Traikutakas were prominent in south Gujarat, north Konkan and parts of Maharashtra from the 4th to the 6th century CE. One of the other dynasties whose inscriptions are relevant to this book is that of the Silaharas of north Konkan who prided themselves as 'lord of Tagara' or Ter, in Osmanabad district, though inscriptions refer to ten families of Silaharas who ruled in Maharashtra and Karnataka. The rule of the Silaharas of north Konkan is dated from 800 to 1260 CE (Figure 36), while the branch that ruled south Konkan comprising parts of Goa and Ratnagiri district held sway for 250 years from 765 to 1024 CE. The inscriptions of many of these rulers were discussed in Chapter 2 from the perspective of royal conceptualization of maritime space and sea battles along the coast.

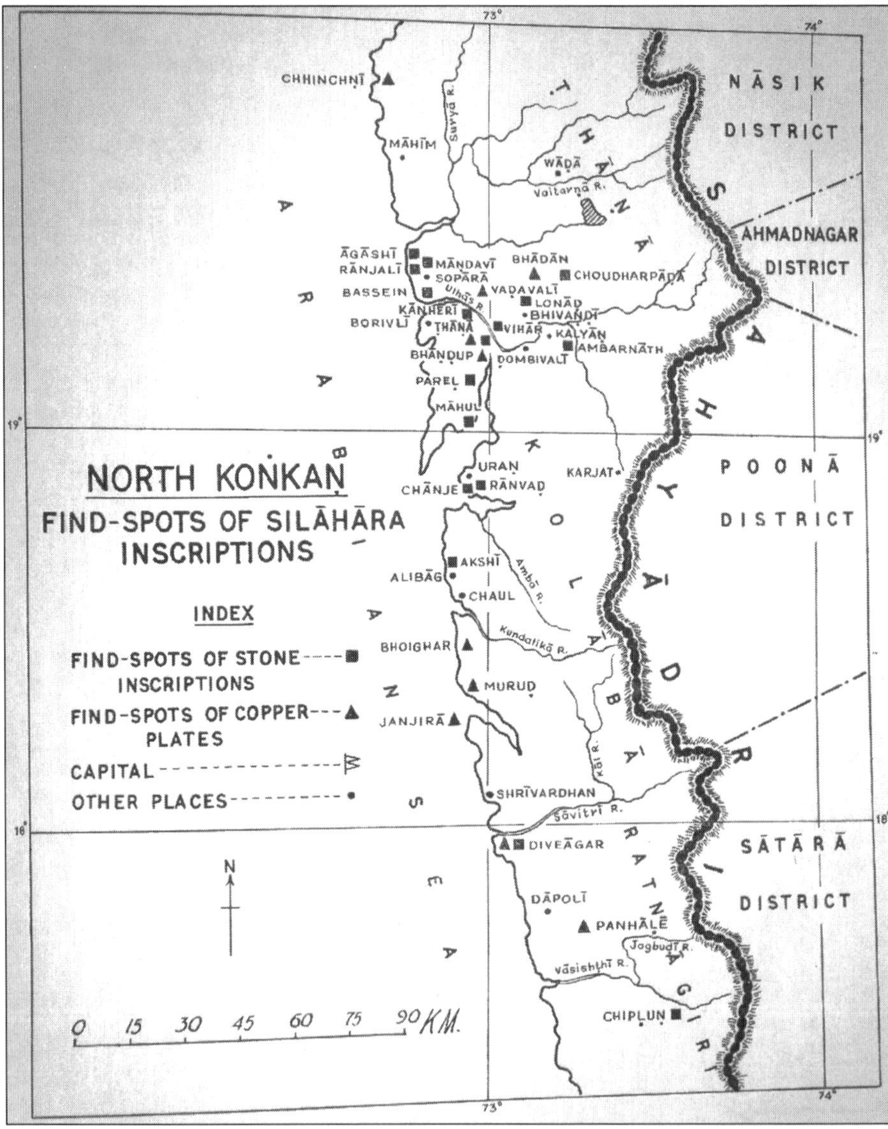

36. Map showing find spots of Silahara inscriptions in north Konkan.

Here we focus on the period from the 10th to 13th century CE to provide a context for a unique document written in Gujarat, i.e. the

Lekhapaddhati already referred to in the fourth chapter. Though the text had its origins in Gujarat, it was adapted to different circumstances during the course of its transmission and dates in the manuscript revised accordingly. Two of the documents in the *Lekhapaddhati* refer specifically to sea trade. One (Document no. 59) refers to the export of slaves; and the other records horses being imported from Hormuz in the Persian Gulf (Document no. 41). By the 10th century Hormuz became the seaport of the province of Kirman, controlling centres on the Arabian littoral of the northern Gulf as well as the Omani coast.

The *Lekhapaddhati* provides two deeds for female slaves, i.e. nos. 58 and 59. The first deed relates to the fair-looking sixteen year old slave Panuti who was brought by Rana Pratap Singh after an attack on another country and sold to a merchant for a price of five hundred and four Visalapriya *drammas*. The merchant then declared to the residents of the towns belonging to the four *varnas* that, in accordance with the prevailing custom, he would provide her unasked, food, clothing and so on while she worked in the merchant's house and her male relatives were not to reclaim her or disrupt her work. The second deed refers to a ten year old girl Sampuri, an orphan from Sirnara village on the banks of the Mahi who herself became a slave to escape hunger, famine and harassment by the *mlecchas*. She approached the merchant Cahada and pleaded for work in his house. He accepted her and she declared at the crossroads in the presence of people of the town that she would be liable to punishment if she either disobeyed the merchant's instructions or left his house.[8]

While there is agreement between the *Lekhapaddhati* and inscriptions in the case of documentation of land grants, we have no such corroboration for several other practices mentioned in the text, such as the issuing of passes for travel across borders, which being fragile in nature would not have survived.[9] How is interaction between these groups and the ruling elite to be categorized? Is the model of patronage provided by the religious centres discussed earlier with reference to Nagapattinam replicated on the west coast or are there deviations from it? An answer to this question provides insights into the differences in the engagement with the sea along the two coasts. We start by discussing the rule of the Chalukyas in order to explicate the setting that led to the need for scribes and model letters compiled in the *Lekhapaddhati*. This text thus forms the first in the history of epistolary in India and underscores the requirement for trained state officials and professional letter writers. The next section underscores developments in Gujarat that nurtured trade and economic prosperity.

GUJARAT UNDER THE CHALUKYAS

Gujarat was ruled by the Chalukyas from 941 to 1297 CE with the capital at Anahilavada Patan, a trading and commercial centre located seventy-eight miles northwest of the present city of Ahmedabad in north Gujarat. The town dates back to the 8th century and there is evidence of it being fortified. The importance of Patan was linked to its position as a trading entrepot, as it was on the routes that linked the cities of the north with the western seaboard both through Kachchh as also the Gulf of Khambat. The road taken by traders from Rajasthan and Patan to ports on the western coast passed through Modhera, Karnavati, Sthambhanaka, Cambay or Khambat and then touching Baroda and Dhaboi went along the coast to Broach and Thana.[10] It is significant that many of these routes were also a part of the itineraries of pilgrims and Jain monks and thus provided major channels of communication.

There are references to both inland and sea trade in the *Lekhapaddhati*. Several agencies involved in the collection of revenues are mentioned, such as *vyapara karana* (trade and commerce department), *velakula karana* (department of harbours), *jalapatha karana* (department of waterways and roads), *mandapika karana* (department of customs) and *tanksala karana* (department of coinage and mints).[11] The text raises two important issues for this study: one is the relationship between the ruler or state and the merchants; and the second is the nature of authority for adjudication of disputes relating to trade. Both of these will be addressed in this chapter, but first an overview of some of the important water structures and shrines at Anahilavada Patan may not be out of place.

The most important monument in the arid environment of the region is the magnificent Rani-ki-vav stepwell, said to been constructed by Queen Udayamati, wife of King Bhimadeva I (1022–1063 CE) (Figure 37). This is the highest watermark of 11th century architecture and was originally constructed of seven stories of which only five are now preserved. The stepwell has a long stepped passage descending down to the underground tank; and the passage walls, pillared pavilions and inner side of the well are all embellished with fine sculptures of gods and goddesses, apsaras and related themes. Other water structures were also constructed around the city of Anhilavada Patan. The Sahastralinga Talav, as the name suggests, was a water body created for the storage of water and had 1000 shrines with Shiva-*lingas* around it. The Khan sarovar (lake) near Patan is another water body that was constructed in the time of Chalukya rule. The location of wells in the vicinity of settlements and on overland routes suggests that these were frequented by travellers and caravans that traversed the region.

At the time of the construction of the Rani-ki-vav, there is evidence for architectural activity in the area of north Gujarat and several temples are known to have been built. King Bhimadeva is credited with the construction of the Surya temple at Modhera, 35 kilometres from Patan, in 1026 CE while his minister was the patron of the Jain temple at Mt. Abu in Rajasthan, about 140 kilometres to the north. Tradition has it that he also built temples at other places in Gujarat, such as Kumbharia, Girnar, Palitana and Shatrunjaya. The Anavada inscription of 1291 CE found near Patan records gifts to a temple dedicated to Krishna by *vanjaras* or itinerant merchants, *nau-vittakas* (merchants knowledgeable about ships) and *mahajanas*, which according to the inscription included *sadhu* or *sahukara*, *sresthi*, *soni* (goldsmith), *thakkura* or *thakura* and *kamsara* or brazier.[12]

37. The richly sculpted wall of Rani ki Vav, Patan.

The ruling house of the Chalukyas was also known for providing patronage to learned teachers or *acaryas*. The polymath Hemacandra's (1089–1172) writings on the wide-ranging themes of dramaturgy, poetics and grammar are fascinating in that they not only provide insights into his incisive intellect, but perhaps what is more relevant for our purposes is that they indicate participation in intellectual rivalry between the courts of the Chalukyas of Gujarat and the Paramaras of central India, especially the 11th century king Bhoja of Dhara the author of *Yuktikalpataru* referred to earlier. The Chalukyas ruled not only over Gujarat, Kachchh and Saurashtra, but also western Malwa and southern Rajasthan. Contemporary inscriptions refer to a network of roads and routes across the region, which included both *rajamargas* or royal roads, as well as feeder paths connecting villages. The primary connection was along the coast from Bhavnagar in the southeast to Somnath and Dwarka, both coastal centres well-known for their magnificent temples, though the beginnings of these sites date to the early centuries of the Common Era. Ahmed Sah's shift of the capital of Gujarat from Patan to his newly founded city of Ahmedabad in 1411 CE resulted in a gradual economic decline of the former from which it has never fully recovered.[13] In the next section we list some of the important towns and cities along the Gujarat coast that participated in the vibrant economic development.

TOWNS AND CITIES

In the early 8th century, especially along the West Coast, there are references to settlements of merchants, as evident from the second set of Anjaneri copper plates found near Trimbak in Nasik district of the ruler Bhoga Sakti, who ruled over the Konkan under the overlordship of the Chalukyas. The inscription begins with a celebration of Visnu's boar avatar, which agitated the ocean and which had the world resting on its projecting right tusk. It declares that the previously deserted Samagiri-pattana, together with its suburb Chandrapuri and along with three villages, which had been devastated, has been resettled and made over to Ela sresthin and Karaputa sresthin and to the entire corporation (*nagara*) of merchants. The merchants were henceforth exempted from paying tolls. There was (to be) no confiscation (by the king) of property (of one dying) without an heir. The residents were not required to provide board and lodging for royal officers. Fines were however imposed for violent crimes though the verdict was left to due deliberation by eight or sixteen senior men of the corporation.[14] It is significant that the inscription refers to settlements of merchants along the coast; and secondly it gives the merchants the right to adjudicate in civic matters and trial by a jury comprising of their own seniors.

Archaeological investigation in western India has provided information on several long-lasting coastal settlements. For example, the site of Mandvi on the estuary of the Rukmavati River at the entrance to the Gulf of Kachchh has been known as a port town with links to both Oman and the East African coast since archaeological exploration conducted in the mid-19th century. In addition to a range of ceramics, important finds include local and regional coins, as well as a Byzantium solidus of Heraclius dated to 638 CE and an Arab Umayyad dinar of 716 CE.[15] Writing in 1836, Alexander Burnes described maritime activities at Mandvi as follows:

> The principal seaport of Kutch is Mandavee, which stands in lat 22° 51'N and long. 69° 34'E close to the Gulf. It has no fewer than 250 vessels belonging to it, and boasts a population of 50,000 souls, which is about one-eighth of that of the whole province of Kutch. It is an open roadstead with a creek. From Mandavee a maritime communication is kept up with Zanguebar and the whole east coast of Africa, with the Red Sea and Arabia and with the Persian Gulf, Mekrom and Sinde and with India as far as Ceylon. The vessels used in this extensive commerce vary in size from 100 to 800 candies or from 25 to 200 tons. They carry a large lateen sail, have two masts and are never decked.[16]

The ethnographic data indicates that the coastal settlements participated in trade with other centres further south and also across the Ocean, though each port specialized in a particular route. Mandvi,

Porbandar and Veraval trade with east Africa, Porbandar and Veraval with south Arabia, Southeast Asia and the Persian Gulf. Thus route specialization is an important aspect of seafaring activity that has far-reaching implications for a study of the past as well.[17]

Bhadresvara was an early site on the coast of Kachchh in Gujarat. It was also the site of a 12th century Jain temple 32 kilometres from the coastal centre of Mundra referred to as *velakula* or harbour.[18] Bhadresvara is at present a small village and a site of pilgrimage, but in ancient times it was a fortified coastal centre. The Sanskrit text *Jagaducarita* records that the town was a city-state run in the 11th and 12th century by a council of Jain merchants under the suzerainty of the Chalukyas of Gujarat. The merchant prince Jagadu is said to have built a mosque here for the Ismaili sect and the local Muslim community with the permission of the Jain Council, but the most notable structure is the shrine of Ibrahim dated on the basis of an *in situ* inscription to 1159–1160 CE, i.e. nearly half a century earlier than the Islamic monuments at Delhi or Ajmer. In Bhadresvara and at several other sites in Gujarat such as Khambat, Somnath and Patan, there are a number of tombstones dated between the mid-12th and early 13th centuries CE. Many of the architectural features at Bhadresvara are also found in a mosque built by early settlers at Junagarh, where an inscription records that the chief merchant and ship-owner Abu'l-Qasim b. 'Ali al-Idhaji built the mosque in 685 AH/1286–7 CE.

Dwarka, located on the north coast of Saurashtra, is another contemporary site with a long period of settlement from the 1st century BCE to almost the present. Its importance stems both from its coastal location as well as the religious significance of its temples and sacred association as a centre of pilgrimage.[19] Other continuously settled sites along the Gujarat coast include Porbandar and Prabhas Patan (Somnath) and Vallabhi at the head of the Gulf of Khambat. At Prabhas Patan, archaeological evidence of historical settlement is dated to the 4th century BCE and its significance as a major fishing harbour has continued well into the present. Religious structures such as temples, however, emerge somewhat later in the 5th–6th centuries CE. The Veraval inscription from Somnath indicates the presence of Muslim merchants at the site in the 12th–13th century CE.

Another important coastal centre was Mangrol, known at present for its fishing industry and for a 14th century mosque. An inscription dated to 1145 CE during the reign of the Chalukya ruler Kumarapala records the foundation of a temple by a subordinate chief of the Guhila family. There are references to a *sulkamandapika* or customs house and trade in grain, betel leaves and salt.[20]

Further south, the main coastal centres on the north Konkan coast were Sopara, Sanjan, Chaul and Thane. An inscription of the Silaharas of 1094 CE refers to Sopara, Chaul and Thana or Sristhanaka as *velakula* or harbours and important centres for import and export. Sanjan is also believed to be the first settlement of the Parsis on arrival in India after they fled the Islamic conquest of the Zoroastrian Sassanid Empire, as described by the 16th century text the *Qesse-ye Sanjan*. The *Qesse-ye Sanjan* (QS), the Story of Sanjan, was written in 1599 CE by Bahman Kay Qobad Sanjana in the Gujarati town of Navsari. He was a Dastur, a Zoroastrian priest who belonged to the community known as the Parsis, ancient emigrants from Iran who fled after the Islamic conquest of the Zoroastrian Sassanid Empire. The QS tells the story of the Parsi community, their flight from Iran to India and their trials and tribulations in their new home. It relates how Parsis came to view themselves in India, "their relationship to the dominant culture, and their historic role within the India context in the 16th century". The sacred fire Iran Shah was established here but had to be removed to protect it from the onslaught of Muslim armies. It was subsequently re-established at Navsari. Archaeological excavations conducted over two seasons have provided evidence of settlement well into the 14th century and the presence of a 10th century *dokma* or Tower of Silence, though there is as yet little proof of Muslim attack and subsequent shift.[21]

Chaul, referred to as Campavati or Revatiksetra in the epics, is mentioned in inscriptions and literary sources from the early centuries of the Common Era to the 17th century. While no systematic archaeological work has been undertaken in the area, villagers digging wells in coconut plantations unearthed crucial information regarding settlement from 250 BCE to 1600 CE, though for a brief period from 250 to 500 CE the site seems to have been unoccupied.[22] Epigraphs dating from the 10th–11th centuries refer to these coastal settlements linked to each other through land routes, as well as to those in the interior.

Archaeological excavations can provide crucial evidence in terms of identifying ancient settlements along the coasts and changes that these may have undergone over time. Along the Saurashtra coast surveys have led to finds of a large number of stone anchors at Dwarka, Bet Dwarka, Miyani, Visawada, Somnath, Mul Dwarka, Hathab and Ghogha, indicating the existence of ancient anchorages. Of these, Ghogha, located in the Gulf of Khambat about 15 kilometres from the town of Bhavnagar, yielded about two dozen stone anchors of the Indo-Arabian type and large quantities of medieval glazed pottery dated from 9th to 12th century.[23] The site is also known for a 10th and 11th century Jain temple. In addition to fulfilling the religious needs of the people, coastal temples and shrines also served as markers for navigators. The Dwarkadhish temple at Dwarka has a height of 78 metres and is visible from at least 20 kilometres out at sea. Similarly, the hilltop temple at Harshad Mata served as a marker of the coastal settlement of Miyani, 40 kilometres east of Dwarka.[24] This brief survey of prominent centres along the west coast shows the presence of a population with multiple religious affiliations. In addition to Hindus, Buddhists and Jains, Muslims and Jewish communities were also settled along the coast. Trade appears as a profitable occupation leading to accumulation of wealth, but also attracting taxes from the king, as evident from the next section.

THE SRENI AND THE ORGANIZATION OF COMMERCE

> The king must protect the conventions of heretics, corporate bodies, guilds, councils, troops, groups and the like in towns and in the countryside.

> Whatever their laws, duties, rules for worship or mode of livelihood, he must permit them.[25]

The *Narada Smrti* places the onus of protecting customary rights of corporate bodies on the king, the one institutional figure that was likely to be the cause of their erosion and thus attempts to minimize the possibility of confrontation between the two. The legal system on the ground in the early medieval period was graded into several levels of law from the rules of the *Dharmasastras* to the regional and community based conventions to localized standards. Several medieval texts on judicial procedure contain discussion on the conventions and legislation by corporate bodies and how these should be handled by the ruler. Writers such as Katyayana, Brhaspati and Manu state that the king was obliged to sanction and enforce those regional conventions that had the consensus of local leaders.[26] This means that local consensus was the real source of *dharma*, as it applied to corporate bodies.

Donald Davis (2005) has explored the increased prominence of intermediate-level corporate groups in the creation and administration of law. The corporate groups in question include, among others, merchants, traders, religious specialists, soldiers, agriculturalists, pastoralists, and castes. Such groups or associations are intermediate in two interrelated ways: 1) they mediate practical legal influences from both highly local sources (villages, families, etc.) and elite-level political rulers, and 2) they mediate theoretical legal influences from local and regional customary law and the elite-level Brahmanical discourses of *Dharmasastra*, the treatises on Hindu law. It is the functioning of these corporate bodies that we explore in this chapter, as also the different partnerships that made medieval trade possible.

The most elaborate of these was the 592 CE record of the Kalachuri king Visnusena from Gujarat who gave a formal order for fixing the seventy-two regulations of the merchant groups as law. By comparing medieval inscriptions with contemporary legal texts, Davis makes a convincing case that despite textual statements against anyone but the ruler or his appointees conducting legal procedures or meting out punishment, corporate groups were authorized to carry out their own trials and to administer punishments.[27] Nevertheless corporate groups were at the same time mandated to seek out the ruler's help when the group's internal processes and punishments were not heeded. In such cases, the texts tell us, rulers should issue decrees that either rectify and reinstate the pre-existing rules of the group or in rare cases proclaim a new set of regulations to be followed by the group.[28]

It is significant that in the case of the inscriptions from Kolhapur, the guilds contributed to Jain temples and Jain ritual worship of the Tirthankara. As discussed in the next section, this was by no means monopolistic control over any one religion instead the practice seems to have been for active engagement between religious shrines and groups of all religious affiliation.

PHILANTHROPY AND PATRONAGE TO TEMPLES

In the 13th century the achievements and philanthropy of two of the merchants close to the ruling elite, viz. Jagadu, the Jain merchant prince of Kachchh and Vastupala, minister of the Vaghela ruler of Gujarat, form the main characters of elaborate poetic compositions. It is significant that many of the authors of the poetic compositions were also scribes of royal inscriptions. For example, Somesvaradeva (1179–1262), the composer of *Kirtikaumudi*, a biography of Vastupala, was also the author of many inscriptions dated from 1241 to 1255 CE, as is evident from one of the epigraphs carrying a verse from the *Kirtikaumudi*. Vastupala, a statesman and warrior, was placed in charge of the administration of Khambat to offer protection and safety to voyaging merchants at Khambat.

The *Jagaducarita* by Sarvananda is a *mahakavya* or epic poem in seven cantos. Sarvananda traces the genealogy of Jagadu from the Srimali group of merchants in southern Marwar and highlights the merchant's anxiety at the absence of a male offspring in spite of his wealth and prominent social position. Prayers to the ocean deity brought the reassurance that all his ships would return safely to port, but offered no hope for a progeny.[29] Nevertheless the ocean deity gave Jagadu excellent jewels from his treasury and with their aid, the merchant went from strength to strength. He had a trusted and reliable agent named Jayantasimha, an Osval, who sailed in one of Jagadu's ships, laden with merchandise, for trade to Ardrapura or Hormuz. On his arrival he presented the lord of the town a valuable *nazrana* or gift and hired a large warehouse. It was at this time that a large stone on the shore attracted his attention and he ordered his servants to take possession of it. This brought him into conflict with a Muslim (Turshka) merchant from Stambha-pura or Khambat, in Gujarat who had also noticed the stone and wanted possession of it. They both then bid for the stone and eventually Jayantasimha deposited three lakh dinaras with the prince of Ardrapura who had meanwhile reached the shore on hearing the altercation. He then returned to Bhadresvara in his now empty ship, but with the stone. On splitting the stone, Jagadu discovered more jewels inside it.

Jagadu is credited with saving the town of Bhadresvara from attack by king Pithadeva by rebuilding the town wall surrounded by a moat and constructing a dwelling of the god Bhadra above the rampart. He then approached the Chalukya ruler for forces to guard the town and this led Pithadeva to flee. Having secured the town of Bhadresvara, Jagadu undertook a pilgrimage to Girnar and Satrunjaya, two holy sites in Gujarat with the Jain community of his town, but before leaving he presented gifts to the ruler of Anahillanagara to obtain his protection. After his return the merchant Jagadu engaged in further works of piety, such as digging wells, donating to temples, restoration of dilapidated shrines, establishment of a mosque and saving the people of the town from famine by distributing grain and building alms houses.[30]

The brothers Tejahpala and Vastupala are two of Jainism's most written about lay devotees, known as able ministers under the Chalukya-Vaghela regime of Gujarat and as patrons of several temples. They are said to come from a prominent merchant family of the Pragvata caste from Patan. Tejahpala built the magnificent temple of Mt. Abu for his dead elder brother if popular legend is to be believed or for his wife and son, as stated in the temple inscriptions praising his illustrious family. According to Jinaharsa's *Vastupalacarita* (1441), Tejapala built a rampart around the town of Dabhoi to protect the residents from constant attack and placed images of deceased Chalukya kings on it. Written sources credit Vastupala with sponsoring several works on Mount Girnar, including the installation of portrait sculptures, though little remains of these. Vastupala is also credited with repulsing an attack by the Muslim merchant Said of Broach and his general Sankha at the port of Khambat, though he lost his general Bhuvanapala in the fight. At the spot where Bhuvanapala fell in battle, Vastupala had a Siva temple erected called Bhuvanapalesvara. Merutunga's *Prabandhacintamani* (1304) refers to a different kind of battle – a battle for control of the Girnar mountain between the Svetambara merchant Dhara and his five sons who had gone on pilgrimage to the site and the local Digambara king who controlled the mountain. In the process, the five sons of the merchant were killed and are said to have been reborn as the protectors or *kshetrapalas* of the mountain.[31]

The multi-religious milieu of the West Coast is reflected in the writings of Hemachandra referred to above and perhaps the most illustrious Jain monk of the period who was both learned and well-travelled and has left a large corpus of writings in Sanskrit and Prakrit. He was born in Dhanduka in the district of Ahmedabad. His parents belonged to the merchant (*vania*) caste, in particular to the sub-caste of Srimodh vanias, so called because they originally came from Modhera. His name was Cangadeva, but at the age of five he was entrusted to the monk Devacandra as his pupil. Devacandra took the boy to Stambhatirtha or present-day Khambat where he probably spent twelve years in study until he ordained as an Acarya and adopted the name of Hemachandra. His first patron in Patan or modern Anahilvad Patan was the Chalukya ruler Jayasimha or Siddharaja (1094–1143) and subsequently his successor Kumarapala (1143–1172). Thanks largely to Hemachandra's influence, Kumarapala's reign remains proverbial among Jains for its patronage and support to the community and to the religion. His last major work was *Trisastisalakapurusa-caritra* or *The Lives of Jain Elders*, which is an epic poem in Sanskrit, written in 3,460 verse couplets divided into 13 cantos of unequal length, about the chief personages of Jainism. The objective was to highlight the teachings of Jaina teachers to their disciples, to provide information of sites of pilgrimage and to validate the claims of Jainism to these.[32]

In his *Trisastisalakapurusa*, Hemacandra describes the travels of several merchants who went from city to city in order to earn money and several rich merchants, such as king Srenika, whose glory was formed by his merchant guilds (canto 1: 22-28), and Dhana (canto 12: 242, 274-80, 292-305) appear as characters of the stories. In the *Parisistaparvan* we have reference to a rich man who lost his possessions, but then went out again to distant lands to make money. The inscriptions also refer to an association termed *desi* that may be translated as a guild of travelling merchants. For example, the Nadlai inscription of 1124 CE records that the *vanajaris* of the villages of Abhinavpuri, Badari and Nadlai having assembled into a guild or *desi* granted rupees two for each twenty *pailas* loaded on bullocks and rupee one for each cart filled with commodities termed *kiranas* for the ascetics of the temple of Mahavira. The term *desi* in the sense of guild occurs in other contemporary inscriptions as well.[33]

Buddhist Centres

As mentioned elsewhere in the book, Kanheri near Mumbai was the largest religious centre along the west coast of India, with one hundred and four caves located in the fertile basin of the Ulhas river dated from 1st to 11th century CE. The single largest group of donors (as mentioned in nineteen inscriptions) comprised of *negamas* (merchants), *vanija* (traders), *suvanakokara* (goldsmiths) and *heranika* (treasurers). This is followed by thirteen inscriptions recording gifts by women and ten by monks and nuns. Merchants travelled to the monastic site from other settlements along the west coast, such as Kalyan, Sopara and Chaul and refer to their donations as *deyadhamma* or obligatory donation made for the welfare of their families. It is significant that these donations are made in association with other members of the family and at least two refer to affiliation with the Sangha and a *thera*.[34] Clearly then traders formed an important segment of the donors of Buddhist sculptural and literary domain in the early historical period.

Kanheri continued to receive patronage from the 1st to the 11th centuries CE. This was in the form of money and land donations in the early centuries of the Common Era, whereas in the early medieval period the pilgrims built votive stupas of brick. Enshrined within these stupas were relic caskets and copper plates or stone tablets bearing the *pratityasamutpada sutra*, the fundamental doctrine of Buddhism,[35] which explains the existence of objects and phenomena as being due to systems of causes and effects. These unbaked clay seals and sealings are ubiquitous at Buddhist sites in the early medieval period and in 19th century literature were often wrongly described as pilgrim's mementoes. Instead they are ritual objects associated with merit making. Based on descriptions provided by the 7th century Chinese pilgrim Xuanzang, it is evident that the production of sealings was linked to merit-making and cleansing of sin. To produce an image of the Buddha or to produce a stupa brought merit. Miniature stupas and images were produced in large numbers and were ceremonially placed inside relic chambers of stupas, which were then sealed. This is an extraordinary practice which can help trace itineraries of ritual or the circulation of cults and ideas. These portable objects formed a crucial part of the universal visual imagery associated with the spread of *dhamma* across Asia and need to be contextualised within local histories for the establishment of shrines. It is significant that these are singularly absent at Buddhist sites on the Tamil coast.

The Hindu temple

The foregoing discussion by no means suggests that Buddhism was the dominant religion along the west coast or that all trading groups owed affiliation to it. On the contrary, the West Coast presented, as at present, a pluralistic society incorporating communities with varied religious affiliations.

The first set of three copper plates from Anjaneri found near Trimbak in Nasik district confirms this position of merchants and entrusts the *nagaram* with the administration of the temple estate, including disposal and investment of the revenues. Bhogashakti grants eight villages for providing materials for worship of the god Narayana, for repairs to the temple and for the maintenance of a *sattra* in the town of Jayapura. The merchants are asked to select five or ten of their number to supervise the great annual festival of the god, which would be attended by many pilgrims from afar and last a whole fortnight in the month of Margasirsa (December). The merchants were in turn exempted from payment of octroi duties and the obligation to pay for the boarding of royal officers. A postscript to the plates records endowments by Tejavarmaraja who donated pasture land in a village to the south of Jayapura. He also deposited a hundred rupakas with the guild of merchants. The interest on this amount was to be used for providing bdellium or *guggulu* for worship of the deity.[36]

The Jaina Temple and the Market Place

Though there is no mention of Jainism in the nearly 100 copper plate grants of the Maitraka period (493–776 CE), Jain literature describes Vallabhi as a great pilgrimage centre (*tirtha*) and archaeological data provides evidence of earlier shrines. Jaina metal and stone images stylistically dated to circa 500–600 CE were found at Akota near Vadodara and from Khedbrahma in north Gujarat. Around the same time, Jaina rock-cut caves were excavated at Dhank in Saurashtra. Somewhat later in the 8th century, a Jaina monastic settlement of Digambara affiliation is known to have existed at Nagasarika or Navasari in southern Gujarat.[37]

The inscriptions from temples in Kolhapur, which were considered sacred by both Jainas and Hindus list the various groups assembled and those who comprised the larger Ainurruvar trade network. It is here that variations are evident as local and regional groups find representation. The *nagaram* or market-place denoted the location where members of the guild interacted with local merchants as evident from the inscriptions above. The location of the inscriptions in the temples at Kolhapur raises questions about the interrelationship between markets, shops and religious shrines. Kolhapur was a major site of pilgrimage for both the Hindus and Jains and, in addition to the temple of tirthankara Parsvanath, was also known for its Mahalakshmi temple. Twelfth century inscriptions are also found incised on beams of the shrine of the temple to Adinatha at Kolhapur, which describes the shrine in graphic detail. It was adorned with "extensive canopies and extraordinarily pleasing with excellent merchants' quarters, with courtesans' houses on both sides, with a large *manastambha*, with a storeyed house, having doors, which had acquired beauty through gold (plating)".[38]

Further proof of the connection between the temple of god Madhavesvara at Sedambal or modern Shedbal in Belgaum district and merchants is evident from the Miraj stone inscription of the reign of Vijayaditya, a Silahara ruler of the Kolhapur branch. The object of the donation was to record gifts made at the meeting of the Friday market held on 28 August, 1142. Those assembled included the Ainurruvar or Ayyavole merchants from the localities of Mirinje, Bage, Donikoda, Tolakale, Kundili and Sedambal, as also two officers of the Silaharas, viz. the *mahapradhana* and the collector of customs and the superintendent of markets. The five hundred heroes and observers of the *vira-bananja* code are described as residents of thirty-two coastal towns, eighteen cities and sixty-four *ghatika-sthanas* or places of assembly of learned men. The assembly agreed to contribute to the worship of lord Madhavesvara at Sedambal and the people of the town also agreed to contribute one *haga* (coin) on each marriage for the festival in Caitra and one *haga* per household to be given by members of the guild of the town for lamps that were to be lit in the festival of Dipavali. Contributions were also confirmed by potters, goldsmiths, shoe-makers, basket-makers and cobblers.[39]

It would seem that contributions were divided between Jain shrines (*basadi*) and temples dedicated to other deities as evident from the Shedbal stone inscription dated 1 March, 1153. In addition, taxes were committed for marriages celebrated with the beating of drums.[40] We have earlier referred to Somnath attaining supra-regional status as an important site of pilgrimage, which was visited by devotees not only along the coastal route, but also across inland centres. In addition to being acts of philanthropy, donations to temples were also a part of creating social status.

The participation of merchants in the construction and maintenance of a variety of projects for the benefit of the community is evident. The temple had become an important institution by the 9th and 10th centuries not only for religious purposes, but in its capacity to further economic growth and social and political integration. This chapter has provided insights into the complexity that developed in the early medieval period in Gujarat in several economic spheres such as the organization of trade activity into corporate bodies. The Law Books and epistolary manuals such as the *Lekhapaddhati* take cognisance of not just customary law of merchant settlements and trading groups, but also of law of joint commercial undertakings that governed partnerships and joint ventures. Vibrant maritime activity is evident from the inscriptions and the texts and is further supported by route specialization of the ports located along the Gujarat coast, such as Mandvi, Porbandar and Veraval, etc. In Chapter 6 we referred to another distinctive feature of maritime activity of Gujarat, viz. the partnership between the *Nakhuda* and local communities as exemplified by the Somnath-Veraval inscription of 1264 CE consisting of two slabs of stone inscribed with a Sanskrit epigraph and two months later an Arabic record. Thus it is evident that the West Coast adopted a different trajectory of engagement with the ocean. This diversity needs to be factored into any study of maritime history.

NOTES AND REFERENCES

1. J. Kurien, Diffusion as a Process: The Case of Plywood Boats in Marine Fishing, *Review of Development and Change*, July-December, 1996: 219-34.
2. R.P. Kangle, *Kautiliya Arthasastra,* Delhi: Motilal Banarsidass, 1988, part III, p. 124.
3. Dilip Rajgor, *Punch-marked Coins of Early Historic India,* California: Reesha Books International, 2001, pp. 63-70.
4. Ashit Boran Paul, The Early Historic Settlement and Subsistence Pattern in the Shetrunji River Basin, Bhavnagar District, Gujarat, *Puratattva* 30, 1999-2000: 99-105.
5. S.R. Rao, *Excavations at Amreli,* Baroda: Museum & Picture Gallery, 1966.
6. R.N. Mehta, Valabhi of the Maitrakas, *Journal of the Oriental Institute*, Baroda, XIII (1963-64): 240-51.
7. The office of the Drangika was peculiar to the Maitrakas and included a number of villages in its jurisdiction, e.g. three grants refer to villages belonging to the Mandali-dranga. The term *petha* has been found in one grant, which refers to Vatagrama in Dipanaka petta in Bilvakhata *sthali*. The conclusion is that a *petha* was larger than a *grama* or village but smaller than a *sthali*. The occurrence of the term *petha* in two copper plate grants from central India and dated to 529 and 533 AD indicates the central Indian connections of Gujarat at this time. K.J. Virji, *Ancient History of Saurashtra,* Bombay: Konkan Institute of Arts and Sciences, 1952, pp. 234-35.
8. Pushpa Prasad, *Lekhapaddhati: Documents of State and Everyday Life from Ancient and Early Medieval Gujarat*, New Delhi: Oxford University Press, 2007, pp. 158-64.
9. Ibid., p. 181.
10. V.K. Jain, *Trade and Traders in Western India*, New Delhi: Munshiram Manoharlal, 1990, pp. 110-14.
11. Pushpa Prasad, op. cit., pp. 20-21.
12. D.R. Bhandarkar, Anavada Stone Inscription of Sarangadeva (Vikrama) Samvat 1348, *Indian Antiquary*, 41, 1929: 20-21.
13. John E. Cort, *Jains in the World: Religious Values and Ideology in India*, Oxford – New York: Oxford University Press, 2001, p. 36.
14. V.V. Mirashi, *Inscriptions of the Kalachuri-Chedi Era*, Corpus Inscriptionum Indicarum, Vol. IV, Government Epigraphist for India, Ootacamund, 1955, pp. 154-59.

15. P.N. Vasa, Find of a Late Byzantine Solidus and Arab Umayyad Dinara from Kutch, *Numismatic Digest*, 14, 1990: 30-33.
16. Alexander Burnes, On the Maritime Communications of India as Carried on by Natives Particularly from Kutch at the Mouth of the Indus, *Journal of the Royal Geographical Society of London*, VI, 1836.
17. Nancy Pinto Orton, Sea-Going Trade in Early Historic Gujarat (c. 100 BC to AD 500), unpublished Ph.D. thesis, University of Pennsylvania, 2001: 100-101.
18. James Burgess, *Archaeological Survey of Western India*, II, 1874-75, pp. 206-07.
19. Z.D. Ansari and M.S. Mate, *Excavation at Dwarka*, Poona: Deccan College Research Institute, 1966.
20. James Burgess, *Lists of the Antiquarian Remains in the Bombay Presidency*, Bombay: Government Central Press, 1885, pp. 179-80.
21. Rukshana Nanji and Homi Dhalla, The Landing of the Zoroastrians at Sanjan: The Archaeological Evidence, in John R. Hinnells and Alan Williams (eds.), *Parsis in India and the Diaspora*, New York: Routledge, 2007, pp. 50-51.
22. V.D. Gogte, Discovery of the Ancient Port of Chaul, *Man and Environment*, 28, 1, 2003: 67-74.
23. A.S. Gaur, Ghogha: An Indo-Arabian Trading Post in the Gulf of Khambhat (Cambay), India, *The International Journal of Nautical Archaeology*, 39, 1, 2010: 146-55.
24. A.S. Gaur, Sundaresh, B.R. Rao, Sila Tripati and V.D. Khedekar, A Possible Medieval Lighthouse at Mul Dwarka (Kodinar), Saurashtra Coast, India, *The International Journal of Nautical Archaeology*, 39, 2, 2010: 418-22.
25. *Narada Smrti* 10.2-3.
26. Richard W. Lariviere, Dharmasastra, Custom, "Real Law" and "Apocryphal" Smrtis, in Bernhard Kölver (ed.), *Recht, Staat und Verwaltung im klassischen Indien*, Munich: R. Oldenbourg, 1997, p. 99.
27. Donald R. Davis, Jr., Intermediate Realms of Law: Corporate Groups and Rulers in Medieval India, *Journal of the Economic and Social History of the Orient*, 48, 1, 2005: 92-117.
28. Donald R. Davis, Jr., *The Spirit of Hindu Law*, Cambridge: Cambridge University Press, 2010, p. 122.
29. G. Bühler, *The Jagaducarita of Sarvananda: A Historical Romance from Gujarat*, Vienna: Akademie der Wissenschaft in Wien, 1892, pp. 28-61.

30. Bühler, *Jagaducarita,* 1892, pp. 15-18.
31. Jack C. Laughlin, Portraiture and Jain Sacred Place: The Patronage of the Ministers Vastupala and Tejahpala, in Phyllis Granoff (ed.), *Pilgrims, Patrons and Place: Locating Sanctity in Asian Religions*, Vancouver: University of British Columbia Press, 2003, pp. 297-331.
32. R.C.C. Fynes, *The Lives of the Jain Elders,* 1998, p. xi.
33. Nadlai Stone Inscription of Rayapaladeva; [Vikrama] Samvat 1202, *Epigraphia Indica*, XI, 1911-12: 42.
34. Himanshu Prabha Ray, *Monastery and Guild: Commerce under the Satavahanas*, New Delhi: Oxford University Press, 1986.
35. *Ye dhamma hetuppabhava tesam hetum tathagato*
    Aha tesan ca yo nirodho evam vadi mahasamano 'ti
    Those dhammas which arise from a cause
    The Tathagata has declared their cause
    And that which is the cessation of them
    Thus the great renunciant has taught.
36. Mirashi, *Inscriptions of the Kalachuri-Chedi Era,* 1955, pp. 146-54.
37. M.A. Dhaky and U.S. Moorty, *The Temples in Kumbhariya*, New Delhi: American Institute of Indian Studies, 2001.
38. V.V. Mirashi, *Inscriptions of Silaharas*, Corpus Inscriptionum Indicarum, VI, New Delhi: Archaeological Survey of India, 1977, pp. 238-39, verse 11.
39. Ibid., pp. 241-46, no. 52.
40. Ibid., pp. 254-56, no. 55.

8

THE SAILING SHIP

Connecting the Sea Lanes of the Indian Ocean

The Sailing Ship: Connecting the Sea Lanes of the Indian Ocean

As discussed in earlier chapters, a distinction is necessary between shipping and maritime trade, though the demarcation is no doubt fine and often the lines get blurred, as sometimes there is evidence for the master mariner transporting his own commodities for trade. In the 16th and 17th centuries, even when Indian ships were owned and controlled by one person, the cargo was not owned by one corporate owner, nor were the men employed by a single individual. It was customary for private merchants and travellers to hire space for their cargo as well as for themselves.[1] The theme may be studied from two perspectives, the two not being mutually exclusive: one, the communities involved in the construction and sailing of water-craft; and second, technology of the craft itself. While the second approach has had a relatively larger following, the literature on boat-building and sailing communities continues to be inadequate. An aspect that requires further attention relates to shipping in the creation of trans-regional communities and cultures and the need to factor in transportation into any discussion on maritime interconnectedness.[2]

Mortimer Wheeler identified so-called 'foreign pottery' such as Rouletted Ware and amphorae during his 1946 excavations at the site of Arikamedu on the Tamil coast of India and dated the former to between the end of 1st century BCE to the beginning of 1st century CE. He used these ceramic finds not only to endorse the nature of trade, i.e. Roman trade, but also the ethnicity of the users and hence suggested an Indo-Roman trading station at the site. More significantly, he started a trend for the study and interpretation of ceramics that has proved surprisingly tenacious.[3] Thus, clearly, 'imports' need to be contextualized within the parameters of patterns of local and regional distribution and consumption. More importantly for this chapter, we need to understand the complex patterns of travel in the pre-colonial period, as also the means of transportation across the waters.

The discussion is divided into two sections: in the first part, I examine archaeological correlates of maritime travel, as also traditional systems of navigation and boat-building; and in the second, I introduce the theme of transformation in maritime networks across the Indian Ocean with the entry of the Europeans. This second section underscores a redefinition of the maritime landscape through the creation of coastal enclaves and transformation in the nature of watercraft employed. This had far reaching implications for interconnectedness across the Indian Ocean and cultural interactions in the region.

THE ARCHAEOLOGY OF MARITIME TRAVEL

Pots were used in the ancient period not only for storing water on voyages, but also for the transportation of commodities and a wide variety were required for this purpose. An analysis of the ceramics from the site of Ras Hafun in the Horn of Africa indicates a mixture of pottery from many settlements acquired along the ship's journey and similar assortments are found in shipwreck assemblages. As such, ceramics neither provide ethnic information regarding the crew nor economic information about the purpose of the voyage.[4]

One of the symbols used on pots is the ship-symbol, which also occurs frequently on coins and sealings.[5] Iconographic representations, such as graffiti on pot-sherds, clay models, illustrations on seals and clay amulets dated to the Harappan period indicate the nature and diversity of boat-types used in the western Indian Ocean in the 3rd millennium BCE. A rectangular stone seal from Mohenjodaro shows a double-ended vessel probably made of reeds bundled with lashings, with a crescent hull and a rectangular structure in the middle of the deck. A similar craft with a small cabin in the centre of the deck is depicted on a clay tablet also found at Mohenjodaro. A graffito from the same site, on the other hand, represents a vessel with a mast and steering oars or side rudders at the stern of the ship. A terracotta boat model from Lothal, in contrast, represents a square-sterned vessel with a sharp bow. A perforation through the bow has been interpreted as a fitting for the rigging, while a second one at the upper edge of the hull is said to be an oar-rest.

Around the beginning of the Common Era, the ship-symbol first occurs on punch-marked copper coins from lower Bengal and thirty-four such coins with representations of a hull have been reported in the collection of the Asutosh Museum, Kolkata. The symbol is more elaborately depicted on unbaked clay sealings and single or double-masted ships are shown often with Kharosthi legends. One of these has been deciphered as 'trapyaga', reminiscent of the trappaga mentioned in the *Periplus Maris Erythraei*. Further representations of two-masted vessels with the rudder shown as a steering oar are to be found on Satavahana coins from the lower Krishna valley. These have been identified as sea-going vessels similar to the *toni* of the Coromandel coast that plied the east coast at the beginning of the last century.[6] These representations continue as evident from the depiction of a single-masted vessel with high prows found in an inscription from Duvegala in Sri Lanka.

In addition to these depictions are representations of so-called 'Roman' vessels. An incomplete graffito on a Rouletted Ware shard from Alagankulam on the Tamil coast is said to represent a 'Roman boat' (Figure 38). Lionel Casson termed it a 'Roman vessel' on the basis of parallels with the mosaic from Ostia,[7] but this analogy has been contested by André Tchernia who identifies the incomplete representation as that of a three-masted vessel which has been referred to in Graeco-Roman texts, but an iconographic representation of which has yet to be found.[8] Another pot-sherd with a ship graffito was recovered during the recent excavations at Berenike in a securely dated deposit of the second half of the 1st century CE. Though the representation has been identified as a characteristic craft of the Mediterranean, a survey of the Red Sea coast in the vicinity of Berenike has provided no evidence for harbour installations much less for any structures similar to those known from Ptolemaic and Roman harbours elsewhere in the Mediterranean.[9] This raises a wider question of the reasons for the choice of the ship-symbol for depiction on pottery and coins. How does this representation reflect engagement with maritime activity? This is not an issue that will be answered here. Instead, the next section shifts to a discussion of traditional methods of navigation in the Indian Ocean region.

38. Potsherd from Alagankulam on the Tamil coast with ship symbol.

NAUTICAL CHARTS IN ANTIQUITY

Traditionally the navigators of the Indian Ocean learnt their routes by identifying natural phenomena and by checking their positions by the stars. Certain routes across the Indian Ocean were more feasible than others were and continued to be in use in the historical period. Stellar navigation made sailing along the latitude possible, though finding the longitude was relatively more difficult. However, longitude tables were theoretically prepared by mathematical computations and early versions of nautical charts were perhaps available for specific routes and sailing schedules. Long-haul direct voyages were known, but these were certainly not the norm.

The *Periplus* refers to several of the navigational techniques adopted in the western Indian Ocean, such as identifying the approaching coast by means of changes in the colour of the water; and the presence of sea-snakes.

Vessels coming from the open sea in the vicinity of these places get an indication that they are approaching land from the snakes that emerge to meet them; these are also black in colour but shorter and with dragon-shaped head and blood-red eyes.[10]

The *Jatakamala* of Aryasura, while listing the qualities of Suparaga, the navigator, describes him as well versed in astronomy and capable of making accurate observations. He could ascertain the precise position of a ship in the ocean by observing the fish, the colour of the water, the species on the ground, birds and rocks.[11] Pliny refers to the Sinhalese who,

> Take no observations of the stars in navigation - indeed, the Great Bear is not visible; but they carry birds on board with them and at fairly frequent intervals set them free, and follow the course they take as they make for the land. They only use four months in the year for voyages, and they particularly avoid the hundred days following midsummer, when those seas are stormy.[12]

This practice of recognising the Indian coast, especially the Gujarat and Konkan coasts, by the abundance of sea snakes is also referred to in Tibbetts' later work and continues to be adopted by local sailors.[13] It is then evident that apprenticeship and experience were essential factors required in the development of navigational skills and the ability to handle a vessel. These skills were generally acquired by starting sailing in a minor position on board a vessel commanded by an experienced skipper and gradually learning the ropes.

While much of this expertise was communicated orally and learnt during years of apprenticeship, there is increasing evidence for the existence of written 'charts' which have unfortunately not survived in the archaeological record. By the late medieval period indigenous nautical charts developed which were comparable to the Portuguese *portolanos.* These were based on a systematic observation of coastal configuration, landmarks easily identifiable from the sea at a distance, bearings in terms of horizon star azimuths and underwater floor features.

Physical evidence of the presence of nautical charts has now been found among the Kachchhi seamen in the form of a *pothi* or manual written in Kachchhi and dated to 1664 CE (now in the National Museum, New Delhi mss. no. 82.263). The manual is not complete and only five maps remain. These are line drawings of limited coastal stretches, often combining silhouette profiles of coastal landscapes as observed from the sea.[14]

An 18th century map painted on cloth measuring 406 x 440 cms. depicts the whole of Gujarat and some parts of Rajasthan and is now in the possession of the Baroda Museum and Picture Gallery. It represents an earlier indigenous tradition known from 15th century textual references and one that was different from the European tradition that originated in Greek cartography. The map when hung shows east on top and all the place names are written bearing this placement in mind. The rivers are shown as zigzag lines, the sea as a large area and the mountains as blocks. The central position in the map is occupied by Ahmedabad shown on the banks of the Sabarmati and the other major towns of Gujarat, such as Surat, Bharuch, Khambat, Baroda, etc. are correctly placed. The main function of the map seems to be to indicate the relative position of the cities and to outline their road system.[15] In addition to nautical charts, indigenous traditions of boat-building in the Indian Ocean are both numerous and diverse. At present a majority of water craft are used for fishing and ferrying passengers across river-crossings, mechanised trawlers having taken over much of the coastal and long-distance transportation by sea. The boat or the ship, the vehicle essential for mobility on the waters, can itself be interpreted as a complex cultural artefact, one which was traded, modified, renamed, and accepted or rejected for a variety of reasons.

SHIP-BUILDING YARDS

Historically the data on boats is sparse and fragmentary in nature. The actual find of a log-boat in Europe dates to the 8th millennium BCE, and that of the earliest plank boat to the 3rd millennium BCE, though there is indirect evidence for the use of water transport as early as 40,000 BCE. In the absence of actual boat remains from India, ethnographic accounts provided by early Europeans are valuable for an understanding of the boat-building traditions of the region. The earliest reference to Indian sewn-plank boats occurs in the 16th century writings of Duarte Barbosa, a Portuguese who worked on the Malabar coast from 1500 to 1515. Those on the east coast were described by the Dutchman, Peter Floris who worked at Masulipatnam on the Coromandel coast in CE 1611.[16]

In his account of the trade of Surat in the first half of the 18th century, Ashin Das Gupta first drew attention to the discussion on Indian shipping in Dutch sources, no Indian evidence of any significance being available for the period. He showed that the strength of Surat's commercial marine at the turn of the 18th century was about one hundred, 'a very impressive fleet for an Indian Ocean port'.[17] Some data is available in the sources on the size of the vessels. This is given in *khandies*, three *khandies* making one ton. The marine *khandy*, probably adapted from the measure used in weighing raw cotton in Gujarat, has continued almost to the present. The problem, of course, is not all the vessels calling at the port of Surat have been listed, nor is it always possible to identify the different types of vessels mentioned in the lists of arrivals. While the larger craft have been generally included, the same is not valid for the single-decked, single-masted craft involved in coastal trade:

> But the entire trade of the Gulf of Cambay was carried by such vessels and Surat's trade with Sind, Kathiawar and much of the west coast was dominated by them.[18]

On the Coromandel coast, Nagore, located five kilometres north of Nagapattinam, was a centre for ship-building from the beginning of the 18th century onwards and also prospered as a centre of free trade under the ruler of Tanjore. Dutch records refer to a three-masted ship, forty-two and a quarter *cobidos* long over the keel (1 *cobido*= 18 inches, hence about 64 feet) built at Nagore for a Marakkayar merchant.[19] In spite of these scattered bits of information available in the sources, a comprehensive delineation is yet to emerge, though several pioneers such as James Hornell have left detailed documentation of the ethnographic data.

JAMES HORNELL (1865–1949): CREATING THE MATERIAL RECORD

James Hornell described distinct boat-building traditions that evolved along the major regions of the Indian coastline based on ethnological studies.[20] Thus the *kotia* is the ocean-going craft of the Kachchh and Kathiawar coast, while along the Konkan, *pattamars* are used for coastal sailing. The dugouts of the Malabar coast are best suited for the extensive inland network. Along the entire east coast, the catamaran is the characteristic fishing craft, the name being derived from the Tamil term *kathu maram* or tied logs, together with the *masula,* also known as *padagu* among Coromandel fishermen. What is intriguing is the distinction in the boat designs along the Palk Straits. On the Tamil side the catamaran and boat canoe alone are used, while on the Sri Lankan side the outrigger canoe called *oruwa* is the dominant type.

In 1946 (reissued in 1970), Hornell published the distillation of a lifetime's work in *Water Transport* in which his major preoccupation was with tracing the evolution of water-craft, as also their common origins and diffusion.[21] Many of Hornell's conclusions continue to be repeated in academic writings: one, regarding the common origin of boat-types and their diffusion around the world; and the second, his emphasis on the evolution of complex boat-types from simpler craft. Thus he traced the beginnings of this evolution of the log-boat or the log-raft and the more advanced stage to the plank built vessels. Another argument put forward by Hornell relates to the common origins of certain boat types and their dispersion through migrations and movements of people, a typical example being the outrigger canoe. The single outrigger is characteristic of the whole of Polynesia and Micronesia and is also found on the coasts of India, Sri Lanka, Madagascar and the Comoro Islands as a result of the voyaging and colonisation by the 'Island people of the Far East'.[22]

Basil Greenhill has countered these arguments in the study first published in 1976 and revised in 1995. Greenhill accepts the diversity of watercraft. He demonstrates that a variety of water-craft ranging from the most basic to the most complex type of floating structure are to be found co-existing at any beach of the world and that this pattern would have prevailed in the ancient period as well.

Hornell had suggested that skeleton construction was of considerable antiquity and was of Mediterranean origin. Subsequent research and documentation of boat-building techniques indicates that boat-builders in antiquity had built boats as a shell with strengthening frames, rather than the other way round, though there was a brief period of skeleton building by the Celts of north-western Europe in the 1st to 3rd centuries CE. The shaping of a vessel by skeleton construction methods is a far more complex process and one that did not develop in Europe until the 7th to 11th centuries CE.[23] Also, scholars are less likely to consider the two methods as distinct systems. It is now accepted that the development of full skeleton construction was a gradual process and that well into 1600s both forms of construction were in use in European ship-building. Vessels continue to be built by the shell method of construction in parts of the east coast of India and in Bangladesh to the present, though in certain regions, such as the Tamil coast, there is increasing evidence for the adoption of the skeleton method of construction.

At this stage we need to shift the focus and to move to the second objective of this paper, i.e. to what extent did these networks change with the entry of the Europeans and especially in the 18th and 19th century with colonization by the East India Company in the Bay of Bengal? How did the East India Company establish control in its maritime empire?

DISCONTINUITIES, CONTROL AND TERRITORIAL EXPANSION

Perhaps the single most significant point of disjunction was the introduction of steamship navigation in the 19th century. Historical evidence indicates that as a result, the indigenous system underwent radical changes. Seafaring activity shifted from being 'fair weather' to 'all weather'. Instead of the traditional communities, liner companies now dominated maritime trade. The skilled manpower required for manning these mechanised vessels could no longer be provided by the littoral sailing communities, and this led to the marginalisation of coastal groups to traditional fishing activities. But before we highlight debates relating to transformation in the 18th century, it is important to discuss the nature of change starting with the arrival of the Portuguese.

The vessel used by the Portuguese for travel down the African coast from about 1436–41 was the *caravela*, widely supposed to derive from Arab fishing craft. It was small and required a relatively modest investment, and significantly no special skills or facilities were necessary for its construction. Also it was small enough for repairs to be carried out by the crew itself should the need arise.[24]

The 15th century was also marked by interchanges between the ship-building tradition of the Europeans with that of the Indian Ocean. Ahsan Jan Qaisar's study assesses the nature, degree and pattern of Indian response in accepting or adapting European technology and remains the only work on this important issue to date.[25] Though the study is broad-based and deals with technology as a whole, an entire section is devoted to ship-building. In addition to the Indian response to European technology, it is also important to understand the extent to which Indian Ocean solutions to problems of the sailing ship were adopted by European shipwrights. This was perhaps one of the factors that led Admiral Paris (1806–93) to undertake detailed documentation of the 'extra-European' craft of the Indian Ocean - a source that continues to be under-utilised.[26] Similarly, the recovery of the wreck of the *Santo Antonio de Tanna* off the coast of Mombasa reveals a very shallow hull 'of a geometric pattern unlike anything recorded in Portuguese documentary sources'.[27] The vessel has been described as a Portuguese 'frigate' built in India in 1681 and lost in 1697. The matter is further complicated by the fact that many of the vessels constructed in India and termed 'frigates' by the English and the Dutch may have been modelled on English ships visiting Goa.[28]

In 1890, sixty-three per cent of the world's combined ship tonnage sailed under the British flag. By late in the 18th century this industrialising country had major centres in Mumbai, Kolkata, Chennai, Penang and beyond the edge of the ocean in Sydney. Over the next fifty years a series of vital ports were taken or created: Colombo in 1796, Cape Town in 1806, Singapore in 1819, Aden in 1839, and beyond the ocean, Hong Kong in 1852.[29]

Michael Pearson goes on to suggest that once the British economy had made the transition from merchant capital to industrial capital, there was a need to control not just the coastal centres, but the entire productive process and hence territorial control and expansion made the vision of the maritime empire a reality. Another development that contributed to the making of the maritime empire was the change to the steam ship, especially in the period from 1850 to 1945. Steam navigation altered the power relations dramatically in the Indian Ocean by pushing local participation to the periphery. Mechanisation of water vessels also resulted in new developments, such as the emergence of ports and dockyards where larger ships could be serviced and commodities loaded. It also enlarged the area of operations by drawing both Australia and the Atlantic into its field of operations. New skills were required, not just for manning the ships, but more so as navigational aids.[30]

Kapil Raj argues that a new development in the 2nd millennium CE was the emergence of cross-cultural mediation as a specialized activity in its own right and autonomous from trading communities. One of the intermediary types suggested by him that is of interest is that of the knowledge broker. Knowledge mediation, Raj argues, gained increasing status throughout the 18th century, especially as a result of sustained European presence in the Indian Ocean region and eventual colonization. The new knowledge that he discusses is generally linked to trade activities such as botany, geography, cartography, navigation, astronomy, ethnography, accounting, law and so on.[31] The new knowledge of interest to this chapter is that of oceanography. This emerging 18th century discipline was unconnected with the requirements of trade, though it was closely linked to colonial expansion and imperial needs to control of the ocean through a study of currents and tides.

The widened canvas of oceanic expansion in the 18th and 19th century was also crucial to the study of oceanography, as is evident through the travels of James Rennell (1742–1830). Rennell is best known for his *Memior of a Map of Hindoostan* and his survey of Bengal, Bihar and Orissa. Scholars have increasingly argued for major contributions of astronomer-pundits from Benares and the sepoy Ghulam Muhammad in the making of this map. "Without their mediation, it is hard to imagine Rennell gaining access to any of the knowledge circuits so crucial to the compilation of his innovative map".[32]

Here I move beyond the making of the *Map* to Rennell's navigational understanding as he surveyed the east coast of India and the overall contributions he made to make shipping safer for British ships. In both these cases, I would maintain that the new forms of knowledge that emerged were radically different from those of the preceding periods. The selection of elements for mapping and their measurement helped establish a new image of the land that could now be governed with ease. Expanding British presence in the Indian Ocean region linked it to the Atlantic and the Mediterranean in the late 18th–early 19th century. It was these newly established networks that facilitated James Rennell's maritime travels and exposed him to a different set of oceanic challenges.

It is no coincidence that interest in the material heritage of Southeast Asia corresponds with British control, starting with the occupation of Penang in the Straits of Malacca by Captain Francis Light in 1786. By 1815, Ceylon became a Crown colony, but soon the English were ousted from Indonesia. Though the Dutch were able to establish control over Java, they had to undertake a hard and bitter campaign for dominance over the northern Sumatran region of Aceh and the island of Bali. There are several similarities between the British experience in India and the emergence of the Dutch as a territorial power in Java, though Dutch control over the Indonesian archipelago was a slower process and was only completed by the early 20th century. In 1819 Sir Thomas Stamford Raffles (1781–1826), the erstwhile Malay translator to the East India Company, established the free port of Singapore.[33] However, the Anglo-Dutch Treaty of 1824 limited the British sphere of influence to the 'Straits Settlements' of Malacca, Penang and Singapore.

Up to the end of the 18th century, Burma had not been the target of European expansion, but this changed with the Treaty of Yandabo in 1826, that gave the East India Company control of Arakan and Tenasserim in lower Burma. The Indian subcontinent came under the British Raj in 1858, after the unsuccessful Revolt of 1857 and thereafter 'British Burma' came into existence, after the defeat of the Burmese king in the Third Burma War (1885–1887). Thus by the late 19th century, the British were able to establish their control over large parts of South Asia and to keep French commercial influence at bay. How did these shifts in the balance of power impact connections across the Bay of Bengal? I will discuss the issue with reference to James Rennell.

JAMES RENNELL (1742–1830): MAPPING THE PRESENT AND THE PAST

Mapping the past is an essential tool for understanding, in a schematic manner, where and when things happened. Is it possible to expect accuracy as regards locations and borders of states/cities/regions in the ancient past and their continued existence into the present? These questions are important as we discuss the contribution of James Rennell. Born in Devonshire close to Chudleigh in England, James Rennell lost his father at a young age. He was then looked after by the Vicar of Chudleigh, the Reverend Gilbert Burrington, in whose house he found a supportive family. The only formal schooling that he had was at the local grammar school, but from a young age he showed a keen interest in making maps. At the age of fourteen he obtained his first naval appointment as the captain's servant in January 1756 at a time when England was going to war with France. In 1758, Rennell made his first plan of St. Cast Bay on the north coast of France, where he saw action and the decimation of a large flank of Grenadiers. In 1760 he secured a place as a midshipman on the frigate *America* and sailed for Madras. After reaching Madras he transferred to another ship and took part in the five month naval blockade of Pondicherry by the British fleet comprising of sixteen ships.

During the rainy season the majority of the ships went to Sri Lanka, and there Rennell made a survey of the harbour of Trincomali. It was no doubt also at this time that he first investigated the chain of sandbanks, known as Adam's Bridge, separating Sri Lanka from the south-eastern extremity of the Coromandel coast, across which he declared that a navigable passage could be maintained by dredging the strait of Ramisseram. It was pointed out in a biographical sketch of Rennell issued in 1842 by Baron de Walkenaer, the secretary of the French Academy, that, though no notice was taken at the time of the suggestions put forward by so young and unknown an officer, the idea was revived some sixty years later.[34]

After six years of meritorious service and having made charts not only of the Tamil coast, but also of the Nicobar Islands, Malacca and northwest Borneo, he left the navy in 1763. The following year he had procured a commission as Surveyor-General of the East India Company's dominions in Bengal.

While in the navy Rennell had lost no opportunity to survey the places at which the ships anchored and had acquired the reputation of an enthusiastic and diligent surveyor. As an employee of the Company, Rennell found a strong supporter in Lord Clive and prepared maps of Bengal, Bihar and Orissa and of the Mughal Empire as far as Delhi, as well as charts of the river Ganga. The actual field-work for the survey took seven years. These maps were then sent back to England and formed the basis for Robert Orme's (1728–1801) study titled *History of the Military Transactions of the British Nation in Indostan from 1745*, which highlighted the military achievements of the English in India and was published in 1763 in three volumes. Thus one aspect of Rennell's work was the delineation of the Company's territories in India in order to publicize, back home, the gains that were made.

Rennell's career may be divided into two periods: the first part was spent as a sailor and surveyor in the navy. It was in this role that he was able to draw the coastline of India with an accuracy that had not been managed before. In this he received the unflinching support of his friend Alexander Dalrymple (1737–1808), the Hydrographer to the East India Company. In 1795, Dalrymple became the first Hydrographer to the Admiralty, a post that he held until his death in 1808. He had made a large collection of maps and charts of the east coast of India and regions further to the east. Other surveyors were also active at this time. Captain Michael Topping (1747–1796) made a chart of the Bay of Bengal in 1788; in 1790 he was employed to make a survey of the Godavari River; and in 1792 he was involved in taking observations for determining the course of the currents in the Bay of Bengal. At his suggestion, the Madras Survey School was established on 17 May, 1794 for training Indians. He died of fever at Masulipatam in 1796, where there is a monument to his memory, with a Latin inscription.[35]

On his long return voyage from India in 1777 round the Cape of Good Hope, Rennell mapped 'the banks and currents at Lagullas'. It was published as the Chart of the Bank and the Current of Cape Lagullas in 1778. His biographer, Clements Markham, considers this 'the very first contribution to the science of oceanography' and rightly calls Rennell 'the father of oceanography'.[36] He undoubtedly benefitted from several improvements in the science of navigation from the 1760s onwards. Perhaps the most significant was the system of finding the longitude at sea by means of a chronometer.

Though the use of stars and certain constellations for finding one's way across the desert or the waters dates to a very early period, scientific astronomical navigation did not appear until the 15th century. "It is, however, customary to regard as astronomical only the type of navigation that is based on observations to obtain the horizontal coordinates of the sun or of a star. This allowed the pilot to select more confidently the direction to be taken for his voyage, once he had determined more closely the position of his ship".[37] By this method it was easier to keep the ship on the same parallel and to travel in an east – west direction. Navigators also found that it was simpler to take observations from the sun and the pole star and to travel along the latitude. Finding the longitude was harder and more problematic. In 1714 an Act of Parliament was passed in Britain, offering rewards from ten to twenty thousand pounds for the discovery of a method for finding the longitude at sea.[38] After the invention of the marine chronometer, knowledge of ocean currents expanded rapidly and Rennell was the first to collect materials for understanding ocean currents in the Atlantic and Indian Oceans.

After his return to England, in 1778, Rennell spent his time in study and research. In 1779, he published the *Bengal Atlas* comprising several large scale maps of Bengal based on his fieldwork and in 1781 he was elected a fellow of the Royal Society. He then started work on the *Memoir of a Map of Hindoostan*, a purely geographical work, though dedicated to the service of the country. The Frontispiece to the Map shows Britannia receiving in her protection the sacred books of the Hindoos presented to her by the pundits or learned brahmanas (Figure 39). Rennell started by defining the boundaries of Hindoostan, which the Europeans have traditionally regarded as lying between the rivers Indus and the Ganga

39. Frontispiece to James Rennell's *Memoir of a Map of Hindoostan*.

with the mountains of Tibet to the north, thereby leaving out the Deccan and south India which were not considered a part of Hindoostan.

The provinces of Hindoostan proper have seldom continued under one head during a period of twenty successive years, from the earliest history down to the reign of Acbar (sic) in the 16th century.[39]

Thus for the *Map of Hindoostan*, Rennell continued to follow the divisions into *subahs* established by Akbar, but for the Deccan and the south he used information made available by several English officials. When discussing the course of the Ganga, Rennell made a long digression to discuss the location of the site of Palibothra mentioned by Pliny, who places it 425 miles below the conflux of the Ganga and the Yamuna and states that "the city meant by Pliny stood on the site of Patna".[40]

Another region that interested Rennell was the Punjab, the region that was traversed by the three great conquerors of India: Alexander, Timur and Nadir Shah. The engagement with the history of Alexander thus appears in a major way in Rennell's writings. To define the surveyor's multi-pronged strategies as he projected the Company's advances and territorial aggrandizements on a map as merely "the will to knowledge" and as a continuation of the Ptolemaic legacy would be to simplify the complex creation of the hegemony of 'colonial' knowledge of mapping the past on to the present.[41]

It was during the second phase of his career, after his return to London that Rennell devoted his time to reading geographical literature of the Greeks and Medieval writers as part of an ambitious study of the geography of West Asia from the Mediterranean to India. The first part of this work was devoted to the geography of Herodotus.[42]

On the subject of Asia, Herodotus has said a great deal....The Asia of Herodotus was in his own idea even *less* than Europe.... Beyond India, Herodotus confesses that he knew nothing.... And hence it must also be inferred, that the Persians of those days had no commercial intercourse with either China or Cathai, as in latter times; otherwise, either Herodotus,

Alexander, or the Seleucidae, would at least have heard of China and Eratosthenes would have noticed it.[43]

Alexander admitted that there was no land beyond the eastern borders of India, though Herodotus had extended a vast desert beyond it. Rennell thus argues that the expedition of Alexander had the effect of falsifying the geography of Asia.[44] Not only was there confusion about lands beyond India, but there was also no clear notion of the Erythraean Sea. Herodotus described it as the entire sea between India, Persia and Arabia, though he pointedly distinguished it from the Arabian Gulf. Arrian, on the other hand, drew his data from the voyage of Nearchus and called the Persian Gulf, the Erythraean Sea.

The source of these errors was the difficulty of adjusting the meridians of different places, previous to the discovery of the polarity of the magnet; and of the improved and facile mode of taking observations of longitude.[45]

In 1793 Rennell presented a paper to the Royal Society titled 'Observations of a current which often prevails to the westward of Sicily, endangering the safety of ships that approach the English Channel'. Until then this information was not known to navigators, often resulting in the loss of ships. As a reward for service rendered to navigation, the current was named after him. His charts of the winds and currents of the Atlantic, the Trade-winds and the Monsoons was however, published after his death by his daughter.

Thus Rennell's reputation rests not only on his work in India, but on his contribution to the science of oceanography. As a sailor he had studied by personal observation the currents of the Atlantic, the Trade-winds, the Monsoons, and their influence on the drift in the ocean, and he assembled over a number of years all the information he could gather from the experience and the log-books of his naval friends. This was clearly made possible by the wide ranging coastal enclaves of the British across the Indian Ocean and the Atlantic in the 19th century.

In the final analysis, how does one explain the enormous explosion of knowledge about archaeology and the study of the past in South and

Southeast Asia, as well as in the understanding of ocean currents and tides in the 19th century? Was there an ideological foundation to the search for this new knowledge? In order to answer these questions, it is important to understand European consciousness that underwrote themes of colonial empire and expansion.

Proponents of the Company's military expansion in the 1760s tended to see landed settlements as necessary adjuncts of an essentially maritime empire, creating self-financing settlements with extra provision against future danger. As the Company's publicists stressed, with the new income from territorial revenues in India after 1757, the Company no longer needed to export bullion to pay for its 'investment' in Indian textiles, rather it would pay for its cotton from local revenue surpluses of silver rupees. "Nor would the Indian territories require a drain of manpower from Britain, unlike the American colonies; silver rupees would pay for Indian troops to police the Company's domains".[46] It is this search for a maritime empire in Asia that radically transformed the landscape of the Indian Ocean from the Bay of Bengal to the South China Sea.

NOTES AND REFERENCES

1. A.J. Qaisar, From Port to Port: Life on Indian Ships in the Sixteenth and Seventeenth Centuries, in A. Das Gupta and M.N. Pearson (eds.), *India and the Indian Ocean 1500-1800*, Calcutta: Oxford University Press, 1987, p. 340.
2. Himanshu Prabha Ray, Introduction, in Satish Chandra and Himanshu Prabha Ray (eds.), *The Sea, Identity and History: From the Bay of Bengal to the South China Sea*, New Delhi: Manohar Publishers, 2013.
3. R.E.M. Wheeler et al., Arikamedu: An Indo-Roman Trading Station on the East Coast of India, *Ancient India*, 2, 1946: 17-124.
4. Mathew C. Smith and Henry T. Wright, The Ceramics from Ras Hafun in Somalia: Notes on a Classical Maritime Site, *Azania*, 23, 1988: 138.
5. Himanshu Prabha Ray, Introduction, in David Parkin and Ruth Barnes (eds.), *Ships and the Development of Maritime Technology in the Indian Ocean*, London: Routledge Curzon, 2002, pp. 1-27.
6. Jean Deloche, Iconographic Evidence on the Development of Boat and Ship Structures in India, in Himanshu Prabha Ray and Jean-François Salles (eds.),

Tradition and Archaeology: Early Maritime Contacts in the Indian Ocean, Delhi: Manohar Publishers, 1996, reissued in 2012.

7. Lionel Casson, Unearthing the Roman Connection, *The Indian Express*, Madras, 10 February, 1997.
8. A. Tchernia, Arikamedu et le Graffito Naval d'Alagankulam', *Topoi* 8/1, 1998: 447-463.
9. S.E. Sidebotham and W.Z. Wendrich (eds.), *Berenike 1995*, Leiden: Research School CNWS, 1996.
10. *Periplus* section 55.
11. *Jatakamala* of Aryasura, chapter XIV.
12. *Natural History*, Book VI: xxiv.
13. G.R. Tibbetts, *Arab Navigation in the Indian Ocean Before the Coming of the Portuguese*, London: Royal Asiatic Society, 1971.
14. B. Arunachalam, Traditional Sea and Sky Wisdom of Indian Seamen, in H.P. Ray and J.-F. Salles (eds.), *Tradition and Archaeology: Early Maritime Contacts in the Indian Ocean*, New Delhi: Manohar Publishers, 1996, reissued in 2012.
15. R.N. Mehta, An Old Map of Gujarat, in S.K. Bhowmik (ed.), *Reflections on Indian Art and Culture*, Vadodara, 1978-79.
16. Sean McGrail, *Boats of the World: From the Stone Age to Medieval Times*, Oxford – New York: Oxford University Press, 2004.
17. Ashin Dasgupta, *Indian Merchants and the Decline of Surat, c. 1700-1750*, Wiesbaden: Franz Steiner Verlag, 1979, p. 289.
18. Ibid., p. 281.
19. B. Bhattacharya, The Dutch East India Company and the Trade of the Chulias in the Bay of Bengal in the Late Eighteenth Century, in Mathew K.S. (ed.), *Mariners, Merchants and Oceans: Studies in Maritime History*, New Delhi: Manohar, 1995, p. 358, footnote 10.
20. J. Hornell, The Origins and Significance of Indian Boat Designs, *Memoirs of the Asiatic Society of Bengal*, 7, 1920: 139-256.
21. James Hornell, *Water Transport*, David & Charles: Newton Abbott, 1970.
22. Hornell, 1970, p. 255.
23. Basil Greenhill, *The Archaeology of Boats and Ships*, London: Conway Maritime Press, 1995, p. 46.
24. R. Barker, Shipshape for Discoveries and Return, *The Mariner's Mirror*, 78, 1992: 4: 433-47.

25. A.J. Qaisar, *The Indian Response to European Technology and Culture*, New Delhi: Oxford University Press, 1982.
26. E. Reith, *Voiliers et Pirogues du monde au debut du xixe siecle*, Du May, Paris, 1993.
27. R. Barker, Perspectives on the 15th Century Ship, *Congress Internacional Bartolomeu Dias E A Sua Epoca*, 2, Porto, 1989: 201-222.
28. C.R. Boxer, Admiral Joao Periera Corte-Real and the Construction of Portuguese East-Indiamen in the 17th Century, *The Mariner's Mirror*, 26, 1940: 396-404.
29. Michael N. Pearson, *The Indian Ocean*, London: Routledge, 2003, p. 191.
30. Ibid., pp. 194-200.
31. Kapil Raj, Mapping Knowledge Go-betweens in Calcutta, 1770-1820, in Simon Schaffer, Lissa Roberts, Kapil Raj and James Delbourgo (eds.), *The Brokered World: Go-Betweens and Global Intelligence, 1770-1820*, Sagamore Beach: Watson Publishing International, 2009, pp. 105-150. Michael N. Pearson, Connecting the Littorals: Cultural Brokers in the Early Modern Indian Ocean, in Pamila Gupta, Isabel Hofmeyr and Michael Pearson (eds.), *Eyes Across the Water: Navigating the Indian Ocean*, Pretoria: Unisa Press, 2010, pp. 32-47.
32. Raj, 2009, pp. 133-34.
33. Thomas Benjamin, *Encyclopedia of Western Colonialism since 1450*, Thomson-Gale, Farmington Hills, 2007: 370.
34. Rennell Rodd, Major James Rennell, *The Geographical Journal*, 75, 4, April 1930: 291.
35. Clements R. Markham, *Major James Rennell*, London – Paris – Melbourne: Cassell and Company, 1895, p. 88.
36. Ibid., p. 212.
37. Armando Corteslo, *History of Portuguese Cartography*, Lisboa: Junta de Investigacoes do Ultramar, 1971, p. 222.
38. Clements R. Markham, op. cit., p. 149.
39. James Rennell, *Memoir of a Map of Hindoostan,* London: M. Brown, 1783, p. 2.
40. Ibid., p. 40.
41. Thomas R. Trautmann, *The Clash of Chronologies: Ancient India in the Modern World*, New Delhi: Yoda Press, 2009, p. 172.
42. Rennell Rodd, op. cit., p. 296.

43. James Rennell, *The Geographical System of Herodotus, Examined and Explained, by a Comparison with those of Other Ancient Authors and with Modern Geography etc.*, London: Bulmer, 1800, pp. 164-68.
44. Ibid., p. 172.
45. Ibid., p. 188.
46. Robert Travers, *Ideology and Empire in Eighteenth Century India: The British in Bengal*, Cambridge: Cambridge University Press, 2007, p. 52.

9

PRESERVING MARITIME HERITAGE

The Path Ahead

Preserving Maritime Heritage: The Path Ahead

The earlier chapters have underscored the need to move beyond the persistent theme of national histories, with a continuing emphasis on trade and European interventions in secondary literature, to focus on cultural routes and channels of communication across the Indian Ocean.[1] Though the seas have been important for the five millennia of human history, they are also the most glossed-over in historical discourse, which has tended to focus on predominantly land-based concerns of agrarian communities. With the focus gradually moving towards World History, the understanding of the Indian Ocean as a cultural, economic and historical trade zone is gaining ground.[2]

In his overview of the history of the Indian Ocean, Michael Pearson wrote of movements of people including traditional groups with trading and banking skills and goods across the waters, as also the spread of religious ideas and migrations of labour.[3] His emphasis was on tracing transformations both spatially and temporally, with the final push being provided in the late 19th and early 20th century that saw radical changes in ideologies of Empire, colonization and the introduction of new technologies in shipping and the establishment of ports at Madras, Calcutta and Bombay by the English East India Company almost from scratch. Equations in the Indian Ocean changed from the mid-18th century when the British began to acquire land in eastern India and steamship navigation altered the balance of power in the region.[4]

Rather than adopt a linear approach, the chapters in this book have underlined the multi-religious and plural landscape of the Indian Ocean that sustained maritime activity. The emphasis was on coastal architecture and shrines as also connections across the seas sustained by sailing communities with multiple trade partners. The unique monsoon system of the Indian Ocean termed *mausam* or Arabic *mawsim* which referred to the season when ships could sail safely was the bedrock of this inter-connectedness. Greek texts of the early centuries of the Common Era credit the ship-captain Hippalus with the 'discovery' of the etesian or annual winds, though Indian and Arab sailors are known to have used the monsoons earlier. The English term *monsoon* came from Portuguese *moncao*, ultimately from *mawsim* in Arabic, perhaps partly via early modern Dutch *monsoon.*

This distinctive wind-system of the Indian Ocean region follows a regular pattern: south west from May to September; and north-east from November to March. Until the 19th century, when steam-powered cargo carriers reduced the reliance on sailing ships, this regular wind system linked the communities of the Indian Ocean.[5] These linkages not only resulted in exchange of commodities, but more importantly of ideas and a shared cultural milieu. This intertwining of natural phenomena such as monsoon winds and the ways in which these were harnessed historically to create cultural routes and networks provides building blocks for contemporary societies, as they work towards universal values and trans-border groupings. As World History acquires centrality and the focus shifts from national histories to globalisation, the history of the sea is discussed as 'connected history' across porous borders, linked through boat-building traditions, community networks and cultural practices (Figure 40).

Thus the book is positioned at two levels: at the macro level it provides an overview of communications in the early period between communities

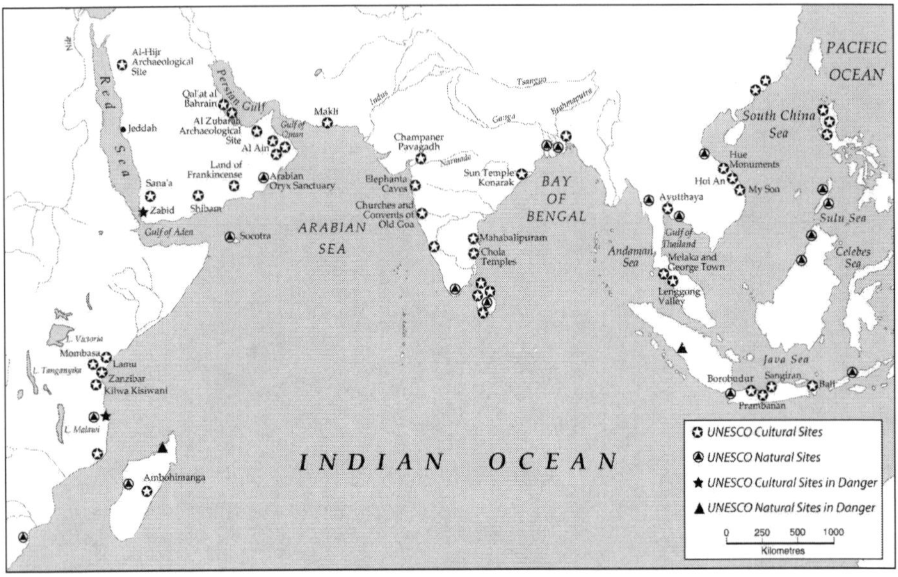

40. Map of Indian Ocean 'World' marking UNESCO's World Heritage Sites.

and regions of the Indian Ocean world; while at the micro level the focus was on understanding the regional and local coastal milieu. Two case studies were discussed: the site of Nagapattinam on the Tamil coast; and the case of early medieval Gujarat, thereby underscoring the differences between historical developments on the east coast of India, as compared to that of the west.

One final point needs to be made, i.e. the urgency to document, record and to preserve maritime heritage for posterity. In defining what constitutes maritime heritage, the approach adopted is the one advocated by the historian Ashin Das Gupta:

> Historians also have to decide what it is they wish to write about when they write the history of the ocean. Maritime History, as it has been developed among the Anglo-Saxons, tends to be written by the sailor for the sailor. While no one doubts the credentials of a sailor in the field, M.N. Pearson has justly argued that it narrows the possibilities of the enquiry unnecessarily.

> The interaction of land and sea rather than life at sea, would seem to be the focus for historians exploring oceanic themes.[6]

In this formulation the coasts acquire centrality and it is here that understanding cultural landscapes and visual topography become key factors. Maritime space cannot be defined solely in terms of geography or the environment; instead it is the product of complex interaction between communities and the landscape. As argued by Peregrine Horden and Nicholas Purcell, the overarching influence of geography over the destiny of man denigrates conscious behaviour and the impact of man on the environment.[7] Besides, the abstract notion of unity of the sea has to be contrasted with a visual ordering of geography. In the context of the sea, this was even more important since it was the coastal features along the shore and the visibility of sea-marks that defined the sailing world in antiquity and created a distinctive maritime milieu. This maritime milieu created coastal enclaves, which dominated communication both across the ocean as well as with the hinterland. Thus historical developments in these coastal enclaves and the links that they forged across the seas, as also with centres further inland become critical to an understanding of maritime heritage.

How does an understanding of the maritime heritage of countries around the Indian Ocean littoral provide a viable model to deepen the knowledge of their own cultural legacy, while at the same time engage with trans-oceanic networks? Legislation and measures for preservation require identification and documentation of the maritime heritage in local and regional contexts. More importantly, its protection draws on national agendas. Can a balance be achieved between national interests and trans-national research networks?

Heritage in this context includes both cultural and natural heritage. Research in several parts of the Indian Ocean has shown a loss of bio-diversity, as well as coastal degradation.[8] Unplanned urban expansion along the coasts has meant marginalization of local communities, including those involved in fishing and utilization of marine resources.[9] By focusing on nautical histories, architecture and archaeology, on the central experience of trans-locality of maritime communities and the mapping and remapping of maritime conceptions of space across two millennia, the book reorients the audience from the conventional linear imperial construct of maritime history as domination, conflict and control to looking at the reality of constant cultural transfer and transmission within the domain of the Indian Ocean world.[10]

Linked to this movement across the waters are the narratives of trans-locality inherent in memories of communities that dot the littoral landscapes of the Indian Ocean. These narratives of travel and pilgrimage across the seas lost their centrality with the development of 'scientific' disciplines such as archaeology and the search of national histories, but are important markers of long-distance pilgrimage and devotional networks that have been an enduring feature of cultural life across the Indian Ocean.

Maritime networks may be identified in the archaeological record by specimens of writing on pottery, seals and sealings and by inscriptions on stone and copper plates showing diversity in the use of scripts, as also languages used by communities who traversed the ocean. A case in point is the evidence from Socotra, an archipelago of four islands at the mouth of the Red Sea. The inhabitants are generally said to be of south Arabian ancestry and traditional occupations are fishing, animal husbandry and date cultivation. A surprise discovery inside a huge cave on the main island was a large number of inscriptions dated from 1st century BCE to the 6th century CE. The majority of the texts are written in the Indian Brahmi script, but there are also inscriptions in South Arabian, Ethiopian, Greek, Palmyrene and Bactrian scripts and languages.

Biological exchanges and transfer of plants, animals and diseases across the Indian Ocean can provide information on agents that helped make these transfers.[11] Data from shipwrecks indicates that pepper had been imported to the Mediterranean at least from the 2nd millennium BCE. It was a critical ingredient in medicines, had culinary applications and was also used in funerary and religious rituals. Pepper has been found at several sites on the Red Sea coast, but perhaps was the most noteworthy import to Berenike and included black pepper, white pepper or black pepper that had ripened and long pepper. Black pepper was a product of south India, while long pepper was cultivated in north India and in all probability shipped from the west coast centre of Bharuch or Barygaza.

Second, the data seems to suggest that social and symbolic factors may have been important, rather than economic.[12] For example, pepper has been found at several sites on the Red Sea coast, but perhaps the most remarkable find was that of two large terracotta jars made in India and recovered from the courtyard floor of the 1st century CE temple of the Graeco-Egyptian god, Serapis. While one of them was empty, the other contained 7.55 kilograms of black pepper-corns.[13] The nature of religious ceremonies where pepper may have been used is not clear, nor are there any explanations in written accounts, though it was also found in the shrine of the Palmyrenes dated from the late 2nd/early 3rd to late 4th/early 5th century CE. Other foods imported into Berenike included sorghum, rice, coconuts, mung beans, amla or Indian gooseberry and sesame seeds and were most likely meant for local consumption. Clearly we need to examine ritual aspects and ceremonial uses of many of the plant remains.

Ideas about religious and ethnic identities often draw from prevailing notions of the past and it is here that the present and the past are inextricably linked not only to individual destinies, but more significantly to the larger meta-narratives of the nation states or as in recent years, the globalising world. A leading historian of Southeast Asia, Oliver Wolters succinctly stated that the purpose of history and the study of the past could well be an enhancement of self-awareness and a better understanding of the present.[14] It is in this complex relationship between the past and the present that monuments and coastal architecture become important, as these speak of the past, but also interact with the communities who live in their vicinity and engage with those across the waters.

Monuments in Asia have generally been studied in terms of architecture and imagery or with regard to chronology and patronage and more recently within debates of generation of colonial knowledge, but seldom with regard to maritime connections, cultural plurality and memory of the community. Thus coastal monuments have been studied as a part of national history linked to political dynasties who patronized art and architecture, rather than relating to the sea around which these are located. The larger issue addressed here underscores the need to include coastal structures such as wharfs, forts, shrines, archaeological sites, etc as a part of the country's maritime heritage and to aid in their preservation for posterity.

Monuments enshrine many kinds of memories: memory of the vision of the builder; memory acquired over time; and finally, the created memory through transformation of the monument, either through its destruction or by altering its context or form. Monuments also become sites for enactment of rituals such as pilgrimage for the replenishment of memory and knowledge of the past. Social carriers of memory are agents for the reproduction and circulation of historical memory and traditionally these have included story-tellers, singers or actors who narrate mythical and past events to a local audience. The social carriers changed with the advent of modernity when the past was 'discovered' as a field of 'objective truth'. The charismatic position of the myth producers was now taken by professional experts. The rise of the expert also affected the relationship between the experts and the lay audience and resulted in the demise of 'public history'. This was further exacerbated by legislation and the narrow focus of what constituted conservation of monuments, as discussed in the next section. It is also being accepted that preservation/protection is a key component of conservation. Thus, to reiterate, preservation is embedded in conservation and the two terms are complementary. They however are not interchangeable.

LEGISLATION AND CONSERVATION OF MONUMENTS

In Britain conservation acquired the status of a specialized activity in the 19th century, requiring the services of an architect. This did not happen in colonial India where provincial Public Works Departments continued to handle conservation work until well into the 1940s, even though conservation had been identified as the main concern of the Archaeological Survey of India (ASI) after the department was reconstituted in 1895, and it is for this purpose that a large part of ASI's budget was earmarked.

In the 19th century, conservation and repair, which were looked after by local governments, had formed no part of the ASI Director-General's responsibilities. Nevertheless several concerned officers submitted memoranda to the Asiatic Society of Bengal urging that the Society appeal to the British Raj to issue some simple administrative rules for better protection of Antiquarian Remains in the various provinces of the country from destruction.

In 1895, after the post of Director-General of the Archaeological Survey of India had lain vacant for some years, the future of the Archaeological Department was re-considered and it was decided to direct it exclusively towards conservation. The Ancient Monuments Preservation Act was passed in 1904 under Lord Curzon, "to provide for the preservation of ancient monuments, for the exercise of control over traffic in antiquities and over excavation in certain places and for the protection and acquisition in certain cases of ancient monuments and of objects of archaeological, historical or artistic interest". In 1923 Sir John Marshall had issued a carefully prepared *Conservation Manual* and it continued in use well into the 1940s.

An outcome of these measures was that monuments of "archaeological, historical or artistic significance" were declared protected monuments and came under the purview of the Central Government.[15] Others that did not fall in this category were left "unprotected" and in the care of Provincial Governments. In addition to these two somewhat ambiguous categories of monuments were the large number of monuments not considered worthy of being protected and this is especially relevant for coastal monuments.

The 1904 Ancient Monuments Preservation Act continued in use even after Indian Independence on 15th August 1947. Article 49 of the Constitution of the Republic of India reinforced the State's responsibility in the protection of the built heritage. "It shall be the obligation of the State to protect every monument or object of artistic or historic interest declared by or under law made by Parliament to be of national importance, from spoliation, disfigurement, destruction, removal, disposal or export as the case may be." Additional legislation was passed in 1958 and 1972 for protection of archaeological sites and antiquities and an ancient monument was defined as any structure, erection or monument, or any tumulus or place of interment, or any cave, rock-sculpture, inscription or monolith which is of historical, archaeological or artistic interest and which has been in existence for not less than 100 years.

Recent amendments to the Ancient Monuments and Archaeological Sites and Remains Act 1958 passed in March 2010 led to the setting up of the National Monuments Authority to identify monuments of 'national importance' and to demarcate prohibited and regulated areas around them. However, the definition of what constitutes a monument of 'national importance' remains unchanged and the amendment 4A (1) now vests power in the National Monuments Authority to identify such structures, rather than the ASI.

Clearly then the ASI merely touches the tip of the iceberg in terms of undertaking conservation work at heritage sites. A critical aspect of conservation that remains unaddressed in the legislation discussed above relates to the definition of the 'monument' itself, its multiple identities; changes and additions over time; and relationship with present communities living in its vicinity or those across the waters. There is no well-defined strategy to engage with these issues, nor do they form a part of public debate in South Asia. Another aspect of this discussion relates to protection being given to monuments of 'national' importance, which leaves out structures and relics of transient communities and groups.

Political boundaries demarcated on geopolitical considerations often split a continuous cultural region, separating places of faith from their followers and traditional cultural landmarks from the communities that used them. The passage of time hardens these man-made partitions, and the memory associated with these once familiar sites is often lost with successive generations. This is nowhere more evident than in the case of the Ocean. The knowledge and use of the monsoon impacted ancient and historical trade, local economies, religion, politics and cultural identity. Centuries of trade, migration, colonialism and modern statecraft transformed these traditional interactions across the Indian Ocean, but present-day national identities and perceptions of the past are deeply interwoven with age-old ties. Revival and cementing of these ties then require international conventions and regulations and this draws UNESCO into the discussion as explained in the next section.

TRANS-NATIONAL NETWORKS: THE WAY FORWARD

The General Conference of the UNESCO in 1972 adopted a Convention concerning Protection of World Cultural and Natural Heritage. The Convention sought to encourage the identification, protection and preservation of cultural and natural heritage around the world considered to be of outstanding value to humanity. India ratified this Convention in November 1977. Of the 812 World Heritage Sites, only thirty are in India and comprise twenty-four cultural and six natural properties. Implicit in the western construction of history is the search for origins and ideas of continuity which reaffirm collective national identities. State-centred histories acquire centrality and the past is discussed as a linear progression of empires or states. What are lost in the process are parallel narratives and multivocality that are inscribed within the monument's multicultural and plural past.

Categories of heritage within the framework of the World Heritage Convention have been broadened over the decades to include cultural landscapes, industrial remains, and heritage routes, which are all now valued as part of our cultural heritage. The World Heritage Committee has also reflected upon such subjects as the need for community involvement, social benefits, heritage as part of sustainable development and the engagement of young people in the World Heritage process.[16] The UNESCO Universal Declaration of Cultural Diversity, adopted in November 2001, states, "Culture takes diverse forms across time and space. This diversity is embodied in the uniqueness and plurality of the identities of the groups and societies making up humankind. As a source of exchange, innovation and creativity, cultural diversity is as necessary for humankind as biodiversity is for nature." The World Heritage Committee sought to redress this at its 29th session held at Durban in 2005 when it was agreed to be 'aware of the need to specify the submission modalities for the nomination of trans-boundary or transnational serial properties on the World Heritage List'.

With all the inherent source of diseconomies, the logical question is: Is the investment in getting a listing of a particular monument or site as World Heritage status worth the tremendous costs to the developing countries? Has the inscription contributed to the ultimate goal of preservation for posterity? Judging by some of the cases in India no clear answer can be given and the way forward continues to be an uphill task. It is challenging, no doubt, but one which requires cooperation across several disciplines and several sectors.

NOTES AND REFERENCES

1. Himanshu Prabha Ray, Writings on the Maritime History of Ancient India, in Sabyasachi Bhattacharya (ed.), *Approaches to History: Essays in Indian Historiography*, New Delhi: Indian Council of Historical Research and Primus Books, 2011, pp. 27-54.
2. http://www.indianoceanhistory.org accessed on 26th November 2014.

3. Michael N. Pearson, *The Indian Ocean*, London – New York: Routledge, 2003, pp. 249-88.
4. Pearson, 2003, p. 148.
5. Himanshu Prabha Ray and J.-F. Salles (eds.), *Tradition and Archaeology: Early Maritime Contacts in the Indian Ocean*, New Delhi: Manohar Publishers, 1996, Updated edition 2012.
6. Uma Das Gupta, compiled, *The World of the Indian Ocean Merchant 1500-1800: Collected Essays of Ashin Das Gupta*, New Delhi: Oxford University Press, 2001, p. 280.
7. P. Horden and N. Purcell, *The Corrupting Sea: A Study of Mediterranean History*, Oxford: Blackwell, 2000.
8. Krish Seetah, Environmental Archaeology in Mauritius, Paper presented at Conference on 'Connecting Continents: Setting an Agenda for A Historical Archaeology of the Indian Ocean World', Stanford Archaeology Centre, 6-7 March 2014. Edgar E. Ribeiro, Legalized Mapping of Heritage of India: Can it be applied to Old Goa? in Himanshu Prabha Ray and Manoj Kumar (eds.), *Indian World Heritage Sites in Context*, New Delhi: National Monuments Authority and Aryan Books International, 2014.
9. Cynthia Chou, Space, Movement and Place: The Sea Nomads, in Satish Chandra and Himanshu Prabha Ray (eds.), *The Sea, Identity and History: From the Bay of Bengal to the South China Sea*, New Delhi: Manohar, 2013, pp. 41-66.
10. Himanshu Prabha Ray, Introduction: Beyond National Histories, in Satish Chandra and Himanshu Prabha Ray (eds.), *The Sea, Identity and History: From the Bay of Bengal to the South China Sea*, New Delhi: Manohar, 2013, pp. 13-40.
11. Tom Hoogervorst, If Only Plants could Talk...Reconstructing Pre-Modern Biological Translocations in the Indian Ocean, in Satish Chandra and Himanshu Prabha Ray (eds.), *The Sea, Identity and History: From The Bay of Bengal to the South China Sea*, Delhi: Manohar Publishers, 2013, pp. 67-92.
12. Nicole Boivin, Perspectives on Indian Ocean and Botanical Exchange, Paper presented at Conference on 'Connecting Continents: Setting an Agenda for A Historical Archaeology of the Indian Ocean World', Stanford Archaeology Centre, 6-7 March 2014.
13. Steven E. Sidebotham, *Berenike and the Ancient Maritime Spice Route*, California World History Library 18. Berkeley – Los Angeles – London: University of California Press, 2011.

14. O.W. Wolters, Southeast Asia as a Southeast Asian Field of Study, *Indonesia*, 58, October 1994: 1-17.
15. Himanshu Prabha Ray, *Colonial Archaeology in South Asia (1944-1948): The Legacy of Sir Mortimer Wheeler in India*, New Delhi: Oxford University Press, 2007: chapter IV.
16. http://whc.unesco.org/archive/2005/whc05-29com-inf09Ae.pdf accessed on 10th May 2014, p. 15.

Bibliography

Abraham, Meera, *Two Medieval Merchant Guilds of South India*, New Delhi: Manohar, 1988.

Agius, Dionisius A., *Classic Ships of Islam: From Mesopotamia to the Indian Ocean*, London – Boston: Brill, 2008.

Amrith, Sunil S., *Crossing the Bay of Bengal: The Furies of Nature and the Fortunes of Migrants*, Harvard University Press, 2013.

Ansari, Z.D. and M.S. Mate, *Excavation at Dwarka*, Poona: Deccan College Research Institute, 1966.

Arunachalam, B., Traditional Sea and Sky Wisdom of Indian Seamen, in H.P. Ray and J.-F. Salles (eds.), *Tradition and Archaeology: Early Maritime Contacts in the Indian Ocean*, New Delhi: Manohar Publishers, 1996; reissued in 2012.

Asher, Catherine B. and Cynthia Talbot, *India Before Europe*, Cambridge: Cambridge University Press, 2006.

Avanzini, Alessandra, Sumhurram: A Hadrami Port in the Indian Ocean, in Eivind Heldaas Seland (ed.), *The Indian Ocean in the Ancient Period*, Oxford: BAR International Series 1593, 2007, pp. 23-31.

Bandyopadhyay, B., *Udayagiri – 2*, New Delhi: Archaeological Survey of India, 2007.

Banerji, R.D., The Bhadreniyaka Grant of Siladitya I, GE 292, *Epigraphia Indica,* XXI, 1931-32: no. 18, 116-19.

Barker, Richard, Perspectives on the 15th Century Ship, *Congress Internacional Bartolomeu Dias E A Sua fpoca*, 2, Porto, 1989: 201-22.

——, Shipshape for Discoveries and Return, *The Mariner's Mirror*, 78, 1992: 4: 433-47.

Barnett, L.D., Bhamodra Mohota Plate of Dronasimha, *Epigraphia Indica,* XVI, 1921-22: 17-19.

Bayly, Susan, *Goddesses and Kings: Muslims and Christians in South Indian Society 1700-1900*, Cambridge University Press, 1989.

Bechert, Heinz, The Beginnings of Buddhist Historiography: Mahavamsa and Political Thinking, in B.L. Smith (ed.), *Religion and Legitimation of Power in Sri Lanka*, Chambersberg: Anima Books, 1978.

Begley, V. et al., *The Ancient Port of Arikamedu: New Excavations and Researches 1989-1992*, Pondicherry: EFEO, 1996.

Benjamin, Thomas, *Encyclopedia of Western Colonialism since 1450*, Farmington Hills: Thomson-Gale, 2007.

Bernet Kempers, A.J., *Ageless Borobudur*, Wassenaar: Servire, 1976.

Bhadkamkar, H.M., Navalakhi Plates of Siladitya I, *Epigraphia Indica*, XI, 1911-12: 174-80.

Bhandarkar, D.R., Plates of Dantivarman of Gujarat, *Epigraphia Indica*, VI, 1900-01: no. 28.

——, Nadol Stone Inscription of Bayapala, *Epigraphia Indica,* XI, 1911-12: 38-9.

——, Anavada Stone Inscription of Sarangadeva (Vikrama) Samvat 1348, *Indian Antiquary*, 41, 1929: 20-1.

Bhattacharya, B., 1995, The Dutch East India Company and the Trade of the Chulias in the Bay of Bengal in the Late Eighteenth Century, in Mathew K.S. (ed.), *Mariners, Merchants and Oceans: Studies in Maritime History*, New Delhi: Manohar.

Boivin, Nicole, Perspectives on Indian Ocean and Botanical Exchange, Paper presented at Conference on 'Connecting Continents: Setting an Agenda for A Historical Archaeology of the Indian Ocean World', Stanford Archaeology Center, 6-7 March 2014.

Boxer, C.R., Admiral João Periera Corte-Real and the Construction of Portuguese East-Indiamen in the 17th Century, *The Mariner's Mirror*, 26, 1940: 396-404.

Bühler, G., A Valabhi grant of Siladitya I, Dated 290, *Indian Antiquary* IX, 1880: 237-0.

——, (trans.), *The Jagaducarita of Sarvananda: A Historical Romance from Gujarat*, Vienna: Akademie der Wissenschaft in Wien, 1892.

Burgess, James, *Lists of the Antiquarian Remains in the Bombay Presidency*, Bombay: Government Central Press, 1885.

Burke, Katherine Strange and Donald Whitcomb, Quseir al-Qadim in the Thirteenth Century, *Ars Orientalis*, 34, 2004: 92.

Burnes, Alexander, On the Maritime Communications of India as Carried on by Natives Particularly from Kutch at the Mouth of the Indus, *Journal of the Royal Geographical Society of London*, VI, 1836.

Casal, J.-M. and G. Casal, *Site urbain et sites funeraires des environs de Pondichery*, Paris: Presses Universitaires de France, 1956.

Casson, Lionel, *The Periplus Maris Erythraei*, Princeton University Press, 1989.

——, Unearthing the Roman Connection, *The Indian Express*, Madras, 10 February, 1997.

Chakrabarti, Dilip K., *The External Trade of the Indus Civilization*, New Delhi: Munshiram Manoharlal, 1990.

Chakravarti, Ranabir (ed.), *Trade in Early India*, New Delhi: Oxford University Press, 2001.

——, *Trade and Traders in Early Indian Society*, New Delhi: Manohar, 2002.

Champakalakshmi, R., *Trade, Ideology and Urbanization: South India 300 BC to AD 1300*, New Delhi: Oxford University Press, 1996.

Chandra, Satish and Himanshu Prabha Ray (ed.), *The Sea, Identity and History: From the Bay of Bengal to the South China Sea*, New Delhi: Manohar Publishers, 2013.

Chattopadhyaya, B.D., *The Making of Early Medieval India*, New Delhi: Oxford University Press, 1994.

Cherian, P.J., Pattanam Excavations and Explorations 2007 & 2008: An Overview, in Stefano Campana, Maurizio Forte and Claudia Liuzza (eds.), *Space, Time and Place*, Oxford: BAR International Series, 2118, 2010, pp. 269-74.

Chhabra, B. Ch., *Expansion of the Indo-Aryan Culture during Pallava Rule*, Delhi: Munshiram Manoharlal, 1965.

——, *Findings in Indian Archaeology*, Delhi: Sundeep Prakashan, 2002.

Chou, Cynthia, Space, Movement and Place: The Sea Nomads, in Satish Chandra and Himanshu Prabha Ray (eds.), *The Sea, Identity and History: From the Bay of Bengal to the South China Sea*, New Delhi: Manohar Publishers, 2013, pp. 41-66.

Christie, Jan Wisseman, State Formation in Early Maritime Southeast Asia: A Consideration of the Theories and the Data, *Bijdragen tot de Taal-, Land- en Volkenkunde*, 151, 2, 1995: 235-88.

——, Javanese Markets and the Asian Sea Trade Boom of the Tenth to Thirteenth Centuries AD, *Journal of the Economic and Social History of the Orient*, 41, 3, 1998.

——, Asian Sea Trade between the Tenth and Thirteenth Centuries and Its Impact on the States of Java and Bali, in Himanshu Prabha Ray (ed.), *Archaeology of Seafaring: The Indian Ocean in the Ancient Period*, ICHR Monograph I, New Delhi: Pragati Publications, 1999, pp. 221-70.

Chutiwongs, Nandana, *The Iconography of Avalokitesvara in Mainland Southeast Asia*, New Delhi: IGNCA and Aryan Books International, 2002.

Cohen, Richard S., Problems in the Writing of Ajanta's History: The Epigraphic Evidence, *Indo-Iranian Journal*, 40, 1997.

Cort, John E., *Jains in the World: Religious Values and Ideology in India*, Oxford – New York: Oxford University Press, 2001.

Cortesão, Armando, *History of Portuguese Cartography*, Lisboa: Junta de Investigacoes do Ultramar, 1971.

Cowell, E.B. (ed.), *The Jataka*, London: Pali Text Society, 1957, Vol. 2.

Daryaee, Touraj, The Persian Gulf Trade in Late Antiquity, *Journal of World History*, Volume 14, no. 1, March, 2003.

Dasgupta, Ashin, *Indian Merchants and the Decline of Surat, c. 1700-1750*, Wiesbaden: Franz Steiner Verlag, 1979.

Dasgupta, Uma, compiled, *The World of the Indian Ocean Merchant 1500-1800: Collected Essays of Ashin Das Gupta*, New Delhi: Oxford University Press, 2001.

Davidson, Ronald M., *Indian Esoteric Buddhism: A Social History of the Tantric Movement*, New York: Columbia University Press, 2002.

Davis Jr., Donald R., *The Boundaries of Hindu Law: Tradition, Custom and Politics in Medieval Kerala*, Torino: CESMEO, 2004.

——, Intermediate Realms of Law: Corporate Groups and Rulers in Medieval India, *Journal of the Economic and Social History of the Orient*, 48, 1, 2005: 92-117.

——, *The Spirit of Hindu Law*, Cambridge: Cambridge University Press, 2010.

De Casparis, J.G., *India and Maritime Southeast Asia: A Lasting Relationship*, Third Sri Lanka Endowment Fund Lecture, 1983.

De Romanis, F., Rome and the Notia of India, in F. De Romanis and A. Tchernia (eds.), *Crossings: Early Mediterranean Contacts with India*, New Delhi: Manohar, 1997.

Deloche, Jean, Konkan Warships of the 11th–15th Centuries as Represented on Memorial Stones, *Bulletin de l'Ecole francaised'Extreme-Orient*, Volume 76, 1987: 165-84.

——, Iconographic Evidence on the Development of Boat and Ship Structures in India, in Himanshu Prabha Ray and Jean-François Salles (eds.), *Tradition and Archaeology: Early Maritime Contacts in the Indian Ocean*, Delhi: Manohar Publishers, 1996; reissued in 2012.

Devahuti, D., *India and Ancient Malaya*, Singapore: Eastern Universities Press, 1965.

Dhaky, M.A. and U.S. Moorti, *The Temples in Kumbhariya*, New Delhi: American Institute of Indian Studies, 2001.

Donaldson, T.E., *Iconography of the Buddhist Sculpture of Orissa,* New Delhi: Indira Gandhi National Centre for the Arts and Abhinav Publications, 2001.

Elliot, Sir Walter, The Edifice Formerly Known as the Chinese or Jaina Pagoda at Negapatam, *The Indian Antiquary*, Vol. 7, 1878: 224-27.

Falk, Harry, *Asokan Sites and Artefacts*, Mainz am Rhein: Verlag Philipp von Zabern, 2006.

Fleet, J.F., Sanskrit and Old Canarese Inscriptions, *Indian Antiquary*, VIII, 1879.

——, Junagadh Rock Inscription of Skandagupta, *Corpus Inscriptionum Indicarum III*, 1886: no. 14.

Fontein, J.,*The Pilgrimage of Sudhana: A Study of Gandavyuha Illustrations in China, Japan and Java*, The Hague: Mouton, 1967, p. 125.

Fynes, R.C.C., *The Lives of the Jain Elders*, Oxford – New York: Oxford University Press, 1998.

Gadre, A.S., Five Vala Copper Plate Grants, *Journal of the University of Bombay*, 3, 1934: 79.

Gaur, A.S., Ghogha: An Indo-Arabian Trading Post in the Gulf of Khambhat (Cambay), India, *The International Journal of Nautical Archaeology*, 39, 1, 2010: 146-55.

Gaur, A.S., Sundaresh, B.R. Rao, Sila Tripati and V.D. Khedekar, A Possible Medieval Lighthouse at Mul Dwarka (Kodinar), Saurashtra Coast, India, *The International Journal of Nautical Archaeology*, 39, 2, 2010: 418-22.

Glover, I.C. and Peter Bellwood, *Southeast Asia: From Prehistory to History*, London – New York: Routledge Curzon, 2004.

Gogte, V.D., Discovery of the Ancient Port of Chaul, *Man and Environment*, 28, 1, 2003: 67-74.

Goitein, S.D., Two Eyewitness Reports on an Expedition of the King of Kish against Aden, *Bulletin of the School of Oriental and African Studies*, 16, 1954: 247-57.

Goitein S.D. and Mordechai Akiva Friedman, *India Traders of the Middle Ages*, Leiden – Boston: Brill, 2008.

Gokhale, Shobhana, *Kanheri Inscriptions*, Pune: Deccan College Post Graduate and Research Institute, 1991.

Greenhill, Basil, *The Archaeology of Boats and Ships*, London: Conway Maritime Press, 1995.

Guo, Li, Arabic Documents from the Red Sea Port of Quseir in the Seventh/Thirteenth Century, Journal of Near Eastern Studies, 58, 3, 1999: 161-90.

Hall, Kenneth R., Trade and Foreign Diplomacy in Early Medieval South India, *Journal of the Economic and Social History of the Orient*, 21, 1, 1978: 75-98.

——, *Maritime Trade and State Development in Early Southeast Asia*, Honolulu: University of Hawaii Press, 1985.

—— (ed.), *Structure and Society in Early South India: Essays in Honour of Noboru Karashima*, New Delhi: Oxford University Press, 2001.

——, Local and International Trade and Traders in the Straits of Melaka Region 600-1500, *Journal of the Economic and Social History of the Orient*, 2004, Volume 47, 2: 213-60.

——, *A History of Early Southeast Asia: Maritime Trade and Societal Development, 100-1500*, Lanham and Plymouth: Rowman & Littlefield Publishers, 2010.

Hart, George L. and Hank Heifetz, *Purananuru* (translated & edited), New York: Columbia University Press, 1999.

Ho, Chuimei, Yue-type and Longquan-type Green Glazed Wares Made Outside Zhejiang Province, in Chuimei Ho (ed.), *New Light on Chinese Yue and Longquan Wares*, The University of Hong Kong, 1994, pp. 103-19.

Holt, John C., *Buddha in the Crown: Avalokitesvara in the Buddhist Traditions of Sri Lanka*, New York: Oxford University Press, 1991.

Hoogervorst, Tom, If Only Plants could Talk...Reconstructing Pre-Modern Biological Translocations in the Indian Ocean, in Satish Chandra and Himanshu Prabha Ray (eds.), *The Sea, Identity and History: From The Bay of Bengal to the South China Sea*, New Delhi: Manohar Publishers, 2013, pp. 67-92.

Horden, P. and N. Purcell, *The Corrupting Sea: A Study of Mediterranean History*, Oxford: Blackwell, 2000.

Hornell, James, Hero Memorial-stones of Kathiawar, *Antiquity*, Volume, 16 Number, 64, 1942: 289–300.

——, The Origins and Significance of Indian Boat Designs, *Memoirs of the Asiatic Society of Bengal*, 7, 1920: 139-256.

——, *Water Transport*, David & Charles: Newton Abbott, 1970.

Hultzsch, E., Palitana Plates of Dharasena II; Gupta Samvat 252, *Epigraphia Indica,* XI, 1911-12: 80-85.

——, Palitana Plates of Simhaditya; the year 255, *Epigraphia Indica,* XI, 1911-12: 16-20.

——, Ganeshgad Plates of Druvasena I, *Epigraphia Indica,* III (1894-95): 322ff.

Huntington, Susan L., *The Art of Ancient India: Buddhist, Hindu, Jaina*, New York – Tokyo: Weatherhill, 1993.

Jacq-Hergoualc'h, Michel, *The Malay Peninsula: Crossroads of the Maritime Silk Road (100 BC – 1300 AD)*, Leiden: Brill, 2002.

Jain, V.K., *Trade and Traders in Western India*, New Delhi: Munshiram Manoharlal, 1990.

Jamkhedkar, A.P., *Vasudevahimdi: A Cultural Study*, Delhi: Agam Kala Prakashan, 1984.

Jones, J.J. (trans.), *Mahavastu*, London: Luzac, 1949-56: Vol. 2.

Kale, M.R. (ed.), *Dasakumaracarita of Dandin*, Delhi: Motilal Banarsidass, 1986.

Kangle, R.P., *Kautiliya Arthasastra,* Delhi: Motilal Banarsidass, 1988.

Karashima, Noboru (ed.), *Ancient and Medieval Commercial Activities in the Indian Ocean: Testimony of Inscriptions and Ceramic Sherds*, Tokyo: Taisho University Press, 2002.

—— (ed.), *In Search of Chinese Ceramic-sherds in South India and Sri Lanka*, Tokyo: Taisho University Press, 2004.

——, South Indian Merchant Guilds in the Indian Ocean and Southeast Asia, in Hermann Kulke, K. Kesavapany and Vijay Sakhuja (ed.), *Nagapattinam to Suvarnadwipa: Reflections on the Chola Naval Expeditions to Southeast Asia*, Singapore: Institute of Southeast Asian Studies, 2009, pp. 135-57.

Kitchen, K.A., *Documentation for Ancient Arabia*, Part I, Liverpool: Liverpool University Press, 1994; Part II, Liverpool: Liverpool University Press, 2000.

Klokke, Marijke J. and Pauline Lunsingh Scheurleer (ed.), *Ancient Indonesian Sculpture*, Leiden: KITLV Press, 1994.

Konow, Sten, Palitana Plates of Dhruvasena I, *Epigraphia Indica* III, 1894-95: 108.

Krishnan, K., Rukshana Nanji and Atusha Irani, *Revisiting Buddhist Gujarat*, Government of Gujarat, 2010.

Kulke, Hermann, *Kings and Cults: State Formation and Legitimation in India and Southeast Asia*, New Delhi: Manohar Publishers, 1993.

Kulke, Hermann, K. Kesavapany and Vijay Sakhuja (ed.), *Nagapattinam to Suvarnadwipa: Reflections on the Chola Naval Expeditions to Southeast Asia*, Singapore: Institute of Southeast Asian Studies, 2009.

Kurien, J., Diffusion as a Process: The Case of Plywood Boats in Marine Fishing, *Review of Development and Change*, July-December, 1996: 219-34.

Lariviere, Richard W., Dharmasastra, Custom, "Real Law" and "Apocryphal" Smrtis, in Bernhard Kölver (ed.), *Recht, Staat und Verwaltung im klassischen Indien*, Munich: R. Oldenbourg, 1997.

Laughlin, Jack C., Portraiture and Jain Sacred Place: The Patronage of the Ministers Vastupala and Tejahpala, in Phyllis Granoff (ed.), *Pilgrims, Patrons and Place: Locating Sanctity in Asian Religions*, Vancouver: University of British Columbia Press, 2003, pp. 297-331.

Leese, M.E., Ellora and the Development of the Litany Scene in Western India, in R. Parimoo et al. (eds.), *Ellora Caves, Sculptures and Architecture*, Delhi: Books and Books, 1988, pp. 164-79.

Majumdar, N.G., A Passage in the Inscription of the Maitrakas of Valabhi, *Indian Antiquary* XLVIII: 207-08.

Malandra, Geri H., *Unfolding a Mandala: The Buddhist Cave Temples at Ellora*, Albany: State University of New York Press, 1993.

Malekandathil, Pius, Winds of Change and Links of Continuity: A Study on the Merchant Groups of Kerala and the Channels of Their Trade, 1000-1800, *Journal of the Economic and Social History of the Orient*, 50, 2-3, 2007: 259-86.

Manguin, Pierre-Yves, The Archaeology of Early Maritime Polities of Southeast Asia, in Ian Glover and Peter Bellwood (eds.), *Southeast Asia: From Prehistory to History*, London – New York: Routledge Curzon, 2004.

Margeriti, Roxani Eleni, Mercantile Networks, Port Cities, and "Pirate" States: Conflict and Competition in the Indian Ocean World of Trade before the Sixteenth Century, *Journal of the Economic and Social History of the Orient*, 51, 2008: 543-77.

Markham, Clements R., *Major James Rennell*, London – Paris – Melbourne: Cassell and Company, 1895.

McCrindle, J.W., *The Christian Topography of Cosmas, an Egyptian Monk*, London: Hakluyt Society, 1897.

McGrail, Sean, *Boats of the World: From the Stone Age to Medieval Times*, Oxford – New York: Oxford University Press, 2004.

McKinnon, E. Edwards, Yue and Longquan Wares in Sumatra, in Chuimei Ho (ed.), *New Light on Chinese Yue and Longquan Wares*, The University of Hong Kong, 1994, pp. 284-98.

McPherson, Kenneth, Maritime Communities: An Overview, in Himanshu Prabha Ray and E.A. Alpers (eds.), *Cross Currents and Community Networks: The History of the Indian Ocean World*, New Delhi: Oxford University Press, 2007.

Meech-Pekarik, Julia, The Flying White Horse: Transmission of the Valahassa Jataka Imagery from India to Japan, *Artibus Asiae*, Vol. 43, no. 1-2, 1981, pp. 111-28.

Mehta, R.N., Valabhi of the Maitrakas, *Journal of the Oriental Institute*, Baroda, XIII, 1963-64: 240-51.

——, An Old Map of Gujarat, in S.K. Bhowmik (ed.), *Reflections on Indian Art and Culture*, Vadodara, 1978-79.

Mehta, R.N. and A.M. Thakkar (eds.), *M.S. University Copper Plates of the Time of Toramana*, Vadodara: M.S. University, 1978.

Mehta, R.N. and S.N. Chowdhary, *Excavation at Devnimori*, Baroda: MS University of Baroda, 1966.

Miksic, John, *Borobudur: Golden Tales of the Buddhas*, Berkeley – Singapore: Periplus Editions, 1990.

Mirashi, V.V., *Inscriptions of the Kalachuri-Chedi Era, Corpus Inscriptionum Indicarum*, Vol. IV, Ootacamund: Government Epigraphist for India, 1955.

——, *Inscriptions of Silaharas, Corpus Inscriptionum Indicarum*, VI, New Delhi: Archaeological Survey of India, 1977.

Mitra, D., *Buddhist Monuments*, Calcutta: Sahitya Sansad, 1980.

——, *Ratnagiri (1958-61)*, Memoirs of the Archaeological Survey of India, no. 80, New Delhi: Archaeological Survey of India, 1981.

Monius, Anne E., *Imagining a Place for Buddhism: Literary Culture and Religious Community in Tamil-Speaking South India*, Oxford – New York: Oxford University Press, 2001.

Mookerji, R.K., *A History of Indian Shipping and Maritime Activities from the Earliest Times*, Bombay – Calcutta – London – New York: Longman's Green and Company, 1912.

Moraes, George M., Sindabur of the Arab Authors, *Journal of Indian History*, 10: 191-95.

——, *The Kadamba Kula: A History of Ancient and Medieval Karnataka*, Bombay: BX Furtado and Sons, 1931, reprinted Asian Educational Services, New Delhi, 1995.

Moti Chandra, *Costumes, Textiles, Cosmetics and Coiffure in Ancient and Medieval India*, New Delhi: Oriental Publishers, 1973.

Nagaraju, S., *Buddhist Architecture of Western India*, Delhi: Agam Kala Prakashan, 1981.

Nanji, Rukshana and Homi Dhalla, The Landing of the Zoroastrians at Sanjan: The Archaeological Evidence, in John R. Hinnells and Alan Williams (eds.), *Parsis in India and the Diaspora*, New York: Routledge, 2007.

Naravane, M.S., *Forts of Maharashtra*, New Delhi: APH Publishing Corporation, 1995.

Orr, Leslie C., Gods and Worshippers on South Indian Sacred Ground, in James Heitzman and Wolfgang Schenkluhn (eds.), *The World in the Year 1000*, Lanham: University of America Press, 2004, pp. 225-54.

Orton, Nancy Pinto, Sea-Going Trade in Early Historic Gujarat (c. 100 BC to AD 500), unpublished Ph.D. thesis, University of Pennsylvania, 2001.

Parker, Grant, *The Making of Roman India*, Cambridge: Cambridge University Press, 2008.

Patel, Alka, Transcending Religion, in Grant Parker and Carla Sinopoli (eds.), *Ancient India in Its Wider World*, Ann Arbor: The University of Michigan Press, 2008.

Paul, Ashit Boran, A Study of the Material Remains of the Early Historic Period Discovered at Padri of Bhavnagar District, Gujarat in India, *Pratnatattva*, Journal of the Department of Archaeology, Jahangirnagar University Vol. 6, June 2000: 53-66.

Pearson, Michael N., *The Indian Ocean*, London – New York: Routledge, 2003.

——, Connecting the Littorals: Cultural Brokers in the Early Modern Indian Ocean, in Pamila Gupta, Isabel Hofmeyr & Michael Pearson (eds.), *Eyes Across the Water: Navigating the Indian Ocean*, Pretoria: Unisa Press, 2010: 32-47.

Prasad, Pushpa, *Lekhapaddhati: Documents of State and Everyday Life from Ancient and Early Medieval Gujarat*, New Delhi: Oxford University Press, 2007.

Prickett-Fernando, Martha, Middlemen and End-Users: The Finds of Yue and Longquan Celadons in Sri Lanka, in Chuimei Ho (ed.), *New Light on Chinese Yue and Longquan Wares*, The University of Hong Kong, 1994: 299-321.

Qaisar, A.J., *The Indian Response to European Technology and Culture*, New Delhi: Oxford University Press, 1982.

——, From Port to Port: Life on Indian Ships in the Sixteenth and Seventeenth Centuries, in A. Das Gupta and M.N. Pearson (eds.), *India and the Indian Ocean 1500-1800*, Calcutta: Oxford University Press, 1987.

Raj, Kapil, Mapping Knowledge Go-betweens in Calcutta, 1770-1820, in Simon Schaffer, Lissa Roberts, Kapil Raj and James Delbourgo (eds.), *The Brokered World: Go-Betweens and Global Intelligence, 1770-1820*, Sagamore Beach: Watson Publishing International, 2009: 105-50.

Rajanubhab, H.R.H. Prince Damrong (translated by J. Crosby), Siamese History Prior to the Founding of Ayuddhaya, *Journal of the Siam Society*, XIII, 1919: 1-66.

Rajgor, Dilip, *Punch-marked Coins of Early Historic India,* California: Reesha Books International, 2001.

Ramachandran, T.N., *The Nagapattinam and Other Buddhist Bronzes in the Madras Museum*, Government Press, Madras, 1954.

Rangaswami, Sarasvati, Political Maxims of the Emperor Poet Krishna Deva Raya, *Journal of Indian History*, 6, 1925: 69 and 72.

Rao, S.R., *Excavations at Amreli,* Baroda: Museum & Picture Gallery, 1966.

Ratnagar, S., *Encounters: The Westerly Trade of the Harappa Civilization*, New Delhi: Oxford University Press, 1981.

——, *The End of the Great Harappan Tradition*, New Delhi: Manohar, 2000.

Ray, Haraprasad, *Trade and Diplomacy in India-China Relations: A Study of Bengal during the Fifteenth Century*, New Delhi: Radiant Publishers, 1993.

Ray, Himanshu Prabha, *Monastery and Guild: Commerce under the Satavahanas*, New Delhi: Oxford University Press, 1986.

——, *The Winds of Change: Buddhism and the Maritime Links of Early South Asia*, New Delhi: Oxford University Press, 1994/ 2000.

——, Accumulation of Knowledge: Pilgrimage as Leitmotif in the Indian Ocean in the Ancient Period, in Frans Hüsken and Dick van der Meij (eds.), *Reading Asia: New Research in Asian Studies*, Richmond: Curzon Press, 2001: 110-27.

——, Shipping in the Indian Ocean: An Overview, in David Parkin and Ruth Barnes (eds.), *Ships and the Development of Maritime Technology in the Indian Ocean*, London: Routledge and Curzon, 2002: 1-27.

——, *The Archaeology of Seafaring in Ancient South Asia*, Cambridge World Archaeology Series, Cambridge University Press, 2003.

——, The Archaeology of Bengal: Trading Networks, Cultural Identities, *Journal of the Economic and Social History of the Orient*, Volume 49, Number 1, 2006: 68-95.

——, Inscribed Pots, Emerging Identities: The Social Milieu of Trade, in Patrick Olivelle (ed.), *Between the Empires: Society in India 300 BCE to 400 CE*, New York: Oxford University Press, 2006: 113-43.

——, *Colonial Archaeology in South Asia (1944-1948): The Legacy of Sir Mortimer Wheeler in India*, New Delhi: Oxford University Press, 2007.

——, The Shrine in Early Hinduism: The Changing Sacred Landscape, *The Journal of Hindu Studies*, 2009, 2, pp. 76-96.

——, Writings on the Maritime History of Ancient India, in Sabyasachi Bhattacharya (ed.), *Approaches to History: Essays in Indian Historiography*, New Delhi: Indian Council of Historical Research and Primus Books, 2011, pp. 27-54.

——, *The Return of the Buddha: Ancient Symbols for a New Nation*, New Delhi: Routledge India, 2013.

——, Introduction: Beyond National Histories, in Satish Chandra and Himanshu Prabha Ray (eds.), *The Sea, Identity and History: From the Bay of Bengal to the South China Sea*, New Delhi: Manohar Publishers, 2013, pp. 13-40.

——, Multi-religious Maritime Linkages Across the Bay of Bengal, in Nicolas Revire and Stephen Murphy (eds.), *Before Siam: Essays in Art and Archaeology*, Bangkok: River Books & The Siam Society, 2014, pp. 132-51.

Ray, Himanshu Prabha and Jean-François Salles (eds.), *Tradition and Archaeology: Early Maritime Contacts in the Indian Ocean*, New Delhi: Manohar Publishers, 1996; reissued 2012.

Reith, Eric, *Voiliers et Pirogues du monde au debut du xixe siecle*, Paris: Du May, 1993.

Rennell, James, *Memoir of a Map of Hindoostan,* London: M. Brown, 1783.

——, *The Geographical System of Herodotus, Examined and Explained, by a Comparison with Those of Other Ancient Authors and with Modern Geography etc.*, London: Bulmer, 1800.

Ribeiro, Edgar E., Legalized Mapping of Heritage of India: Can it be Applied to Old Goa? in Himanshu Prabha Ray and Manoj Kumar (eds.), *Indian World Heritage Sites in Context*, New Delhi: National Monuments Authority and Aryan Books International, 2014.

Rougelle, A., Medieval Trade Networks in the Western Indian Ocean, in H.P. Ray and J.-F. Salles (eds.), *Tradition and Archaeology: Early Maritime Contacts in the Indian Ocean*, New Delhi: Manohar, 1996, pp. 159-80.

Sachau, Edward Carl, *Alberuni's India. An Account of the Religion, Philosophy, Literature, Geography, Chronology, Astronomy, Customs, Laws and Astrology of India about AD 1030. Vol. I-II,* New Delhi: Munshiram Manoharlal.

Salomon, R., *Indian Epigraphy*, New York: Oxford University Press, 1998.

Sankalia, H.D., A Unioque Wooden Idol of the Buddhist Goddess Tara from Kanheri Caves, *Journal of the Asiatic Society of Bombay*, Volumes 56-59, 1981-84: 296-99.

Sastri, K.A.N., *The Colas*, Madras: University of Madras, 1955.

Schalk, Peter (ed.), *Buddhism among Tamils in Pre-Colonial Tamilakam and Ilam*, Stockholm: Uppsala University, Volume II, 2002.

Schlingloff, Dieter, *Studies in Ajanta Paintings*, Delhi: Ajanta Publications, 1988.

Sedov, Alexander, The Port of Qana' and the Incense Trade, in David Peacock and David Williams (eds.), *Food for the Gods: New Light on the Ancient Incense Trade*, Oxford: Oxbow Books, 2007.

Seetah, Krish, Environmental Archaeology in Mauritius, Paper presented at Conference on 'Connecting Continents: Setting an Agenda for A Historical Archaeology of the Indian Ocean World', Stanford Archaeology Center, 6-7 March 2014.

Seland, Eivind Heldaas, Archaeology of Trade in the Western Indian Ocean, 300 BC–AD 700, *Journal of Archaeological Research*, published online 2nd April 2014.

Sen, Tansen, In Search of Longevity and Good Karma, *Journal of World History*, Volume 12, no. 1, 2001: 1-28.

——, *Buddhism, Diplomacy and Trade: The Realignment of Sino-Indian Relations 600-1400*, New Delhi: Manohar Publishers, 2004.

Senart, E., The Inscriptions in the Caves at Nasik, *Epigraphia Indica*, VIII, New Delhi: Archaeological Survey of India, 1905-06, pp. 59-65.

Seshadri, Gokul, New Perspectives on Nagapattinam, in Hermann Kulke, K. Kesavapany, Vijay Sakhuja (eds.), *Nagapattinam to Suvarnadwipa: Reflections on the Chola Naval Expeditions*, Singapore: Institute of Southeast Asian Studies, 2009.

Sharma, R.S., *Indian Feudalism c. AD 300 – 1200*, New Delhi: Macmillan, 1965.

Shastri, Hiranand, The Nalanda Copper Plate of Devapaladeva, *Epigraphia Indica*, 17, 7, 1924: 310-27.

Shinde, V.S., The Earliest Temple of Lajjagauri? The Recent Evidence from Padri in Gujarat, *East and West*, IsMEO 44 (2-4), 1994, pp. 481-85.

Sidebotham, Steven E., *Berenike and the Ancient Maritime Spice Route*, Los Angeles and London: California World History Library 18. Berkeley: University of California Press, 2011.

Sidebotham, S.E. and W.Z. Wendrich (eds.), *Berenike 1995*, Leiden: Research School CNWS, 1996.

Sircar, D.C., Charter of Visnusena Samvat 649, *Epigraphia Indica,* XXX, 1953-54: no. 30, 163-81.

——, More Inscriptions from Nagarjunikonda, *Epigraphia Indica*, Vol. XXV, 1963-1964: 1-7.

Smith, Mathew C. and Henry T. Wright, The Ceramics from Ras Hafun in Somalia: Notes on a Classical Maritime Site, *Azania*, 23, 1988: 138.

Sonam, Ruth (trans. and ed.), *Atisha's Lamp for the Path*, Ithaca, New York: Snow Lion Publications, 1997.

Sonawane, V.H., Some Remarkable Sculptures of Lajjagauri from Gujarat, *Lalit Kala*, Journal of Oriental Art, 23, 1977-78: 27-35.

Soundara Rajan, K.V., *Junagadh*, New Delhi: Archaeological Survey of India, 1985.

Spencer, G.W., The Politics of Plunder: The Cholas in Eleventh Century Ceylon, *Journal of Asian Studies*, 1976, 35: 403-19.

Spink, Walter M., *Ajanta: History and Development*, Volume 3, *The Arrival of the Uninvited*, Leiden: Brill, 2005.

——, *Ajanta: History and Development*, Volume 2, Leiden: Brill, 2006.

——, *Ajanta: History and Development*, Volume 5, Leiden: Brill, 2007.

——, *Ajanta: History and Development*, Volume 4: *Painting, Sculpture, Architecture*, Leiden: Brill, 2009.

Srinivasan, K.R., *Cave Temples of the Pallavas*, New Delhi: Archaeological Survey of India, 1964.

Srisuchat, Amara, Discovering Chinese Yue and Longquan Green Glazed Wares and Reconsidering their Socio-Economic Roles in the Development of Ancient Communities in Thailand, in Chuimei Ho (ed.), *New Light on Chinese Yue and Longquan Wares*, The University of Hong Kong, 1994, pp. 213-28.

Stillman, Norman A., The Eleventh Century Merchant House of Ibn 'Awkal (A Geniza Study), *Journal of the Economic and Social History of the Orient*, 16, 1973: 15-88.

Strauch, Ingo, *Foreign Sailors on Socotra: The Inscriptions and Drawings from the Cave Hoq*, Bremen: Hempen Verlag, 2012.

Subramanian, T.S., Stunning Indicators of Nagapattinam's Buddhist Legacy, *The Hindu*, Dec 25, 2011.

Tampoe, M., *Maritime Trade between China and the West*, Oxford: BAR International Series 555, 1989.

Tatelman, Joel, *The Heavenly Exploits: Buddhist Biographies from the Divyavadana*, The Clay Sanskrit Library, New York University Press, 2005.

Tchernia, A., Arikamedu et le Graffito Naval d'Alagankulam' *Topoi* 8/1, 1998: 447-463.

Tibbetts, G.R., *Arab Navigation in the Indian Ocean before the Coming of the Portuguese*, London: Royal Asiatic Society, 1971.

Tomber, Roberta, *Indo-Roman Trade: From Pots to Pepper*, London: Duckworth, 2008.

Trautmann, Thomas R., *The Clash of Chronologies: Ancient India in the Modern World*, New Delhi: Yoda Press, 2009.

Travers, Robert, *Ideology and Empire in Eighteenth Century India: The British in Bengal*, Cambridge: Cambridge University Press, 2007.

Tubb, Gary A., Hemacandra and Sanskrit Poetics, in John E. Cort (ed.), *Open Boundaries: Jain Communities and Cultures in Indian History*, Albany: State University of New York Press, 1998.

Vallet, Eric, Yemeni 'Oceanic Policy' at the end of the 13th century, in Rob Carter and St John Simpson (eds.), *Proceedings of the Seminar for Arabian Studies,* Volume 36, Papers from the thirty-ninth meeting of the Seminar for Arabian Studies, held in London in July 2005 is date of paper presentation; 2008 is date of publication.

Vasa, P.N., Find of a Late Byzantine Solidus and Arab Umayyad Dinara from Kutch, *Numismatic Digest*, 14, 1990: 30-33.

Virji, Krishnakumari Jethabhai, *Ancient History of Saurashtra: Being a Study of the Maitrakas of Valabhi V to VIII centuries A.D.*, Bombay: Konkan Institute of Arts and Sciences, 1955.

Vogel, J. Ph., Seals of Buddhist Monasteries in Ancient India, *Journal of the Ceylon Branch of the Royal Asiatic Society*, Centenary Volume, New Series, Vol. I, 1845-1945: 27-32.

Wade, Geoff, The Pre-Modern East Asian Maritime Realm: An Overview of European Language Studies, in Satish Chandra and Himanshu Prabha Ray (eds.), *The Sea, Identity and History: From the Bay of Bengal to the South China Sea*, New Delhi: Manohar, 2013, pp. 107-15.

——, *The Zheng He Voyages: A Reassessment*, Asia Research Institute Working Paper Series, 31, 2004.

Wenzel, H., A Jataka Tale from the Tibetan, *Journal of the Royal Asiatic Society*, New Series, Volume XX, 1888: 503-510.

Westerdahl, C., The Maritime Cultural Landscape, *International Journal of Nautical Archaeology*, 21, 1, 1992.

Wheatley, Paul, *The Golden Khersonese*, Westport: Greenwood Press, 1973 (first published 1961).

Wheeler, R.E.M., A. Ghosh and Krishna Deva, Arikamedu: An Indo-Roman Trading Station on the East Coast of India, *Ancient India*, 2, 1946: 17-124.

Whitehouse, David, Siraf: A Sasanian Port, *Antiquity* XLV, 1971: 262-67.

Wicks, Robert S., *Money, Markets, and Trade in Early Southeast Asia*, Ithaca: Cornell University Studies on Southeast Asia, 1992.

Wink, Andre, *Al-Hind: The Making of an Indo-Islamic World*, New Delhi: Oxford University Press, 1990.

Wolters, Oliver W., *Early Indonesian Commerce: A Study of the Origins of Srivijaya*, Cornell: Cornell University Press, 1967.

——, Southeast Asia as a Southeast Asian Field of Study, *Indonesia*, 58, October 1994: 1-17.

Woodward, Hiram, Esoteric Buddhism in Southeast Asia in the Light of Recent Scholarship, *Journal of Southeast Asian Studies*, 35, 2, June 2004.

Wu, Peiyi, An Ambivalent Pilgrim to T'ai Shan in the Seventeenth Century, in Susan Naquin and Chun-fang Yü (eds.), *Pilgrims and Sacred Sites in China*, Berkeley: University of California Press, 1992, pp. 65-88.

Index

Abbasid Caliphate 39, 96
Adam's Bridge 197
Aden 83, 92, 97, 98, 138, 147-50
Adulis 143
Agastya 60
Agius, Dionisius 8
Ainurruvar or Ayyavole 68, 176-77
Ajanta 17, 77, 110-12, 131
Akhbar al-Sin wa-l Hind 82
Akota 34, 176
Alagankulam 186-87
Alberuni 27
Alexander 129, 134, 201-02
Alexandria 83, 141
Amaravati 105-06, 109
Amreli 159
Anahilavada 147
Anahilavada Patan 162-64, 173
Anchor – stone 169
Anchorage 169
Ancient Monuments Preservation Act 1904 215-16
Ancient Monuments and Archaeological Sites and Remains Act 1958 216
Andamans 89
Andhra 134
Angkor 88-89, 117
Anjuvanam 68
Anuradhapura 54, 94
Apollodotus 134
Appar 53, 65
Arab 5, 6, 8, 27, 135, 136, 193
Arabian peninsula 128, 131, 139-40
Arabic 8, 11, 81-83, 95, 129, 144, 151-52, 178
Aramaic 8
Archaeological Survey of India 215
Arikamedu 54-55, 136, 184-85
Arthasastra 28, 137, 158
Asoka 17, 34, 105-06, 119, 120, 121
Atisa Dipankara 61-62
Aurangabad 110, 114
Avalokitesvara 20, 57, 105, 109-17

Baba Pyara 34-35, 107
Bali 69, 86-87, 196
Balipattana 38-39
Banigrama 69

Bankot 38
Barbarikon 133
Barbosa, Duarte 190
Ben Yiju 147-49
Bengal 85, 88, 91, 92, 156, 186
Berenike 54, 157, 187, 213
Beyt Dwarka island 26, 169
Bhadresvara 167, 172
Bharadhavasa or *Bharatam varsam* 17
Bharuch/ Broach or Barygaza 23, 27, 118, 132-37, 141, 173, 189, 213
Bhatkal 41
Bhoja 5
Bodh Gaya 90, 92, 93
Bodhisattva 119, 121
Borneo 84, 89, 197
Borobudur 62, 93, 118, 120
Brahmagiri 17
Buddha 57, 59-60, 62, 85, 91, 107, 111, 113, 115, 118, 121
Buddhagupta 85
Buddhism 5, 77, 89, 91, 123, 174-75
Buddhist bronze 49, 107
Buddhist caves 107
Buddhist vihara or monastery 31, 36, 51, 56, 107-09
Bujang valley 93
Burma 69, 87-88, 96, 196
Burnes, Alexander 166

Cairo 143, 146-49
Calicut 84
Cambay or Stambhatirtha 27
Cambodia 88, 89
Canton 40, 90, 91
Casal, J.M. 55
Casson, Lionel 186
Caste 2
Chaiya 85
Chalukya 23, 80
Chalukya (Gujarat) 162-65
Champa 48, 88
Chandor 38-39, 122
Chaul 38, 40, 168, 174
China 11, 40, 48, 53-54, 60, 65, 67-69, 81-82, 84, 86, 88, 89, 91, 92, 109, 113, 119, 128, 201
Chinese ceramics 11, 84-87, 93-96
  Celadon 95
  Chansha 95
  Dusun 95
  Longquan ware 93-94
  Yue ware 93-95
Chinese cloth 133
Chinese inscriptions 92
Chinese Pagoda 56
Chinese pilgrims 89-93
Chola 6, 11, 48, 53, 91, 156
Christian 83, 141
Christian Topography 129, 142
Chronometer 199
Chutiwongs, Nandana 121
Cinnabar 139
Coins – punch marked 186
Commodities 131
Conservation 215-17
Constantine 143
Constantinople 143
Cosmas Indicopleustes 129, 138, 141-43
Cudamani vihara 53, 55-62
Cunningham, Alexander 89
Curzon, Lord George Nathaniel 215

Dabhoi 173
Dabhol 38
Dandin 29
Das, Sarat Chandra 62
Das Gupta, Ashin 190, 210
Dasakumaracaritam 29
Davidson, Ronald M. 61
Davis, Jr., Donald R. 170
Desi or guild 174
Devnimori 34
Dhammaceti 56
Dhank 34, 176
Dharmakirti 62
Dharmasastras 5, 170
Dhauli 105
Dhow 150
Divyavadana 19, 77, 110
Dunhuang 109
Dutch East India Company 65
Dwarka 106, 167, 169
Dwarkadhish temple 169

East Africa 130-31
East India Company 193, 196-98
Eksar 24
Elliot, Walter 56
Ellora 110, 114, 117
Epic 18, 24

Failaka 141-42
Faxian 20, 89
Feudalism 4, 61
Fishing grounds 157-58
Floris, Peter 190
Fort 10, 16, 37-39
Fustat 148-49

Gandavyuha 62, 111, 119
Ganesa 31
Gaur/Gauda 87, 113
Geniza 132, 143-44
Ghulam Muhammad 195
Girnar 33, 106-07, 158, 163, 172, 173
Goa 24-26, 38, 39-41, 84, 194
Gogha 169
Gop 31
Greek 4, 8, 129, 132-34, 136, 140, 142-43, 189, 201, 209
Greenhill, Basil 192
Gupta 34

Hadramawt 138
Hall, Kenneth 9, 67
Harappan 4, 6, 186
Hathab 159, 169
Hathigumpha 17
Haribhadra Suri 37, 78
Hemachandra 78, 165, 174 – 174
Herodotus 201
Hippalus 209
Honavar 40
Hoq cave 141
Horden, Peregrine 211
Hormuz 81, 97, 151, 161, 172
Hornell, James 25, 191-92
Horse 161
Hoysala 40

Ibn Battuta 40, 82-84
Ibn Majid 82
Ikshvaku 135
Indigo 30, 132

Indo-Roman trade 5, 7 (also see Roman)
Indonesia 54, 61, 62, 81, 88, 157
Intwa 34
Islam 4, 6, 8, 81-83

Jagaducarita 79, 167, 171-72
Jaigarh 38
Jain 34, 37, 41, 77-79, 123, 152, 163, 165, 167, 169, 171
Jambi 49, 53, 91, 92, 93, 94
Jambudvipa 17, 88
Java 69, 86-88, 96, 117, 119
Jesuit 56
Jew 83, 144, 146-49, 169
Junagarh 28-29, 33-35, 106-07, 158, 167
Junnar 135

Kadambas of Goa 24, 27, 96
Kadia Dungar 107
Kalyan 38, 113, 137, 142, 174
Kalyankarin, prince 111-12
Kalyani inscription 56
Kampong Sungai Mas 85
Kanchipuram 54
Kanheri 106, 109-12, 135, 174-75
Karandavyuha sutra 20
Kateshwar 107
Kaveripumpattinam 49-51, 54, 67
Kayarohanaswami temple 63-65
Kedah 49, 65, 85, 91, 92
Khambat 84, 152, 173, 189
Khapra Kodia 34-35, 106-07
Kharavela 17
Kharosthi 186
Khedbrahma 34
Khok Phanom Di 10
Khmer 88
Kish/Qays 97
Kitab aja'ib al-Hind 82
Kizil 22
Kling 88
Kolhapur 176
Kollam or Quilon 38
Korkai 54, 55
Kota Cina 94
Kshatrapa 17, 22
Kumaragupta 32
Kuvalayamalakaha 37

Lajja-gauri 30-31
Lalitagiri 108, 114-15
Lalitavistara 62
Langudi 108
Lebdi, Joseph b. David 147-49
Lekhapaddhati 37, 79-80, 161-62, 178
Leyden plates 55-56
Li, Guo 144-45
Lohata 29
Lokesvara 57-58
Lothal 186

Madagaram 53
Madurai 68
Mahabharata 17, 61
Mahabodhi 90
Mahasena 22
Mahavamsa 20
Mahavastu 20
Maitraka 28-37, 159, 176
Maitreya 90
Majumdar, Ramesh Chandra 48

Malabar 83, 92, 98, 133, 142, 190, 191
Malay peninsula 81, 85, 86, 91
Mamallapuram 54, 67, 122
Mamluk 39-40, 96
Mandasor 32
Mandvi 166, 178
Mangalore 84, 142, 148
Mangrol 168
Manigramam 68
Mantai 94
Mantrayana 61
Maratha 41
Margeriti, Roxani 150
Maritime Heritage 211
Markham, Clements R. 198
Marshall, Sir John 215
Masulipatnam 190, 198
Mataram 86-88
Mathura, Bhuteshwar mound 21-22
Maurya 33
Mecca 145-46, 151
Mediterranean 130, 137, 192
Megalithic 7, 55
Memoir of a Map of Hindoostan 199-201
Memorial stone/ hero stone or *viragal* 10, 24-26, 69
Memory 214
Menander 134
Mesopotamia 6
Ming dynasty 40
Mleccha 24, 161
Modhera 163
Mohenjodaro 186
Mongkut, king 119
Mongol 39-40
Monius, Anne 66
Monument 214-17
Mookerji, Radha Kumud 5
Musi river 86
Muziris 77, 133

Nabatean 137
Nagapattinam 11, 48-70, 104, 161, 191, 210
Nagaram 176-77
Nagarjunakonda 107, 134, 135
Nagore 53, 65, 191
Nakhuda 150-52, 178
Nalagiri 60
Nalanda 61, 113, 117
Nagarakertagama 88
Nakorn Pathom 119-21
Nanadesi 68
Narada Smrti 170
Nasik 17, 19, 113, 135
National Monuments Authority 216
Nautical chart 189
Navsari 34, 168
Nayak 65
Neak Pean, Angkor 22-23
Nelkynda 133
Neolithic 53-54
Nestorian Christian 141-43
Nilakantha Sastri, K.A. 48

Oman 81-83, 138, 140, 166
Outrigger 192

Padri 30, 159
Pagan 22, 69
Pahlavi 112

Pala 61
Palembang 49, 91, 93
Pallava 54, 122
Paramara 165
Paris, Admiral 193
Parsi 168
Patan 167, 172
Patel, Alka 152
Pattana 137
Pattanam 8
Pearson, Michael N. 194, 208
Pepper 130-31, 142, 149, 212-13
Periplus Maris Erythraei 7, 22, 38, 129-36, 186, 188
Persia/Persian 4, 5, 8, 84, 140-43
Phanigiri 17
Philippines 87, 93
Pilgrimage 122, 145, 212, 214
Pitalkhora 110
Pliny the Elder 128, 129, 201
Polonaruwa 94
Pondicherry 197
Porbandar 167, 178
Port/market centre/harbour 136-37
Public History 214
Purananuru 76
Purcell, Nicholas 211
Purnavadana 111
Pushpavanam 52

Qaisar, Ahsan Jan 193
Qana (Bi'r 'Ali) 138
Qays 97-98
Qesse-ye Sanjan 168
Quanzhou 69
Quilon 40 (also see Kollam)
Quseir al-Qadim 143-46

Raj, Kapil 194
Rajbadidanga 85
Rani-ki-vav 163-65
Ra's al Hamra 9
Ras Hafun 185
Rashtrakuta 36
Rasulid Sultanate 97
Ratnagiri 106, 109, 114-17
Rawlinson, H.G. 7
Ray, Harprasad 9
Red Polished Ware 7
Red Sea 130-31, 136, 144-46, 157
Rennell, James 195-202
Roman 4, 7, 55, 186
Roman coins 8, 133-35
Roman Empire 128
Rouletted Ware 7, 55, 156, 184-86
Rudradaman 159

Saddharmapundarika Sutra 109-10
Sadhanamala 117
Sailendra 48, 56
Salihundam 54
Samaraiccakaha 37, 78
Sambandar 53
Sangam 7
Sanjan 168
Sanskrit 8, 11, 56, 77, 78, 84-86, 151-52, 173, 174
Sarnath 60
Sasanian 80, 95
Satavahana 17-18, 22, 186

Schalk, Peter 60
Scheurleer, Pauline 59
Schlingloff, Dieter 104, 110, 111
Schopen, Gregory 110
Schouten, Wouter 56
Sea battle 10, 16, 27
Sea snakes 188
Sen, Tansen 9, 67
Serapis 213
Sharma, Ram Sharan 61
Ship symbol 185
Sigiriya 94
Silahara 24, 27, 38, 159-60, 168, 177
Sima charters 87
Simhala 20
Simhala vijaya 19, 111, 112
Sinbad 82
Siraf 80-81, 95
Siva 31, 34, 59, 61, 64-65, 94, 123
Siyot 107
Skandagupta 28, 32
Slave 161
Socotra 131, 136, 137-41, 212
Sohar 81
Somnath 27, 107, 152, 167, 169
Somnath – Veraval inscription 151, 178
Sopara 38, 105, 168, 174
Soutokeny 55
Spink, Walter 19, 111, 117
Sreni 169-71
Sri Lanka 6, 20, 53, 54, 82, 84, 87, 89, 94, 96, 111, 129, 142-43, 156, 186, 191, 192, 197
Sriwijaya 48-70, 85, 92
Sthanu Ravi 38
Sudhana 119
Sumatra 49, 53, 60, 61, 62, 69, 84, 85, 87, 89, 91, 93-94, 96, 196
Sumhurram 138
Supparaka Jataka 117-20
Surat 189, 190
Surya 32
Syria 38

Tabo 62
Takuapa 85
Talaja 107
Tamil 11, 48-57, 65, 76-77, 95, 137, 157, 175, 184, 186, 191, 192, 197
Tamil – Brahmi 54
Tamil – inscriptions in Southeast Asia 69, 87
Tamralipti 91
Tang Annals 8, 9
Tara 109, 112-17
Tchernia, André 186
Tejahpala 172
Thailand 93-94
Thana 27, 168
Thanjavur 68
Tibet 62
Tibbetts, G.R. 188
Tiruchirapalli 65, 68
Toramana 28-29, 33
Tortoise shell 131, 139
Trimbak 176
Turushka 172

Udaigiri 114-15
UNESCO 217-18
Uperkot 34-35, 107

Vadrapalli 29
Vajrayana 116
Valahassa Jataka 20-22
Valentyn, François 56
Vallabhi 10, 27-29, 32, 34, 36, 159, 167, 176
Vallet, Eric 97
Vasavasamudram 55
Vastupala 172
Vastupalacarita 173
Vedic 5
Velankanni 53
Veraval 167
Vietnam 157
Vijaya 20-21
Vijayadurg 38, 41
Vijayanagar 40-41
Vikramshila 62
Viracoliyam 60, 66
Visnu 31, 34, 59, 61, 85, 123, 165
Visnusena 29-30, 170
Votive stupa 60

Waqf 152
Warmington, E.H. 7
Wheeler, R.E.M. 55, 184
Wink, André 4
Wolters, Oliver 48, 67, 86, 213
Woodward, Hiram 61
World Heritage Convention 217-18
Writing 212
Wutai, Mount 68

Xuanzang 89-90, 175

Yavana 24
Yemen 84, 97-98, 133, 135, 137, 139, 145
Yijing 91-92
Yogini Tantra 61
Yuktikalpataru 5, 78-79

Zanzibar 80
Zheng He 40, 92, 95-96
Zoroastrian 168